Tammy has gained a wealth of knowledge
she desires to share it so others can learn fr
This book contains an amazing amount of
to be prepared for a tight situation.

Kate Asbury

Tammy Price is one of the most resourceful people I have ever met. Her enthusiasm for being self-sufficient is contagious!

Teresa Eyre

I love Tammy's easy meal planning method for figuring her food storage needs. Now after learning her simple approach, I feel like I was doing it all backwards! With her help, I am motivated to assess my family's needs and plan according to our everyday menu plan. She has also taught me how to bake some fantastic dinner rolls! Thanks Tammy for your sweet testimony of food storage, you are a light for all of us!

Tiffani Winward

Tammy has put her whole heart into learning about each area of provident living. Her knowledge is sharp, her teaching is helpful and patient, and her testimony is sweet. Her willingness to help others learn what she knows is a blessing.

Katie Turley

Saving for a rainy day is a goal many aspire to, but few are able to achieve. Tammy's financial expertise offers a simple approach to what many find daunting...setting up a family budget. A lifetime of experience conveyed throughout this book gives readers a gift of empowerment and when practiced, eliminates the stress of financial pressures.

Jill Gardner

When Tammy does something, she does it well. Her knowledge and personal application of provident living have been a great example and blessing to all who are lucky enough to be in her reach. So glad she's passing it along in a book so all can enjoy!

Becky Sattler

All Things Provident

Inspiring ideas to help use your food storage, manage your finances, and prepare for emergencies.

By Tamara Price

Illustrated by Katie Ormond

> For new recipes, additional tips, and tutorials check out:
>
> # allthingsprovident.blogspot.com

Written Copyright © 2011, Tamara Price

Illustrations Copyright © 2011, Katie Ormond

All rights reserved. No part of this book may be reproduced or transmitted in any form or by any means, graphic, electronic, or mechanical, without permission in writing from the publisher.

ISBN 978-0-9832677-0-6

Published by Lightning Creek Press
www.lightningcreekpress.com

Acknowledgement

I want to thank all the friends and family over the years who have passed recipes my way and encouraged me through this entire experience. Little comments or tips on things that worked in the homes of others have encouraged me to search for more options as we've organized our home. I am inspired by the stories I have learned of families that have lived through catastrophes because they were prepared. All these things have provided motivation for me to keep working at incorporating principles of provident living into daily life.

Living providently takes consistent and repeated effort. Without the inspiration and encouragement we receive from others, it is too easy to give in to the temptation to not worry about being prepared. I have been blessed with a wonderful husband who supports me in taking the steps to be temporally prepared. This includes all the areas of food storage, finances and emergency preparedness. My children have also been great motivators. I know they are counting on me to take care of their needs every day. I want to be able to do that regardless of what major challenge we may be facing.

I especially want to thank my husband and children who have sat down to an adventurous dinner quite often over the years as I've learned to cook with food that can store—and loved it!

Contents

Introduction 1

Food Storage 7
    Food Storage Hurdles 9
    Creating a 3-Month Meal Plan 19
    Using Your Freezer 33
    Storable Meals 49
    Storable Snacks 89
    Storable Desserts 101
    Cooking with Whole Wheat 115
    Bread Making 123
    Pantry Mix Recipes 143
    Cooking with Dry Beans 154
    Using Powdered Milk 165
    White Sauce Mix Recipes 177
    Using Garden Produce 187
    Preserving Your Harvest 195
    Just for Kids 211

Finances 217
    Organizing Your Family's Finances 219
    Paying Your Tithing 223
    Spending Less Than You Earn 225
    Learning to Save 231
    Honoring Your Financial Obligations 243
    Teaching Your Children to Follow Your Example 245

Emergency Preparedness 248
    Preparing For Emergencies 251
    72-Hour Kits 253
    Preparing for an Emergency at Home 259

First Aid/CPR 267

"Just in Case" 269

Getting It All done 271

Appendix 277

Recipe Index 295

Introduction

We've all had times of our lives that feel harried and out of control. Perhaps your craziest times fall during soccer season or the holidays when there really is more on the calendar than there should be. Maybe it feels crazy when you are asked to serve in a new calling at church that requires far more time than you have ever given before. Perhaps someone in your family is diagnosed with, or struggling through a health challenge. Another big challenge that many face sometime in their lives is a job change or layoff. All these events affect our families and our ability to care for their basic needs.

Many of us have decided that food storage and provident living principles are only for times of mass destruction and utter chaos. We do not realize that incorporating these principles and organizing ourselves during the calmer moments of our lives will allow us to care for the needs of our families even in the events described above.

I grew up in a home with parents who wanted to obey the counsel to store a year supply of food, stay out of debt, and prepare for emergencies. They worked hard to carefully budget their income to allow for this. There are nine kids in my family so a year supply for eleven people was a staggering amount! Little by little, we made it and I remember the peace we felt in our home knowing we were ready. I can remember the Family Night when my dad was so excited to present to us a framed copy of the deed to our home that they had just paid off. Our parents encouraged us to help in the efforts. We have fond memories of canning peaches together with peach juice dripping down our arms to our elbows. One summer we canned 22 bushels of fruit! This gave us about 450 quarts of fruit and was pretty typical. We used to lay the fruit out in a single layer on the garage floor to ripen. It covered the entire two-car garage!

I've learned over the years that you stand on the shoulders of those who came before. Because I grew up in a home that lived these provident principles, I had a good foundation and understanding going into my marriage. I also have a very supportive husband who avoids debt and is willing to let me channel budget money into gathering our storage and other preparedness items.

Each family has different challenges. Our main challenge to this point has been bringing babies here. We have five children, all of whom came prematurely and had to spend time in the NICU after birth. My pregnancies have been very challenging with severe morning sickness, reduced activity, and bed rest required in all five of them. My third pregnancy was the most challenging. I began full bed rest at 19 weeks along because of pre-term labor. I spent four months in bed unable to be a mom to the two young children I already had. It was during this significant challenge that Heavenly Father helped me understand the power that comes from being prepared.

As hard as this challenge was, we knew we had taken steps to be prepared. We had a lot of food in the house which simplified things for my husband. As long as I could think of what recipe to make with what we had, he could quickly mix something up when he got home. Even though the grocery stores were still functioning, it added one more thing to his list to have to shop. It was much easier to limit his trips so he could be home. The other thing we had done was build up our emergency fund to cover the extra costs associated with this situation. We were able to pay for a nanny to come in and help with the kids during the day so my husband could continue working. We also had enough saved to cover the out-of-pocket maximum payment required by our insurance company to meet the staggering medical bills.

As I lay in bed for four months, I had a lot of time to think. One thing I felt inspired to consider and ponder on was my food storage. (I know that sounds crazy, but I really feel Heavenly Father was helping me use my time in a way that I could eventually help and inspire others.) I had a lot of food, but would it really last a year? How would I know that my kids were getting the nutrition they needed? Did my husband and I both know how to cook what we had at the house?

I came to understand that food storage and financial preparedness were meant to get us through everyday life, not just catastrophes. We had done a pretty decent job of pulling through a challenging pregnancy. But we also learned areas that we were lacking in. By developing our talents in the areas of provident living, we could support our families through just about any stressful time regardless of the source of the stress. These thoughts inspired me to do more.

As soon as I was able to be up and doing, I took an inventory of the food we had left. (We really had eaten a lot of it during my pregnancy.) I decided that to be sure we were getting the nutrition we needed from our food storage and to know just how long it would last, I should make a list of storable meals. These meals would be ones that would allow me to store *all* the required ingredients at my home. By doing this, I could be sure that I had all the ingredients to make a full meal instead of just cooking wheat or rice for dinner. If I purchased enough ingredients to make these meals multiple times during the year, I could store an entire year supply this way.

> *My goal is that you will walk away from this book with a renewed desire to live the counsel we have received to prepare our families.*

This idea made so much sense to me! I did menu planning every day. This was just taking the idea a big step farther. I began going through our family recipe book for inspiration and ideas. Most of the meals for my menu plan came directly from that book. I just needed to make a few small changes to the recipe, such as using dehydrated vegetables or powdered milk in place of the fresh items. I knew we liked these recipes since we ate them all the time already. When the most recent counsel came out to store a 3-month supply of what we eat on a regular basis, this verified that what the Holy Ghost had directed me to do was right on track. I have a year's worth of meals instead of just 3 months' worth. (I realize that as my kids grow it will shrink to a 6-month supply pretty quickly.)

I made a list of goals about what I needed to learn more about, such as using powdered milk and cooking with dry beans. These are items I had in my food storage so I worked them into my meal plan, but I had never actually cooked with them since getting married. I then decided I would work on one main goal each year. (Remember that the Prophets have asked us to collect and prepare a little at a time until we reach our goals.) This made the task seem doable. Each year became a new adventure. My children often asked as they sat down to dinner, "Mom, is this another experiment?"

The other thing my husband and I did was set some goals to organize our finances a little better. (I had pondered on this part of our life as well during all those months in bed.) We had always lived below our means and saved for a rainy day, but I felt we could do more to be sure we were really ready for what may come and for retirement one day.

This book is a collection of the knowledge we have gained during these adventures over the years. We've come to understand that provident living principles go way beyond food storage. We've learned so many lessons on finances and emergency preparedness in addition to what I now know about food storage.

I know that the bulk of this book covers food storage topics. This is because we can never stop thinking about food. As soon as you have cleared the kitchen up from one meal it is time to begin thinking about the next. Finances and emergency preparedness are a little easier to get a handle on. Once you have a good system in place, you can just follow it.

I realize that there are many books printed on these topics. I hope you find mine inspiring. My goal is that you will walk away from reading or thumbing through this book with a renewed desire to live the counsel we have received. Great peace will fill your life as you do so.

Don't bite off more than you can chew—choose one thing to try now. It may be as simple as trying a new recipe. Each week or each month, pick the book up again and try something else. I hope this is a book you will want to return to again and again for a new tip you are ready to try.

You will be amazed at how much peace you will feel just because you are doing something to get a little more prepared. If you go to the work of putting together a 2-week menu plan and purchase what you need to get through 3 months, you will feel even greater peace. You'll find yourself feeling like you have a restaurant menu to select from for every meal since you have all the ingredients at your house. Soccer season or any other busy time of your life won't feel so harried when you can pull from any of 14 meals for dinner since you know you have all of the ingredients.

You will be better able to serve those around you *knowing* your family has done all you can do to have your house in order. When a new challenge arises, because you know it will, you can go in confidence to Heavenly Father and ask Him for the assistance you need. He will be there to support you and the challenge will not feel so large since you are prepared.

Food Storage Hurdles

Hurdle #1: Gaining a Testimony - The very first and highest hurdle to overcome is gaining a personal testimony that food storage is essential. It doesn't matter how many times we've heard others talk on the importance of preparing our families, or how many quotes from Prophets or other leaders that are shared with us, until *we* decide that it is important for *us* to do we will always be able to come up with excuses or reasons that it just really isn't important to think about or focus on at the moment.

To overcome this hurdle, we must first "desire to believe" as Alma teaches us in the Book of Mormon. We must begin with a desire to live *all* the counsel we are given by wise leaders not just the counsel that seems easy or important at the time. We need to change the question we are repeating in our minds.

Instead of asking, "Why should I obey this counsel," we should ask, "How can I do it?"

The questions we are asking help to develop our attitude and the attitude we have opens or closes our hearts to receiving guidance from the Holy Ghost. When we make a conscious decision to follow *all* the counsel and grow in our desire to gather food storage, we begin to have our eyes opened to how best to do this. The other blessing is that all the excuses we've come up with over the years begin to melt away because our hearts have changed. The Holy Ghost helps us jump all the other hurdles and just get it done.

Hurdle #2: Motivation - After we know it is something we want to do, the next big hurdle is motivating ourselves to move it to the top of our to-do list. James and I got married in 1999 and, you may remember, the big push that year was Y2K. The Church leaders were continuing to counsel us to prepare ourselves, but as the turn of the century approached, all the news media and civic leaders also spoke on the subject constantly. This made it easier to keep it on the top of our minds. We set a goal to have a year supply by our first anniversary. This gave us a deadline to work with. Over the course of that first year, we collected lists of what we needed and budgeted to acquire the basics. This got us off to a very good start.

Give yourself a deadline. Be realistic knowing what you already have and what you need to purchase. Once you have a deadline, break your to-do list into steps that can be done each month or two depending on what will work best for you. Assign other members of the family to do their part. It doesn't all have to rest on your shoulders. If you are single, gather a group of single friends together and encourage each other in this endeavor. You could assign each person a responsibility and then check back each month. Spread the responsibility around. If you have children, ask one of them to create a visual aide such as a thermometer or a path to your goal that you can color in as your family makes progress. You could assign one of the parents to research the best price for wheat in your area and then go together to pick up the 300 lbs you decided you needed. I'm always the one to check prices and my husband is the one to stop and pick up the big items that require a good back for lifting. If you have older teenagers, they can go to the LDS cannery with you to help package items into #10 cans. They have to be at least 16 years old to do this. Our whole family gets in on the canning and organizing of the storage room. Everyone can do something. You can make it a fun experience as you also show by example your willingness to follow the Prophet.

Hurdle #3: Space to store it - When we have a testimony of storing the food, we somehow figure out ways to find space for it. Let me share a personal story. When I was a young girl, my father was in graduate school. My parents lived in a tiny two-bedroom apartment with three children. Upon graduation, my father joined the military and we were being stationed in Germany. This meant the military would be moving us. The movers came one day to take a quick look at the apartment to get an idea of how long it would take to pack everything. They figured it would take about three hours—there really wasn't much room at all. They finally finished packing everything three *days* later! They made the mistake of not looking in the closets and under the beds when they made their quick walk through. My parents had a testimony of needing to store a year supply. They found the space even in their tiny apartment.

This story has always inspired me and I hope it does the same for you. When you set a goal to collect the food that your family will need, other things become less important and you do without so the space can be filled with the food you are storing.

A year supply of food for one person can fit under a twin size bed. If your focus is a 3-month supply, then you could fit four people's food under that same bed. When I completed my meal plan and collected all I would need to make a year's worth of meals it took up far less space than I was first thinking. Work on gaining a testimony of needing it and then you will somehow figure out where to put it.

 Before we had a house with a separate storage room, I tried to assign certain items to certain rooms. One closet was where we put all the pasta and tomato products, one closet held all the canned fruits and vegetables, under one bed was all the #10 cans from the cannery. We stacked 8 boxes of canned wheat to create our TV stand. I just made a cute tablecloth to cover them. The items, such as wheat, that have a longer shelf-life, we put in the harder to get to places. The boxes of #10 cans from the cannery fit very well on the floor in standard size closets. We just made a false floor and put our shoes on top of the boxes. Ask around and see how others have done it. The Spirit will help you see space you didn't think you had.

Hurdle #4: How to afford it - This may not be a challenge for some, but for many of us, we feel this is a huge hurdle. You need to look closely at where your money is being spent. It really doesn't have to cost a lot. For just $5 a week you can make great progress. At the time of this printing, for $5 I can purchase a box of hot cereal, a package of pasta and a can of spaghetti sauce. This adds up to 5 meals for our family. The box of hot cereal will make enough for 4 days of breakfast and then the spaghetti can cover one simple lunch or dinner. If $5 a week is all you can afford, you can start setting that much aside and as it grows, you can purchase more costly items. If you can dedicate $20 a week to storable ingredients, then you will be able to reach your goal even faster. Skip ahead to the section on finances and saving on your groceries for even more ideas of how to make those few dollars stretch. Many families can find the money they need in the grocery budget they are using already. It just takes a little more discipline in how you are spending the funds you have already allocated to food.

I have found that when we are focused on a righteous goal, Heavenly Father helps us figure out a way to accomplish it. Some items that we thought were important, we decide to do without, or an opportunity to earn just a little extra presents itself. Remember that you are not in this alone. Heavenly Father, like any loving father, does not want to see His children suffer. Through His prophets, He has told us what we need to do. He will help us.

Hurdle #5: How to cook with it - The bulk of this book will help you clear this hurdle. There are many recipes and simple suggestions to help you gain skills and knowledge in this area. Don't pass up the opportunities you are given through Relief Society to learn these skills from others. Communities often offer classes through their community education programs on Dutch Oven cooking, bread making, etc. The other place to check for classes would be a local preparedness store that sells dehydrated fruits and vegetables or other storable food items. They often offer classes or are willing to share recipes. The internet is also an amazing resource.

Give yourself credit for what you already know how to do! Maybe you don't know how to cook dry beans—just store canned ones until you figure out cooking your own. Because you can be in charge of what recipes you choose to include in your meal plan, you can choose ones you already know how to cook. With a little focused thinking and some hints from the recipes in this book, you'll be able to put together a 2-week menu plan made mostly of meals you already know how to do.

You have to grasp the idea that now is your time to experiment. If you try cooking something new for dinner and it flops (we've all had those experiences), you can always pull out cold cereal. When you are in a situation where you are living off of your storage, you don't want to be experimenting! You want to have built confidence in your abilities to cook what you are storing long before the emergency hits.

Hurdle #6: Rotating it - This hurdle is taken care of when you store items to make the recipes you are already eating. If you serve one of your food storage meals a couple days a week, you'll rotate through your food in plenty of time before any of it loses its nutritional value. This hurdle basically disappears.

I cook my food storage meals pretty regularly, but I also pull from my stored items to make other meals all the time. For this reason, I do an inventory every 6 months and then restock what I need. Most of the items I store you can purchase at any grocery store. I've tried to limit the "specialty items" I have to purchase other places because I know it's more difficult to work that into my schedule. The internet makes these more available since I can order what I need and have it shipped right to my house.

When I purchase items, I actually purchase a little more than I truly need for my year supply of meals. This lets me feel that I am free to use what I need to and not worry about doing inventory every month. If a true emergency hits and I'm a little low on a few things, I will be okay. Our family will improvise.

Hurdle #7: How long to store it - Recent studies have shown that food holds its nutritional value lots longer than first believed. The following information comes from www.providentliving.org. Check out this great resource for more information on how best to package and store your food.

Food	Shelf-life Estimates (in years)
Wheat	30+
White rice	30+
Corn	30+
Sugar	30+
Pinto beans	30
Rolled oats	30
Pasta	30
Potato flakes	30
Apple slices	30
Non-fat powdered milk	20
Dehydrated carrots	20

Commercially canned products such as Del Monte or Libby's brand fruits and vegetables also last well past their "best by" dates. If the can is dented or bulging, throw it away. After storing for many years, the color and texture may change slightly but this does not mean the food has spoiled.

After all I've read and learned from experience, (my mom has things in her storage room that are quite old but are still good when we open them) I've decided to stop worrying too much about shelf-life since things store so very long. Since I store items that I use in my recipes on a regular basis they are rotated well before the 20- or 30-year mark.

Hurdle #7: How much to store - The current recommendation is to store 3 months' worth of what you eat on a regular basis and a year supply of the basics. By going through the steps to create your 2-week menu plan you will know how much to store for 3 months' worth of meals. Take inventory every 6 months and restock the items that you need.

The recommendation on calculating the amount of basics to store can be found at www. providentliving.org. You need 25 lbs of grain per month per person and 5 lbs of dry beans per month per person. So for 12 months for one person, you would need 25x12 or 300 lbs of grains (you pick whatever grains you want) and 5x12 or 60 lbs of dry beans. If you gather the 3 months needed for your menu plan then you only need to store 9 months of grains and beans per person. It really has been simplified a lot over past lists.

I store my grains and beans in #10 cans with oxygen absorbers so they are ready for the next 30 years. I don't open these cans on a regular basis. I figure at about the 25-year mark, I'll start working them into what I am using. I don't want to go through the time or expense to can these items every year. Instead, I keep a certain amount of basics in 5-gallon buckets that I pull from on a daily basis. I just fill these up as needed to keep my 3-month supply stocked.

Hurdle #8: Hard to store items -

Eggs - For your long-term storage, you can store powdered eggs. These are a little pricey so many people shy away from them, but they work well in all of your baking. You need to remember that one can holds the equivalent of 80+ eggs so it is like buying 7 dozen at once. They have a shelf-life of at least 10 years, unopened.

To substitute in any recipe calling for eggs: 1 egg = 2 Tbsp dried egg powder + ¼ cup water. If you are mixing a recipe with dry ingredients, you can just add the egg powder with the dry ingredients and add the water with the wet ingredients without having to actually mix the egg up.

For shorter-term storage, you have two options. The FDA has determined that eggs are good for 10 weeks in the refrigerator. This means you can store almost all the eggs you need for a 3-month supply in your fridge. So you can change your buying habits and just make sure you have plenty of eggs at all times. The other option is to freeze eggs. Frozen eggs work just like fresh eggs once they are thawed out. You can even fry them up for breakfast!

To freeze eggs, crack them out of their shell and store in an airtight container. I use ½ cup-size freezer containers. One egg fits in each container very easily. They stack well in my freezer and it is easy to determine how many eggs I have. I can grab one or more depending on my recipe. I let them sit in a sink of hot water to thaw and then use just like a fresh egg.

Don't let the idea of storing eggs keep you from putting certain recipes into your meal plan. If French toast is something you eat on a regular basis, you can easily store what you need to make it again and again.

Fruits/Vegetables - Many of us have been taught to choose fresh over frozen or canned products whenever possible. In all the reading I have done, even health magazines suggest that fresh is not always best. If fruits or vegetables are processed at their peak of ripeness, they actually can have higher levels of vitamins than if they are picked and shipped before they are fully ripe. A slight decrease in vitamin levels, especially vitamin C, occurs during the processing of fruits and vegetables. Since ripe fruits or vegetables are so much higher in these levels to begin with, they remain higher even after processing than "fresh" products picked too early.

It is great to get into the habit of eating from your garden or local farmers' markets when items are in season and then eating from your freezer or pantry during the off season. You can learn how to preserve these fresh products yourself and then you will know you have the best products possible. (Check out the section on Preserving Your Harvest for information on how to do this.)

The other option for storing fruits and vegetables is to use dehydrated or freeze-dried varieties. I especially love the dehydrated vegetables for soups and stews through the winter. I save so much time since I don't have to peel and chop all my onions, carrots, etc. When using dehydrated items, remember that they will double in size when you rehydrate them. They will rehydrate faster if you soak them in warm water, which is why I just drop them into my soups or stews and adjust the water amounts as needed. Freeze-dried varieties do not change size when rehydrated. Both dehydrated and freeze-dried varieties store for 20+ years.

I love using dehydrated vegetables—they save me so much chopping time!

Rehydrating Vegetables

Place dry vegetables in a pan. Cover them with enough water that they can double in size and still be covered. Bring water to a boil and then cover the pan and turn the heat off. Allow the vegetables to sit for 15–20 minutes until tender. Drain off any remaining water and use in your recipe. If making a soup, just drop the dry vegetables in the pot and allow to simmer along with the soup. For just a tablespoon or two of onions or peppers, place them in a small glass dish and fill it with water. Microwave for 30 seconds and drain off any excess water.

Meats - You can store quite a bit of meat in the freezer. This is the perfect way to store what you need for your 3-month supply. Obviously, you need to have a generator and some fuel to be sure you can keep your freezer cold during a lengthy power outage.

The other options for storing meats are in canned form. Chicken, beef, tuna, salmon, etc. all come canned and have 3–5 year shelf lives. You can also choose to store some TVP (textured vegetable protein sold by food storage retailers) or freeze-dried meats for your longer-term storage. These store 20+ years and so you would not need to rotate or use them on a regular basis.

For those who really want to make everything themselves, you can actually make a meat substitute out of your wheat. It is actually made from the gluten in the wheat which is the protein portion of wheat. You can purchase gluten flour which works well in bread baking, but also gives you a shortcut for making "wheat meat" as we call it in our family. For any who are interested, a quick search of the internet will take you to plenty of sites that teach how to do this. This book is meant to focus more on the concept of storing what we eat on a regular basis and for most of us, "wheat meat" does not fall in this category. I do store extra wheat and gluten flour in case I reach a point that I deplete all my other options and I need to feed my family in this way.

Dairy Products - Cheese, sour cream, cream cheese, yogurt, and ice cream…all the things that make everything so tasty can be difficult to store until you figure out using powdered milk. There is an entire section and many recipes on using powdered milk to help you realize that these products can work into your meal plan of storable recipes.

I use powdered milk in my baking and cooking on a daily basis. I make yogurt all the time and then use it as a sour cream and cream cheese substitute. It really helps me rotate through my powdered milk and it tastes great and is fat free! I know how to make cheeses and I store the items to do so, but this is not something I do regularly. But I know I'm ready if I need to.

For my meals, I store Parmesan cheese in the pantry. Cheddar and mozzarella I store shredded in the freezer. Cream cheese actually stores quite well in the refrigerator for at least 3 months so I always keep a good amount of it on hand. I also keep 3–4 bricks of cheese in the fridge for slicing and using on sandwiches. These are all good options for the shorter term. Change your habits and buy in bulk so your needs are covered for much longer than a week or two.

Hurdle #9: Accommodating a special diet -

Babies - If you are in a season of your life that you have babies around, you need to think of their special needs when it comes to food storage and emergency preparedness. Buy extra formula and diapers to be ready for what may come. Because a baby grows so quickly, I try to think a month out for their needs. I keep enough formula and diapers at the house to get through a month. (I do store cloth diapers for my 72 hour kit since I can fold them to fit any size baby.) I also plan ahead on the fruits and vegetables we have stored during the year we have a young baby. It is much more cost effective to make your own baby food than to purchase the little bottles at the store. I grind a bottle of peaches or make up a little more mashed potatoes when I am making them for the family and then freeze baby food size portions. It really isn't difficult to plan for the needs of a baby.

Allergies - Our extended family fights many allergies so the traditional food storage lists don't work for them at all. The food storage meal plan presented in this book addresses their needs quite easily. You just store the items you are using on a regular basis. You know your family can eat them, and you know how to cook with them. As you follow the steps to create your food storage meal plan, you will be able to determine your own list of recipes that work for the special needs of your family. There are many recipes in this book that are egg-free. You can also store powdered soy or rice milk to use for those who are allergic to dairy. It will substitute nicely in most of the recipes calling for powdered milk in this book. Although, it will not make yogurt or cheese. Even though some of the recipes in this book may not work, I hope they can serve as inspiration for you as you work to find ones that will feed your family.

Creating a 3-Month Meal Plan

Many of us get overwhelmed with the idea of food storage. How much do I need to have? Where can I store it? Can I cook with it? Will my family even eat it if we had to? These are all questions we've asked ourselves over the years. Church and government leaders continue to counsel us to store some food to help our families weather emergencies. The most recent counsel from the leaders in the Church of Jesus Christ of Latter-day Saints is to store 3 months' worth of what your family eats on a regular basis and a year supply of the basics such as beans, rice, and wheat.

As I've thought about this counsel, the solution that makes the most sense to me is to store ingredients to make the recipes my family loves. With this thought in mind, I went in search of recipes that I was already making that contained storable ingredients. I determined that with a few slight changes, many of the recipes I was making on a regular basis could be stored.

I decided to put together a food storage meal plan and determine just how much of each ingredient I would need to make these meals enough times to give my family a year supply of food. (I did this before the counsel changed to 3 months instead of a year. My kids were young when I put my plan together, so I figure as their appetites increase, what used to be a year supply will shrink into 6 months or less by the time they are teenagers. I also figure that it never hurts to store more than 3 months of what we eat so I haven't gone through to refigure the amounts.) I focused on recipes that included ingredients I already had since I had been collecting food storage. I really wanted to make use of all that wheat, rice, beans, and spaghetti sauce.

This chapter focuses on the basics of putting a meal plan together that is personalized to your family's likes and your cooking habits. By serving food storage meals twice a week, you will rotate an entire year supply in 3 ½ years! If you store a 3-month supply of meals and serve one food storage meal each week, you will rotate through your storage in about 1 ½ years. Everything can be rotated well before it reaches its shelf-life. You will know how to cook what you are storing and your family will actually like it!

There are other amazing benefits that I have recognized over the last few years since we have implemented this approach. My fear of hardships and challenges has diminished and is actually almost non-existent. I am confident that what we have stored at the house will keep my entire family fed for at least a year. Being at peace is a HUGE benefit. I can also say that I'm spending less time planning meals, and my trips to the grocery store are spread out so I have more time to do other things. We are also saving money on our food budget since I purchase storage items in bulk when they are on sale for a great price. I know we are eating healthier as well since I am cooking more from scratch and incorporating whole grains into our diet.

> *If you only have an extra $5 a week, you can begin to collect food storage.*

Before you decide this plan seems too difficult, give your mind a few more minutes to think about some options. What are your "go to" meals—you know, the ones that you end up fixing when 5:00 P.M. rolls around and you realize you haven't planned dinner yet? Spaghetti is an easy one. We probably all have a package of pasta and a can of spaghetti sauce in the pantry. Pancakes are another quick option. How about canned soup or chili? We all have a few meals if we begin to think about it. You can skip ahead at this point to the Storable Meals chapter for a lot of other ideas. It won't take long at all to come up with a 2-week menu of recipes to try.

Some people define food storage as food that can be stored for long periods of time without the help of the fridge or freezer. It is definitely important to have some items and meals that fall in this category. Over the years, I have come to realize that very few emergencies take all power away for long periods though. Most of the emergencies that hit our families involve a drop in family income, a long-term medical challenge, an extra busy month or two at work that make menu planning and shopping fall to the bottom of our list, or something similar. I have decided that I feel fine using my freezer as part of my long-term food storage plan since we have a generator and we store enough fuel to get us through a couple weeks of a power outage.

By using my freezer as part of the plan, my options expand greatly. I have such a testimony of having food storage that I want everyone to realize that they *can* do it. If you rely on frozen pizza and lasagna on a regular basis, then start budgeting for a new freezer so you can buy 12 lasagnas! You <u>can</u> store what you eat and you <u>can</u> eat what you store! In America, the only limitation is our attitude. Income is not even an excuse if you plan very carefully—it only takes $5 a week to build a year supply a little at a time. Five dollars will purchase one box of hot cereal, a package of pasta and a can of spaghetti sauce if you watch for a sale price. It will also buy 25 lbs of wheat, as another example. If you can only spare $5 each week, you can still do it. With careful planning, you'll reach your goal of a 3-month supply in no time!

Putting Together a Food Storage Meal Plan

The easiest way to be sure you have a food supply that *your* family will eat and you know how to fix is to base it around recipes you already use.

1. Collect recipes for breakfast, lunch, dinner, and snacks that can be converted to fully storable meals. (Check out the suggestion lists in this chapter as well as the other chapters in this section for ideas.)
2. Fill in your 2-week menu plan. (A form has been included at the end of the chapter.) You will need to store enough ingredients to make each meal 6 times. (You can repeat some meals over the 2-week menu plan. If you want to serve pancakes 3 days a week, you can. It is completely up to you.)
3. Multiply the ingredient amounts by the number of times you will serve the recipe and record the totals in the table provided at the end of this chapter.
4. Use your table as your shopping list. Take inventory every 6 months and update amounts.
5. Keep in mind that you should incorporate all food groups over the course of the day, not necessarily in every meal.

Things to think about when choosing recipes:

- Cost of the items in the recipe
- Limit the amount of items that are harder to store (i.e. eggs, meat, cheese)
- Ease of preparation. Some recipes should be simple enough to make without electricity in case you are in a situation where no power is available for a few days. I keep two weeks of meals that fall in this category.
- Shelf-life recommendations are not throw-away dates. There is plenty of nutrition left in the food. Open it and start using it. If there is an odd smell or color change, or the can is bulging, then throw it away.

- Remember that you still need a few "fancy" meals in your plan. Even if your family is in a situation to be living off your food storage, you will still want to prepare a nice meal when company comes or on special occasions. It can also lift everyone's spirits to have a simple meal served on fancy dishes.

Math Helps

As you begin trying to total all of your ingredients, it becomes a huge math problem. Thank goodness for a calculator! Here are a few ideas to help you know just how many pounds of items to purchase since your recipes are in cups, but you purchase the items by the pound.

Conversions (amounts are approximate):

1 lb dry beans = 2 cups	1 lb sugar = 2 ¼ cups
1 lb cornmeal = 3 cups	1 lb brown sugar = 2 ½ cups
1 lb flour = 3.6 cups	1 lb wheat = 2 cups
1 gal honey = 16 cups	1 lb wheat = 4 cups flour
1 lb non-instant powdered milk = 1 gal milk, mixed	1 lb yeast = 29 Tbsp
	1 cup = 16 Tbsp = 48 Tsp

Amount in #10 can (from www.providentliving.org)

Beans, Black 5.5 lbs	Carrots 2.8 lbs
Beans, Pinto 5.2 lbs	Macaroni 3.4 lbs
Beans, White 5.3 lbs	Oats, quick 2.6 lbs
Milk, nonfat dry 4.1 lbs	Oats, regular 2.7 lbs
Rice, White 5.7 lbs	Onions, dry 2.8 lbs
Sugar, Granulated 6.1 lbs	Potato Flakes 1.8 lbs
Wheat, Hard Red 5.8 lbs	Spaghetti 4.3 lbs
Wheat, Hard White 5.8 lbs	White Flour 4.8 lbs
Apple slices 1 lb	

To help you see the process, here is an example of how you can fill out the meal plan. I have only filled out the meals for one day.

A sample day's worth of storable meals:

Breakfast	Pancakes, syrup, canned fruit and milk
Snack	Granola bars
Lunch	Soup and grilled cheese
Snack	Dried fruit
Dinner	Chicken Caesar Tetrazzini, French bread and green beans

Now record all the storable ingredients needed for the recipes in your 2-week menu. (Listing the ingredients in alphabetical order helps you to be able to find it again when you have another recipe that calls for the same ingredient. You can just increase the total amount needed on your master sheet until you have completed adding in all of the recipes you have chosen for your meal plan.) Remember that when you figure out the total amount needed to complete your 3-month supply you need to multiply the amount you would use for one meal by 6 since you need to store enough ingredients to make this meal 6 times. This will give you 12 weeks' worth of ingredients to make your meals. Below you'll see the table filled out for the sample breakfast listed above. Repeat this process with all of the meals you have chosen for your meal plan.

Storage Item	Amount I need	Amount I have	Amount I need to buy
Canned fruit	6 quarts	4 quarts	2 quarts
Pancake mix	18 cups	4 cups	14 cups
Powdered milk	6 quarts = 4.5 cups milk powder	1 #10 can (about 12 cups)	--
Syrup	1 quart	1 gallon	--

When your master list of ingredients is complete, you will know just how much of all the ingredients you need down to the very teaspoon in some cases. When you follow through and purchase enough of these ingredients, you will know you can feed your family meals they will enjoy and look forward to for a period of 3 months without having to worry. What a tremendous blessing!

Many of the recipes you are already making can be stored. Take a little time to explore the chapters of this book that are full of recipes that are storable. You may need to use powdered milk or dehydrated vegetables in some of your favorite recipes. Give them a try. You may be pleasantly surprised by how good they taste.

Before adding a meal to your 2-week plan, try cooking it the fully storable way first. Determine that your family really does like it this way before you store enough ingredients to make it 6 times. There are many recipes in this book to inspire you. They have all been tested by my family and my kids have given me the "thumbs up." I know you'll find some that your family will enjoy also.

2-Week Storable Breakfast Suggestions

Keep in mind that you want nutrition over the course of the day and you don't have to hit all the food groups each meal. To start with, I would recommend storing the basics for a meal and then working to add the extras. For example, store pancake mix, syrup and powdered milk to start with and then add your fruit or hash browns once you have a 3-month supply of the basics.

Breakfasts - (could also be used for dinner sometimes)

Hot cereal, toast, jam, milk

Cold cereal, canned fruit, milk

Homemade granola with dried fruit, milk

Pancakes, syrup, canned fruit, milk or juice

Biscuits and sausage gravy, frozen or dehydrated hash browns, juice

Waffles, jam, syrup, canned fruit, milk or juice

Muffins/fruit bread, yogurt smoothie with homemade yogurt and frozen fruit

Cinnamon rolls/Monkey bread, canned fruit, hot cocoa

Maple bars, yogurt smoothie with homemade yogurt and frozen fruit

Scones, canned fruit, milk

Carnation Instant Breakfast, milk

Rice pudding, toast, milk

Mix and match these ideas to fit the way your family eats. If your family eats cold cereal 5 days a week, then stock up when it's on sale and find a place to stash it. You will need 60 days' worth. We go through a box every 2 days at our house so that would mean storing 30 boxes. If I served pancakes or waffles once each week, I would need 3 cups of mix a week. That makes 36 cups in 3 months. A 10 lb bag of Krusteaz mix holds 40 cups, so one bag is my 3-month supply.

2-Week Storable Lunch Suggestions

Pay attention to what you planned for breakfast as you fill in your lunch menus to make sure you cover the nutrition needs of the family.

Lunches -(could also be used for dinner sometimes)

Main Dish Options

Alfredo Pasta	Pizza/calzone
Macaroni and Cheese	Sloppy Joes
Quesadillas with Homemade Tortillas	Tuna/Chicken/Hamburger Helper
Soup and Grilled Cheese	Canned Ravioli/Spaghetti
Tuna Fish/Salmon Sandwiches	Potato Pancakes (Latkes)
Chicken Salad Sandwiches or Wraps	Rice Pilaf
Peanut Butter Sandwiches	Fried Rice
Tacos or Nachos	Pasta Salad
Chili	

Side Dish Options

Canned Fruit	Pretzels
Canned Vegetables	Baked Apples
Mashed Potatoes	Jello
Fried Potatoes	Pudding
Yogurt Smoothie	Baked Beans
Breadsticks	Pork 'n' Beans
Crackers	

Hopefully these ideas can inspire you as you fill in your 2-week menu. Be sure and customize them to fit the way your family eats. We eat leftovers for lunch 3–4 times each week so I only need 6 days' worth of lunch menus to complete a 2-week menu. If you have a generator and fuel, then you can count your freezer as part of your food storage options which really expands your possibilities.

2-Week Storable Snack Suggestions

No day goes by without me needing to grab a snack for me or my kids. Snacks are a big part of our eating habits. You can't really feel done with your food storage plan until you have taken some time to consider snacks. For the shorter-term of a 3-month supply, many of the premade store-bought snacks work just fine. These are probably what many of you are pulling from on a regular basis already. Just think about purchasing enough to get your family through 3 months. For the longer-term of a year supply, you will need to store the ingredients to make snacks if you needed to. This list is intended to give you ideas. You will find recipes scattered throughout the sections of this book that will work for snacks. You probably have some you use in your own collection as well.

Muffins	Cinnamon Toast	Chips and Salsa
Dried Fruit	Toast and Jam	Tortilla Roll-ups
Snack Mix	Yogurt Smoothies	Instant Pudding
Popcorn	Soft Pretzels	Cold Cereal
Caramel Corn	Pretzels	Potato Chips
Granola Bars	Crackers	Rice Cakes
Cookies	Cheese Ball	Maple Bars
Brownies	Tortilla Chips	
Rice Krispie Treats		

2-Week Storable Dinner Suggestions

Remember that you want nutrition over the course of the day. I filled in my dinner menus first on my meal plan, knowing they would need to be the most substantial meal of the day. After I determined what food groups would be covered with dinner, I filled in the other slots on the menu plan to be sure we had a nutritious day. Just as with lunches, I would recommend storing the items to make the main dish to start with and then add your side dishes once you have a 3-month supply of your main dish ingredients.

The recipe sections of this book are full of recipe ideas for meals that would work for dinner. You are more than welcome to use them in your meal plan. Hopefully this list of main dishes will inspire you and help you realize how many options there really are for dinner. Because of what we store at the house, I can make any one of these fabulous meals any night of the year! It's like having a restaurant menu to choose from every night without worrying if I have the right ingredients. These are only some of the recipes you will find in this book. Are your taste buds aroused yet?

Mexican

Black Bean Soup
Taco Soup
Mexican Lasagna
Mexican Rice
Nachos
Mexican Sweet Pork
Bean and Rice Burritos
Chicken Enchiladas (w/white beans)
Beef Enchiladas
Soft Shell Tacos
White Chicken Chili
Tortilla Soup
Taco Cups

American/Casseroles

Chicken Pot Pie
Potato Casserole
Panquecas
Chicken and Broccoli Casserole
Shepherd's Pie
Rice Casserole
Scalloped Potatoes
Rice Haystacks
Meatballs in Mushroom Gravy
Creamy Italian Chicken

Italian/Pasta

Fettuccine
Alfredo Pasta
Pasta Primavera
Hays' Special/Stove Top Lasagna
Spaghetti
Mediterranean Chicken
Beef Stroganoff
Pasta with Sour Cream Sauce
Chicken Caesar Tetrazzini
Saucy Tarragon Chicken
Pasta Carbonara
Lasagna

Pizza
Chicken Bistro Twist
Pizza Pinwheels
French Bread Pizza

Soups

Potato Cheese Soup
Broccoli Cheese Soup
Clam Chowder
Creamy Chicken Rice Soup
Creamy Chicken Noodle Soup
Navy Bean Soup
Hearty Bean Soup
Lentil Soup
Split Pea Soup
Tortellini Soup
Chili
Beef Stew
Hobo Stew

Chinese

Fried Rice
Stir Fry Noodles
Sweet and Sour Chicken
Orange Chicken
Lemon Chicken

Storing Spices

When I finished calculating what I needed for my meal plan, I found I was very low on most of the spices I needed. Don't hesitate to store spices in larger containers such as pint or quart jars. We have a local grocery store that sells spices and bouillon in bulk so it is very inexpensive to stock up. Keep spices in a cool, dark place to lengthen their shelf-life. They never go bad. Most spices just lose some of their flavor over time so you may need to use a little more than normal. A few spices, such as cayenne pepper, actually become stronger with time so be careful about how much you use.

Feel free to exchange different varieties of the same spice. If you do not have dried, minced onion, then use onion powder, for example. Just season to taste with the variety that you have. If you really hit a period where you need to live off your storage, you will be so very grateful for some chili powder or cumin to give some variety to all the beans you will be eating! Depending on the recipes you choose, there are definitely spices you would miss. Stock up now and know you can serve some flavorful meals any time.

2-Week Menu Plan Form

	Sun	Mon	Tues	Wed	Thurs	Fri	Sat
Breakfast							
Snack							
Lunch							
Snack							
Dinner							

	Sun	Mon	Tues	Wed	Thurs	Fri	Sat
Breakfast							
Snack							
Lunch							
Snack							
Dinner							

Ingredients Master List

Storage Item	Amount I need	Amount I have	Amount I need to buy

Using Your Freezer

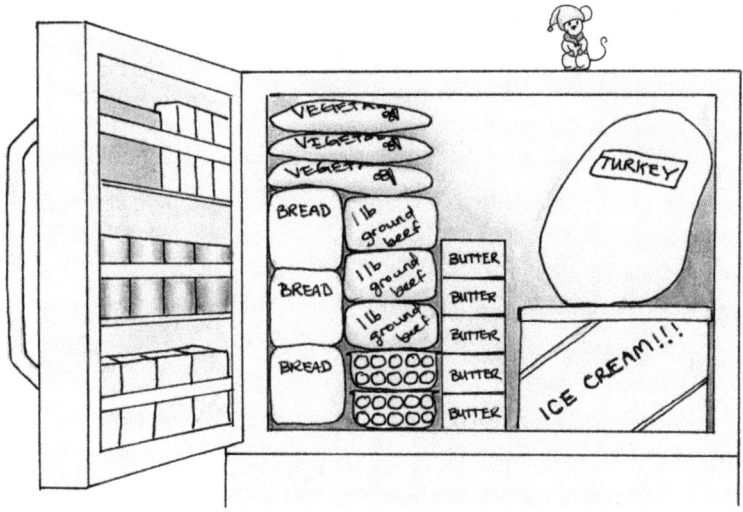

A freezer is a great tool that can make your life so much easier. It's actually the first big item we saved for after getting married. Having a freezer allows you to stock up on items when they are on sale, preserve some of your garden harvest, and cook or bake ahead for busy nights. Our freezer is what got us through five pregnancies that all required bed rest for me for a certain number of months! Over the years, we have experimented to determine what dishes freeze well. Throughout the book, I have noted if a particular recipe freezes well. This section is full of additional freezer ideas.

You have to consider your freezer a necessity when you are thinking about a 3-month supply of food that you eat on a *regular* basis (unless your family loves TVP or canned meats.) With this in mind, you need to have a generator and some gasoline stored to keep your freezer going during a power outage. There are books available to teach the concept of cooking for a day and eating for a month. I've never been able to do an entire day of marathon cooking. My philosophy is to double or triple the batch of something that I know freezes well when I am already making it for a meal. This has worked very well for us. My freezer is always full, but being rotated pretty regularly.

The dinner time rush—which is an intense mothering time of day—goes so much better if I have at least a portion of our meal already precooked and in the freezer.

Some items need to be pulled out in advance and other items I can grab right as I'm preparing the meal.

What I keep in the freezer at all times:

1 large turkey	Lunch meat	Grated zucchini
1 large ham	California style veggies	Bananas
Chicken	Stir fry veggies	Berries
Hamburger	Mixed vegetables	Freezer jam
Meatballs	Green beans	Yeast
Pork/beef roast	Peas	A variety of juices
Pork ribs	Corn	Bread
Pork chops	Peas/carrots combo	Butter
Sausage	Broccoli	Margarine
Hot dogs	Pumpkin	Cool whip

I prefer an upright freezer to a chest freezer because I use it every day. I know that chest freezers are more energy efficient, but I also know I would lose food in the bottom and so the convenience factor is worth the energy trade off. I organize my freezer by dedicating one shelf to premade meals or convenience foods, one shelf to meats, one to fruits and vegetables, etc. This helps me keep on top of what I have and what I may be getting low on.

The more you start thinking in bulk so you can have the food storage you need, the more you will rely on your freezer. You'll be surprised at how much money you save also by purchasing when items are on sale and not grabbing fast food since you have something prepared ahead for those crazy nights.

Some people have asked me about the nutritional value of frozen or canned produce compared to fresh. I've done a fair amount of reading on this topic since I want to be sure I am doing what is nutritionally best for my family. Everything I've read suggests that frozen or canned produce preserved at its peak of ripeness can actually have more vitamins than fresh produce that was picked early and shipped before it was truly ripe. With this in mind, we eat from our garden through the summer months and then preserve what we can to pull us through the winter months. I do purchase a few fresh items when I go shopping, but I do not worry about eating frozen or canned produce on a regular basis. Any produce is better than no produce, which is what we would have in a long-term emergency situation if we hadn't prepared ahead of time.

Precooked Meats

Having meat already precooked can shave 20–30 minutes off of the dinner prep time. Cook your meat in large quantities and package in ziplock bags, label, and freeze. When you need to use some in a recipe, thaw the meat out in the microwave just long enough to break the portion you need out of the ziplock bag. Return the remaining partially frozen meat to the freezer to use another time and continue thawing what you will use for dinner.

To precook hamburger, you can fry two or three pans full on the stove or you can place a large amount in a roasting pan in the oven. Cook at 350° F until it is no longer pink. Break it apart periodically as it cooks.

To precook chicken, you can fill your crockpot and cook until done. This works well if you want shredded chicken for chicken salad or tacos. Sometimes I let it cook too long to dice very well without shredding. You can place a single layer of chicken breasts on a baking sheet and cook in the oven at 350° F until done. You can also dice and cook in a frying pan on the stove. I just can't do as big of a batch that way.

To precook sausage, follow the directions for hamburger.

To precook pork roast for making pulled pork, place in a crockpot and cook on low for 10–12 hours. I usually do it overnight. When it shreds easily with a fork it is done. Remove roast from the crockpot to a baking sheet and pull apart using two forks. It pulls apart easiest when it is still warm. Discard any fat and freeze for later.

To precook ham, turkey, or beef roast, I wait until I am serving it for dinner and then I just plan to freeze the leftovers.

If you freeze precooked hamburger, then you can make:

- Mexican Lasagna
- Taco Filling
- Beef Stroganoff
- Hamburger Helper
- Hays' Special/Stove Top Lasagna
- Sloppy Joes
- Chili
- Taco Soup
- Shepherd's Pie
- Spaghetti
- Tater Tot Casserole
- Warm Bean Dip
- Hobo Stew
- Mashed Potato Casserole

If you freeze precooked chicken, then you can make:

- Homemade Chicken Noodle Soup
- Chicken Tacos
- Rice Haystacks
- Mediterranean Chicken
- Chicken Helper
- Sweet and Sour Chicken
- Chicken Enchiladas
- Chicken Dumplings
- Chicken Pot Pie
- Chicken and Broccoli Casserole

If you freeze pulled pork, then you can make:

>Pulled Pork Sandwiches
>
>Pork Tacos or Enchiladas
>
>Mexican Sweet Pork

If you freeze precooked ham, then you can make:

>Omelets or Quiche
>
>Ham and Corn Chowder
>
>Scalloped Potatoes and Ham
>
>Scrambled Eggs with Ham
>
>Hearty Bean Soup

If you freeze precooked sausage, then you can make:

>Biscuits and Sausage Gravy
>
>Spaghetti/Lasagna
>
>Mountain Man Breakfast
>
>Split Pea Soup
>
>Sausage and White Bean Soup
>
>Breakfast Empanadas

Simple breakfasts that freeze well

>**Pancakes** - Freeze flat on a cookie sheet so they don't stick together, then store in ziplock bags. Heat in the toaster.
>
>**Waffles** – Freeze like pancakes.
>
>**Muffins/fruit bread** – Package in ziplock bags. Take out the night before to thaw.

These are just some ideas to get you thinking. Precooked meats really give you lots of options for fast and easy meals. There are also many recipes available online or in other recipe books that freeze well. Don't be afraid to try a few and pick some of your favorites. Here are some of our family's favorites. We hope you enjoy them.

Breakfast Burritos
A favorite for the entire family!

Eggs, slightly beaten with a little water
Potatoes, peeled and diced (can use frozen)
Salsa
Sour cream
Cheddar cheese, grated
Flour tortillas

Cook potatoes in a small amount of oil. Add eggs and scramble until done. Stir in some salsa. Spread a little sour cream down the center of a flour tortilla. Add some of the egg mixture. Top with cheese. Roll into a burrito and enjoy. **To freeze:** Wrap burritos in paper towel and then place in ziplock bags. **To eat:** Heat in microwave.

Breakfast Empanadas
Feel free to experiment with different fillings to create other "hot pocket" flavors.

Dough:
½ cup butter, softened
3 oz cream cheese, softened
1 cup all-purpose flour

Filling:
6 oz cream cheese, softened
Chopped onions, chives, and green peppers
⅔ cup shredded cheese
5 large eggs, scrambled
Precooked sausage or bacon, crumbled

To make the dough: Cream together the butter and cream cheese. Add the flour and mix until you have a smooth ball. Wrap in plastic wrap and refrigerate a few hours or up to a week. To make filling: Mix cream cheese, chopped onions, chives, peppers, and shredded cheese. Scramble the eggs and stir in sausage or bacon. To assemble empanadas: Roll chilled dough thin and cut into 5-inch circles, using a small bowl as a cutter. Spread cream cheese mixture over each dough circle, leaving a little border around the edge. Top with scrambled egg mixture. Fold each circle in half, pinching edges to seal. Bake on greased baking sheet at 375° F for 15–20 minutes or until golden brown. **To freeze:** Wrap cooled empanadas in paper towel and then place in ziplock bags. Reheat in microwave. You can also freeze these before baking. Just thaw and bake as above.

Breakfast Sandwiches

My husband makes his co-workers' mouths water when he brings these in.

Bagels or English muffins
Eggs, fried
Sausage patty or ham slice, optional
Cheddar cheese, sliced

Fry eggs. Place an egg, meat slice, and cheese slice on each bagel or English muffin. If eating right away, toast bagels or muffins in the oven while frying the eggs. **To freeze:** Wrap sandwiches in paper towel and then place in ziplock bags. Heat in microwave.

Quiche

This is fun to take as a baby gift to give the new mom a quick meal!

1 (9-inch) unbaked pie crust
1 ½ cups shredded cheese
4 tsp all-purpose flour
½ cup cooked ham or sausage
2 eggs, beaten
1 ½ cups evaporated milk
¼ tsp pepper
¼ tsp salt
¼ tsp ground dry mustard
2 tsp dried, minced onion

Prepare pie crust using the recipe found in the storable desserts section. Toss cheese with the flour until it is well coated. Place cheese in the bottom of the pie crust. Sprinkle meat on top of cheese. At this point, you can add ½ cup of additional fillings such as frozen, chopped broccoli or frozen spinach (squeeze dry first.) Combine remaining ingredients in a bowl and mix well. I always make an evaporated milk substitute by mixing ½ cup dry milk powder with 1½ cups warm water. Pour mixture over fillings in pie crust. Bake immediately or freeze for later. **To bake immediately:** Bake at 350° F for 40 minutes or until a knife inserted in the center comes out clean. Cover just the edges of the crust with foil during the last 10 minutes of cooking if it is browning too quickly. **To freeze:** Cover with plastic wrap and then foil. Seal well around the edges and place on a level shelf in the freezer. **To use frozen quiche:** Remove plastic wrap and foil. Cover just the edges of the crust with foil to prevent it from browning too quickly. Bake at 400° F for 60 minutes or until a knife inserted in the center comes out clean.

Chicken Dumplings

Having these dumplings in the freezer gives me a quick dinner option.

3 chicken breasts
1 (8 oz) pkg cream cheese
1 small tub cream cheese, onion & chives
1 small can mushrooms, drained
4 cans refrigerator crescent rolls

Gravy:
½ cup butter
½ cup all-purpose flour
2 cups chicken broth
½ cup reconstituted powdered milk

Dice and cook chicken breasts. Mix cream cheese and mushrooms together. When unrolling crescent rolls, leave two triangles connected to form a square. Place one spoonful of mixture on each dough square. Fold dough over filling and seal all seams. Freeze on a cookie sheet until firm and then store in a freezer bag. **To use frozen dumplings:** Thaw in refrigerator and bake on a cookie sheet at 350° F for 15 minutes. To make gravy, melt butter and add flour. Slowly pour in chicken broth and milk. Stir until smooth over medium high heat. Pour gravy over dumplings before serving. Use 2 cups of water and 2 tsp chicken bouillon to substitute for the broth.

Beef Enchiladas

You can use pulled pork or chicken in place of the hamburger and you can also add cooked dry beans to stretch your meat. We've loved all the combinations.

2 ½ lbs ground beef
⅓ cup dried, minced onion, rehydrated
2 (15 oz) cans red enchilada sauce
1 can cream of mushroom soup

1 can condensed tomato soup
20 flour tortillas
2 ½ cups shredded cheddar cheese
Additional shredded cheddar cheese

In a skillet, cook meat and onion until beef is no longer pink; drain. Combine enchilada sauce and soups; pour about 1 cup into two greased 9x13-inch pans. Stir 1 ½ cups sauce into meat mixture; set remaining sauce aside. Spoon ¼ cup of beef mixture down the center of each tortilla. Top with 2 Tbsp cheese. Roll up tightly; place 10 tortillas seam side down in each pan. Top with remaining sauce. Cover and freeze one pan for up to 3 months. Cover and bake second pan at 350° F for 25–30 minutes. Uncover; sprinkle with additional cheese. Bake 5–10 minutes longer or until cheese is melted. **To use frozen enchiladas:** Thaw in the refrigerator overnight and bake as directed.

Chicken Enchiladas

I freeze this in lunch-size portions for my husband. It is one of his favorites!

12 small flour tortillas
5–6 cups chicken, cooked and cubed
2 cans cream of chicken soup
1 (4 oz) can diced green chilies
2 cups sour cream (plain yogurt)
¾ lb cheddar cheese, grated
¾ lb Monterey jack cheese, grated
1 can black olives, sliced
Chopped onion as desired (rehydrate dried onion)

Combine chicken, soup, chilies, sour cream, olives, onion, and most of the cheese. Spoon ¼ cup of mixture down the center of each tortilla. Roll up tightly; place tortillas seam side down in a 9x13-inch pan. Top with remaining mixture. Sprinkle cheese on top. Cover and freeze for up to 3 months. **To use frozen enchiladas:** Thaw in refrigerator and bake at 350° F for 45–50 minutes or heat in the microwave. I stretch the filling by using rice and white beans instead of all chicken. It still freezes very well. Many times I stack this similar to lasagna to make the prep go faster.

Green Sauce Enchiladas

I experimented after tasting a similar dish at a potluck—it's a new family favorite!

7–8 large flour tortillas
2 cups chicken, cooked and cubed
4 cups cooked navy beans
1 (4 oz) can diced green chilies
1 (8 oz) pkg cream cheese
2 cups cheddar cheese, grated
2–3 Tbsp dried, minced onion, rehydrated
1 large can green enchilada sauce

To make filling, combine chicken, beans, chilies, cream cheese, 1 cup cheese and onion. Add ¼ of the can of enchilada sauce and mix well. Put 2–3 Tbsp enchilada sauce in the bottom of a 9x13-inch pan. Spoon filling down the center of each tortilla. Roll up tightly; place tortillas seam side down in pan. Top with remaining enchilada sauce. Sprinkle remaining cheese on top. Cover and freeze for up to 3 months. **To use frozen enchiladas:** Thaw in refrigerator and bake at 350° F for 45–50 minutes or heat in the microwave.

Chicken Caesar Tetrazzini

This is one of the "fancy" meals I like to store the items to make so we can be ready for unexpected company in a flash. Everyone loves it!

8 oz spaghetti, cooked
2 cups chicken, cooked
1 cup chicken broth
1 cup Caesar salad dressing
1 (4 oz) can mushrooms, drained
½ cup Parmesan cheese
2 Tbsp dry bread crumbs

Combine noodles with chicken. Add broth, dressing, and mushrooms. Mix. Place in a 2 qt casserole dish. Cover and freeze for up to 3 months. **To use frozen pasta:** Thaw. Mix together Parmesan cheese and bread crumbs and sprinkle on top. Bake at 350° F for 25 minutes or heat in the microwave. If using the microwave, wait to put the crumbs on top until just before serving. You can also use 1 cup of water and 1 tsp chicken bouillon to substitute for the broth.

Manicotti with Cheese Stuffing

I often use homemade cottage cheese in this dish. It is delicious!

½ lb mozzarella cheese, diced or grated
2 lbs ricotta or cottage cheese
2 eggs, slightly beaten
½ cup grated Parmesan cheese
1 tsp dried parsley
1 tsp salt
1 tsp sugar
¼ tsp pepper
21 Manicotti noodles
Spaghetti sauce

Boil noodles with 1 Tbsp of oil in the water just until pliable. Combine ingredients to form cheese filling. Stuff each noodle. Place a small amount of sauce in the bottom of a 9x13-inch pan to prevent sticking. Place stuffed noodles on top. Cover with additional sauce. Cover pan with plastic wrap and then foil and freeze for up to 3 months. **To use frozen manicotti:** Thaw in refrigerator. Remove from refrigerator 30 minutes before baking. Remove plastic wrap and replace foil. Bake at 350° F 40–50 minutes or until heated through.

Sausage Spaghetti Pie

I give this as gifts quite often. Everyone loves it!

1 (16 oz) pkg spaghetti
4 eggs, beaten
⅔ cup Parmesan cheese
⅓ cup dried, minced onion, rehydrated
2 cups sour cream (plain yogurt)
2 tsp Italian seasoning

2 lbs pork sausage
2 cups water
2 (6 oz) cans tomato paste
Oregano, basil, garlic (to taste)
1 cup shredded mozzarella cheese
½ cup shredded cheddar cheese

Cook spaghetti according to package directions; drain and place in a large bowl. Add eggs and Parmesan cheese. Transfer to three greased 9-inch pie plates; press mixture onto the bottom and up the sides to form a crust. Set aside. Mix together onions, sour cream and Italian seasoning. Spoon into crusts. In a skillet, cook the sausage over medium heat until no longer pink; drain. Stir in water, tomato paste, and spices. Simmer, uncovered for 5–10 minutes or until thickened. Spoon over sour cream mixture. Sprinkle with cheeses. Cover and freeze for up to 3 months. **To use frozen pies:** Completely thaw in refrigerator. Remove from refrigerator 30 minutes before baking. Bake at 350° F for 35–40 minutes or until heated through.

Sweet and Sour Chicken

By the time your rice is cooked, dinner can be thawed and on the table.

5 chicken breasts
2 medium onions
2 medium green peppers
1 (20 oz) can pineapple chunks

Sauce:
¼ cup cornstarch
¾ cup sugar

¾ cup red wine vinegar
¾ cup chicken broth
6 Tbsp catsup
3 Tbsp soy sauce
1 ½ tsp ground ginger
¾ tsp salt
¾ tsp crushed red pepper

Dice chicken breasts. Fry in 1 Tbsp oil until done. Set aside. Slice onions and peppers in thin strips. Fry in 1 Tbsp oil until tender. Set aside. Stir sauce ingredients together in a pan. Add pineapple chunks juice and all. Stir until sauce boils and thickens. Add chicken and vegetables to sauce. Freeze in containers. **To use frozen sauce:** Thaw and reheat in microwave. Serve over rice.

Lasagna

When I go to the work to make lasagna, I always make more than one.

1 (8 oz) pkg lasagna noodles
3 eggs, beaten
¾ cup Parmesan cheese
6 cups cottage cheese
1 ½ tsp dried parsley

1 ½ lbs sausage or hamburger, browned
1 (6 oz) can tomato paste
5 cups spaghetti sauce
Carrots, zucchini, black olives, spinach
4 cups shredded cheese

Prepare two 8x11-inch pans by spraying them with cooking oil. Combine eggs, Parmesan cheese, cottage cheese, and parsley. In a separate bowl, combine meat, tomato paste, spaghetti sauce and any vegetables you would like to add. (Precook your vegetables before adding. I usually add 3–4 cups of vegetables. You can use fresh, frozen, or dehydrated.) Place 1 cup of sauce mixture in the bottom of each pan. Top with a layer of noodles. Spread ¼ of the cottage cheese mixture on top of the noodles in each pan. Top with ¼ of the sauce mixture. Sprinkle with 1 cup of cheese in each pan. Repeat layers. Cover with plastic wrap and then foil. Freeze for up to 3 months. **To use frozen lasagna:** Thaw in refrigerator. Remove from refrigerator 30 minutes before baking. Remove plastic wrap and replace foil. Bake at 375° F for 35–40 minutes. Uncover and bake an additional 10 minutes. Let stand 5–10 minutes before serving. Or, bake frozen lasagna about 1 hour and 20 minutes. Remove foil and bake an additional 10 minutes. Let stand 5–10 minutes before serving. I often use homemade cottage cheese in this dish.

Party Meatballs

No one can ever guess the ingredients in this simple dish—it's always a hit!

Grape jelly
Heinz Chili sauce

Frozen meatballs

Combine equal parts of jelly and chili sauce in a pan. Heat until melted. Combine precooked meatballs and sauce in a crockpot and simmer until it is time to serve. This is great for potluck dinners. Just bring toothpicks. You can get chili sauce by the ketchup in most grocery stores. You can also substitute Little Smokies for the meatballs.

Meatloaf, Meatballs, or Hamburgers

Stock up on hamburger when it is on sale and then make a large batch of this mixture. You will have many quick dinners ready to go.

3 lbs hamburger, thawed
1 ½–2 cups quick oats
3 Tbsp dried, minced onion, rehydrated
1 Tbsp dried, minced garlic, rehydrated

½ cup dehydrated carrots, rehydrated
3 eggs
Salt and pepper to taste

Combine all ingredients in a large bowl. Mix well. You can use 2 carrots, grated to replace the dehydrated carrots. You can also use bread crumbs, cracker crumbs, or pretzel crumbs to replace the oatmeal. Choose hamburger with 15% fat for the best tasting option.

For meatloaf: Shape into large loaf and cook in loaf pan at 350° F for 40–50 minutes or until cooked through. Make individual size meatloaves for a quicker dinner. Place side by side in rectangular baking dish and cook at 350° F for 20–25 minutes or until cooked through. We always top our meatloaf with a thin layer of tomato sauce or ketchup just before serving. You can freeze before cooking for later use. To use frozen meatloaf, thaw and then bake as above.

For meatballs: Shape into balls and place side by side on baking sheet. Bake at 350° F for 15–20 minutes or until cooked through. Cool, package in ziplock bags and freeze for later use.

For hamburger patties: Shape into patties and freeze in a single layer on a baking sheet. When frozen, transfer to a ziplock bag and freeze for later use. When ready to cook, thaw slightly and then grill or cook as usual. You can cook before freezing if you need to be able to heat and eat quickly.

Meatballs in Mushroom Gravy
Simple and delicious!

10–12 frozen meatballs
1 can cream of mushroom soup
2 tsp dried, minced onion
2 tsp dried, minced garlic
Salt and pepper to taste
1 (4 oz) can mushrooms, optional

Combine all ingredients in saucepan or crockpot. Cook until meatballs are thawed and heated through. Add a little water if gravy is too thick. Serve over rice or egg noodles. You can stir in a spoonful of sour cream or plain yogurt just before serving to achieve a stroganoff flavor.

Twice Baked Potatoes
Always a hit at our house. I make a large batch knowing they freeze so well.

8–10 large potatoes
2 cups sour cream (plain yogurt)
1 cup reconstituted powdered milk
1 stick butter or margarine
2 cups cheddar cheese, grated
½ cup fully cooked bacon bits
Salt and pepper to taste
Green onions, sliced (optional)

Bake potatoes. Allow to cool for 10–15 minutes. Slice in half lengthwise and scoop out the insides, creating potato boats. Add sour cream, milk, butter, 1 cup cheese, bacon, salt and pepper to the insides. Add some green onions if desired. Mix with a mixer until smooth and creamy. Spoon this mixture back into the potato boats. Sprinkle the remaining cheese on top and add a few green onions for color. Place in foil pan. Cover and freeze for up to 3 months. **To use frozen potatoes:** Thaw in refrigerator. Bake at 350° F 30–45 minutes, until heated through. May also be heated in the microwave.

Potato Dish (a.k.a. Funeral Potatoes)

This is a favorite of adults and kids alike.

8–10 potatoes
2 cans cream of chicken soup
2 cups sour cream (plain yogurt)
1 cup cheddar cheese, grated
Salt, onion powder – to taste
Crushed corn flakes and butter

Bake potatoes then peel and grate. Mix soup, sour cream, cheese and seasonings together. Stir in potatoes. Push into 9x13-inch pan. Cover and freeze for up to 3 months. **To use frozen potatoes:** Thaw in refrigerator. Melt butter and stir corn flakes into it. Put corn flakes on top of potato mixture. Cover pan with foil and bake at 350° F 30–45 minutes, until heated through. May also be heated in the microwave. Wait to add cornflakes until hot if heating in the microwave.

Angel Food Cake Roll

This is the perfect dessert to serve at a shower—even diabetics can enjoy a slice if you use sugar-free pudding.

1 (16 oz) angel food cake mix
powdered sugar
1 (8 oz) carton strawberry yogurt
1 pkg instant vanilla pudding
3 drops red food coloring, optional
Milk (use reconstituted powdered milk)
2 cups frozen whipped topping, thawed

Line a jelly-roll pan with waxed paper. Prepare cake according to package directions. Pour batter into prepared pan. Bake at 350° F for 15–20 minutes or until cake springs back when lightly touched. Cool for 5 minutes. Turn cake out onto a kitchen towel dusted with powdered sugar. Gently peel off waxed paper. Roll up jelly-roll style in the towel, starting with a short side. Cool on a wire rack. In a bowl, whisk the yogurt, pudding mix and food coloring. Add enough milk to make a thick, creamy texture. Fold in whipped topping. Unroll cake; spread filling evenly over cake to within ½ inch of edges. Roll up. Roll in plastic wrap and freeze. Remove from freezer 30 minutes before slicing. Allow slices to thaw a little longer before serving.

Ice Cream Crunch

Pick your favorite ice cream flavor and dress it up a little with this easy recipe.

½ cup butter or margarine
½ cup brown sugar, packed
3 cups Rice Krispies cereal

2 cups flaked coconut
1 cup chopped nuts
½ gallon ice cream, softened (any flavor)

In a pan over medium heat, cook butter and brown sugar until butter is melted and sugar is dissolved. Stir in remaining ingredients. Press half of mixture into greased 9x13-inch pan. Spread ice cream over crust and top with remaining mixture. Freeze until firm. To serve, allow to soften slightly and cut into squares.

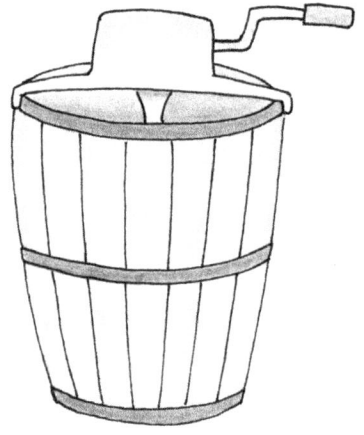

Snickerdoodles

Many cookies freeze well in the dough form—here is just one of our favorites!

½ cup butter
½ cup shortening
1 ½ cups sugar
2 eggs

2 ¾ cups all-purpose flour
¼ tsp salt
1 tsp baking soda

Cream butter, shortening, sugar, and eggs. Add dry ingredients. Roll into balls and place on cookie sheet to freeze. Transfer to ziplock bag when frozen. **To use frozen dough:** Take out as many as you want to bake. Thaw just until sticky. Roll in cinnamon and sugar. Place on a greased cookie sheet to thaw a little longer; press down lightly. Bake at 400° F 8–10 minutes.

Storable Meals

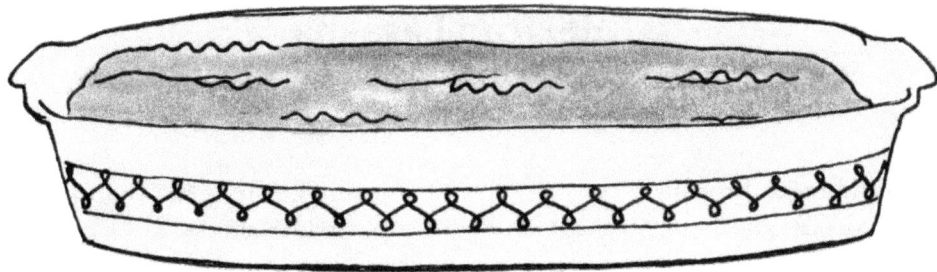

All the ingredients for the recipes in this section can either be stored in your pantry or freezer. They are all kid friendly and most of them can be done in 30 minutes or less. The bulk of these recipes would be good for lunch or dinner. There are a few at the end of the section that we use for breakfast. There are plenty of other ideas throughout the other sections of this book. It's pretty amazing to think that with what I store, I have the option of making over 50 complete meals at anytime. It's like choosing from a restaurant menu every meal. A well-stocked pantry and freezer give you limitless possibilities!

To make a recipe storable, you usually only need to make a few changes. Substitute reconstituted powdered milk for the milk, and use dehydrated, canned, or frozen fruits and vegetables instead of fresh. I'm sure that as you look through your own collection of recipes with these thoughts in mind you'll find many of your family's favorites are more storable than you thought.

There are a few items I've discovered over the years that I just love because they are storable and they speed up my time in the kitchen. I love the bottled minced garlic since I don't have to wait for the dried, minced garlic to rehydrate. It tastes just as good as fresh garlic in my opinion. I also love the precooked real bacon bits. I hardly ever cook bacon anymore and don't have to bother with the mess. It is so easy to drop bacon into soups and salads. It gives us a little bit of protein and a whole lot of flavor. I also find myself using dehydrated vegetables often. I love that I don't have to spend my time peeling and chopping all the vegetables for the soup. I really go through more dehydrated vegetables in the winter months when I make more soup. I just drop a handful into the pot and let them rehydrate as the soup simmers. These same vegetables work well in casseroles and sauces too. I just rehydrate them in a small amount of hot water before adding them to the recipe.

Mexican-Style Meals

Mexican Lasagna

If you have precooked hamburger, this can be done and on the table in less than 15 minutes!

½ lb hamburger, browned
6 flour tortillas
1 can refried beans
1 cup sour cream (plain yogurt)
1 cup cheddar cheese
1 cup salsa

Layer in a round pan like you would lasagna. Start with salsa on the bottom so nothing sticks to the pan. Top with cheese. Cover with foil and bake at 350° F for 30 minutes or until heated through. You can also heat in the microwave. This freezes very well. Just thaw and heat when needed. We love this made with the whole wheat flour tortillas.

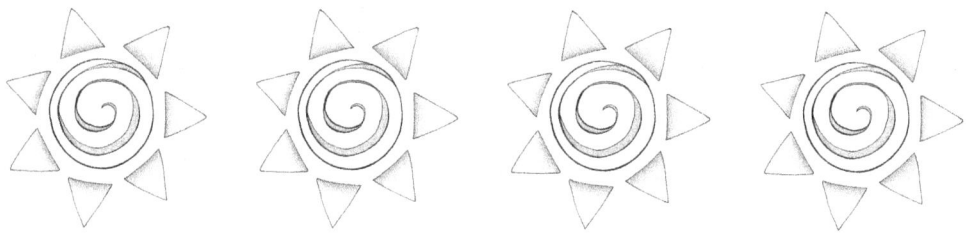

Chicken Tacos

This is a fun recipe shared by my sister. It is an easy one to take to a potluck.

2–3 frozen chicken breast halves
1 pkg fajita seasoning mix
1 can corn, drained
1 can kidney beans, rinsed
1 can black beans, rinsed
1 can sliced black olives, optional

Combine the chicken and the fajita seasoning in a crockpot. Cook on high for 3 hours. Remove from crockpot and cut chicken into bite-size pieces. Add back to crockpot with the remaining ingredients. Cook on low for an additional 30 minutes or until heated through. Use as filling for tortillas or serve over tortilla chips. Top with your favorite taco toppings. You can substitute 1 ½ cups of cooked kidney beans and 1 ½ cups of cooked black beans for the canned beans. The leftovers freeze very well.

Taco Soup

Serve with a dollop of sour cream and shredded cheese, if available, for a tasty winter meal.

2 (15 oz) cans kidney beans, rinsed
2 (15 oz) cans diced tomatoes
1 (15 oz) can corn, drained
1 lb hamburger
1–2 tsp taco seasoning
1 Ranch seasoning packet, optional
¼ cup dry onions

Combine all ingredients in a pan or crockpot. Add water depending on how much liquid you like. Heat through. You can use 3 cups precooked dry beans—kidney, pinto, or red beans work equally as well. The leftovers freeze very well.

Flour Tortillas

Making tortillas is a fun activity for our family. All the kids like to take turns rolling them out.

3 cups all-purpose flour
1 ½ tsp baking powder
1 ½ tsp salt
2 Tbsp shortening
1 cup warm water

Mix flour, baking powder, salt, and shortening together with your hands. Add warm water. Work into a soft, pliable dough. It should not be sticky, but you may need to add a little more water. Divide into several small balls and place on a tray. Cover with a moist paper towel and allow to sit for at least one hour or up to 8 hours. This makes them much easier to roll out. Cut the seams off a gallon-size ziplock bag creating two pieces of heavier plastic. Roll each ball out between the two pieces of plastic as thin as possible. Cook on a hot, ungreased griddle like you would pancakes. Usually the first one is ready to turn about when the second one is rolled out. Cover with a kitchen towel or place in a tortilla warmer until ready to serve.

Corn Tortillas
You can't beat a homemade tortilla!

1 cup cornmeal
1 cup all-purpose flour
¾ tsp salt

¼ cup shortening
⅔ cup hot water

Mix dry ingredients in a bowl. Cut in shortening, leaving walnut size chunks. Stir in water and knead for 1 minute. Divide dough into 12 equal pieces. Cover with a moist paper towel and allow to sit for at least one hour or up to 8 hours. This makes them much easier to roll out. Cut the seams off a gallon-size ziplock bag creating two pieces of heavier plastic. Roll each ball out between the two pieces of plastic as thin as possible. Cook on a hot, ungreased griddle 30 seconds each side. For chips: Cut tortillas into quarters and fry in hot oil until crisp. Salt if desired.

Whole Wheat Flour Tortillas
We love these in the Mexican Lasagna recipe so I usually whip one together with the leftover tortillas and freeze the entire lasagna for later.

4 cups whole wheat flour
1 cup all-purpose flour
2 tsp salt

½ – ¾ cup shortening
1 ½ cups boiling water

Mix dry ingredients together in a large bowl. Rub the shortening in by hand until the dough is the texture of oatmeal. Make a well in the center and pour in the boiling water. Mix with a fork until the water is all mixed in. Sprinkle with a little additional flour and knead with your hands until the dough does not stick to your fingers. Divide into balls about the size of golf balls and place on a tray. Cover with a moist paper towel and allow to sit for at least one hour or up to 8 hours. This makes them much easier to roll out. Cut the seams off a gallon-size ziplock bag creating two pieces of heavier plastic. Roll each ball out between the two pieces of plastic as thin as possible. Place a tortilla on a hot griddle. As soon as you see a bubble on top (in about 10 seconds) flip the tortilla over. Cook for about 30 seconds. Flip and cook the other side for an additional 30 seconds. Roll out the next tortilla while you wait for one to cook. Continue until all the balls are done. Store your cooked tortillas between two kitchen towels to keep them warm and soft before serving. These freeze well.

Taco Filling

You are only limited by your imagination as to what you put together to fill a tortilla.

There are lots of options for taco fillings. Just make a mix of items your family likes. Possible options are: black beans, pinto beans, kidney beans, refried beans, rice, hamburger, chicken, pulled pork, corn, onions, peppers, salsa, diced tomatoes, tomato sauce, taco seasoning, fajita seasoning, or chili powder. Wrap in your favorite tortillas or serve as a taco salad over chips.

Taco Cups or Taco Nests

The kids call these nests since they resemble bird's nests when filled.

3 cups biscuit mix
Taco filling
Salsa

Lettuce, if available
Shredded cheese

Mix biscuit mix with approx. 1 cup of water to form dough that is not too sticky. Divide into 12 pieces. Roll each piece out into a 3 ½-inch circle. Turn muffin pan upside down and spray with oil. Press each biscuit over a muffin cup. Bake at 350° F 10–12 minutes or until lightly browned. Fill each cup with taco filling and add any toppings you like.

Warm Bean Dip

A friend brought this for dinner one of the times I was on bed rest. She knew just what our family would love!

1 lb hamburger, browned
1 can refried beans
Salsa

Sour cream (plain yogurt)
Shredded cheese
Sliced black olives

Layer hamburger, refried beans, salsa, sour cream, cheese, and sliced olives. Heat and top with fresh tomatoes if desired. Serve with tortilla chips.

Soft Shell Tacos
So simple, yet delicious!

Shell:
2 cups cold water
2 eggs
1 cup corn meal
1 cup all-purpose flour
¼ tsp salt

Filling:
2 cans pork 'n beans
½ lb hamburger, browned
Taco seasoning
Shredded cheese

Use dried or frozen eggs, if needed. Mix and pour a small amount into a non-stick frying pan. Spread out into a very thin pancake, similar to how you cook crepes. Flip once to complete cooking. Fill with taco filling made from pork 'n beans and hamburger, seasoned with taco seasoning. Top with shredded cheese before rolling up. These must be eaten with a fork. You cannot pick them up.

Mexican Sweet Pork
This becomes a speedy dinner if you already have pulled pork cooked and frozen in the freezer.

1 pork picnic roast
1 cup medium salsa
1 cup brown sugar, packed
½ cup chicken broth, optional

Place pork roast in a crockpot and cook on low for 12–15 hours. I usually put the roast in just before going to bed. Test the pork by stabbing it with a fork and twisting. If the meat shreds easily, it is ready. Remove from the crockpot and place on a baking sheet. Using two forks, pull the pork apart and separate out all the visible fat and bone pieces. It pulls apart more easily when it is still warm. Combine 4 cups of the shredded pork with the salsa, and brown sugar. Add a small amount of pork juices or chicken broth if the mixture seems too dry. Return this all to the crockpot. Heat through and serve wrapped in tortillas or top a taco salad with it.

Tamale Casserole

You can find canned tamales near the canned chili at our local grocery stores. Sometimes they are in a Hispanic isle. I've always used the Hormel brand.

2 cans of tamales
2 cups rice, cooked
2 cans chili

Grated cheese
Sour cream or plain yogurt

Empty the cans of tamales into a 9x13-inch pan or two 8x8-inch pans. Remove and discard papers then cut into bite sized pieces. Spread evenly in the pan. Cover evenly with cooked rice. Spread the 2 cans of chili over the rice and top with cheese. Bake at 375° F for 30–45 minutes or heat in the microwave. Top with a dollop of sour cream or plain yogurt when serving. This freezes very well.

Tortilla Soup

This is a fun soup that you can turn into a mix to give away to a friend.

1 cup rice
8–10 cups water
1 can diced tomatoes with green chilies
1 can chicken breast
2 Tbsp chicken bouillon
2 tsp sweetened lemonade drink mix
1 tsp lemon pepper

1 tsp dried cilantro
½ tsp garlic powder
½ tsp cumin
½ tsp salt
¼ cup dried, minced onion
2+ cups slightly crushed tortilla chips

In a large soup pot, add the rice and water. Adjust the water amount depending on how much broth you like. Add the can of diced tomatoes and green chilies, the can of chicken, and the seasonings. Bring to a boil; lower the heat, cover and simmer for 20–30 minutes until rice is tender. Add tortilla chips and simmer 5 more minutes. You can use 1 Tbsp of lemon juice to replace the lemonade drink mix. By using the drink mix, you can turn this into a mix and combine all the seasonings in a small ziplock bag just ready to speed up dinner prep one night.

American-Style Dinners

Chicken Pot Pie

Use the biscuit mix recipe found in the Pantry Mix section of this book to give you an inexpensive alternative to store-bought mix.

2 cups diced vegetables, fresh or frozen
1 cup chicken, cooked and cubed
1 can cream of chicken soup
1 cup biscuit mix
½ cup milk
1 egg

Combine vegetables, chicken, and soup in ungreased 9 inch pie pan. Stir remaining ingredients together with a fork and pour over vegetable mixture. Bake at 400° F for 30–45 minutes or until golden brown. I often use dehydrated vegetables. Just rehydrate them first. Reconstitute powdered milk to substitute for the milk and use dried or frozen eggs, if needed, without any change in flavor. Also, check out the recipes for making your own biscuit mix and cream of chicken soup substitute in later sections of this book. I make this recipe with these substitutes all the time.

Potato/Tater Tot Casserole

This is a favorite of my boys. I am always met with, "Oh, yum!" when I tell them what's for dinner.

4 cups dry hash browns
1 lb hamburger
1 can green beans, drained
2 Tbsp dried, minced onion
1 can cream of mushroom soup
1 cup sour cream (plain yogurt)
2 cups reconstituted powdered milk
Garlic, salt and pepper

Cover hash browns with water in a large pan. Bring to a boil and then turn off the heat. Allow hash browns to soak for 15–20 minutes. Place in 9x13-inch pan. Add meat, beans, and onions. Mix soup, sour cream, milk, and seasonings to make a gravy. Pour over potatoes. Cover and bake at 350° F 45–60 minutes or until bubbly and potatoes are tender. This also cooks well in the microwave or the crockpot. Just stir a few times while it is heating. I use reconstituted powdered milk in place of the milk all the time. We also love this casserole made with a 32 oz bag of tater tots instead of the hash browns.

Chicken and Broccoli Casserole

This has been a family recipe for years—it is true comfort food.

1–2 lbs chicken, cooked and cubed
2 cups frozen broccoli
2 cans cream of chicken soup
½ cup mayonnaise
½ cup sour cream (plain yogurt)
1 Tbsp lemon juice
1–2 tsp lemon pepper
1 cup bread crumbs
1 cup cheddar cheese, grated

Mix soup, mayonnaise, sour cream and seasonings together. Layer chicken, broccoli, soup mixture and cheese in a 9x13-inch pan. Top with bread crumbs. Cover with foil and bake at 325° F 30–45 minutes. This also cooks well in the microwave or crockpot. Stir a few times while it is heating. Sprinkle bread crumbs and cheese on top just before serving. We love this served over rice. This casserole freezes well. Thaw and then bake as above.

Tips for Using a Crockpot

Many dishes can be cooked in a crockpot or slow cooker. I learned to love my crockpot when I had two young children. They would both take naps in the afternoon and then seem to *need* me constantly during the time that I should have been preparing dinner. I learned that if I put something in the crockpot during their nap time we could eat on schedule. Now I rely on it to have dinner ready even when I have to run kids to scouts or soccer practice, etc.

Soups, stews, and casseroles with gravy or sauce do well in the crockpot. If the traditional recipe suggests cooking or baking for 25–30 minutes, cook it in the crockpot on high for 2–3 hours or on low for 5–6 hours. Soups and stews can just slowly cook without any stirring. I have found that casseroles cook on the outside first so I remove the lid and stir a couple of times during the cooking cycle so we don't end up with a crusty outside and a cold middle. If my recipe calls for a breadcrumb topping or something similar, I sprinkle that on just before serving. Check online for more suggestions on converting recipes for use in a slow cooker.

Creamy Italian Chicken

Enjoyed by adults and kids alike—you can serve it over rice or pasta.

1–2 lbs chicken, cooked and cubed
2 cans cream of chicken soup
1 ½ cups plain yogurt

1 pkg dry Italian Salad dressing mix
⅓ cup dehydrated celery
Cooked rice or pasta

Mix soup, yogurt, salad dressing packet and celery together. Place chicken in a casserole dish or crockpot. You can also heat this in a pan on the stove or in the microwave. Cover chicken with soup mixture and heat through, stirring occasionally. On the stove top or in the microwave it takes 10 minutes or less. In the oven, cover with foil and bake at 325° F for 30–45 minutes. In the crockpot, cook on low for 3–4 hours or on high for 1–2 hours. Stir a few times while it is heating in the crockpot to prevent it from getting overdone on the sides and bottom. Serve over rice or pasta. This casserole freezes well. Thaw and then bake as above.

Poppy Seed Chicken

This is a favorite of many families. Using homemade plain yogurt in place of sour cream makes it fully storable.

1–2 lbs chicken, cooked and cubed
2 cans cream of chicken soup
1 ½ cups plain yogurt
Onion and garlic powder to taste

1 Tbsp poppy seeds
1 sleeve Ritz crackers, crushed
¼–½ cup melted butter
Cooked rice or pasta

Mix soup, yogurt, and seasonings together. Place chicken in a casserole dish or crockpot. You can also heat this in a pan on the stove or in the microwave. Cover chicken with soup mixture and heat through, stirring occasionally. On the stove top or in the microwave it takes 10 minutes or less. In the oven, cover with foil and bake at 325° F for 30–45 minutes. In the crockpot, cook on low for 3–4 hours or on high for 1–2 hours. Stir a few times while it is heating in the crockpot to prevent it from getting overdone on the sides and bottom. When warm, combine crushed crackers with melted butter and poppy seeds. Sprinkle across the top. We also enjoy this made without the crackers. I just add the poppy seeds to the soup mixture instead. Serve over rice or pasta. This casserole freezes well. Thaw and then bake as above.

Mashed Potato Casserole

My boys often request this meal for their birthdays. I never complain because it is so simple.

1 lb hamburger, browned
2 cans cream of mushroom soup
1 can green beans, drained

Mashed potatoes (2 cups potato pearls)
Cheddar cheese, grated

Layer ingredients in the order listed in a 9x13-inch pan. Cover with foil and bake at 350° F for 30–45 minutes or cover with plastic wrap and heat in the microwave. For the mashed potatoes, I love the potato pearls that are available at the LDS cannery, but you can use any instant potatoes. Just make 3–4 cups to cover your pan.

Pork Chop Supper

I love meals I can do in the crockpot. It frees up my hands to help with homework or gives me the time I need to run kids to their activities.

2–3 potatoes, quartered
4–5 carrots, cut in sticks
4 pork loin chops

1 medium onion, quartered
1 can cream of mushroom soup
¼ cup water

Place potatoes and carrots in slow cooker. Top with pork chops and onions. You can use ¼ cup dried, minced onion in place of a fresh onion. Stir soup and water together and pour over the top. Cook on low for 6–8 hours.

Rice Casserole

This is another meal from my youth. Simple and quick is the theme to most of the meals my mom served as she tried to keep 11 of us fed.

2 cups rice
2 cans cream of mushroom soup
2 cans green beans, drained

½ lb hamburger, browned, optional
½ tsp cumin
Onion, garlic, salt, and pepper to taste

Cook the rice. Stir in remaining ingredients. Heat through and serve.

Slick Rock Chicken

Over the years, I have come to realize that some of the pickiest kids will try something new if you can come up with a fun name for it.

3–4 chicken breasts
1 can cream of mushroom soup
1 cup sour cream (plain yogurt)
1 box chicken flavored stuffing mix

Mix stuffing according to package instructions. Combine soup and sour cream or plain yogurt. Place chicken in 9x13-inch pan or crockpot. Top with soup mixture and then with prepared stuffing. Cover with foil and bake at 350° F for 45 minutes or cook in crockpot on high for 3–4 hours. Sometimes I use cubed, precooked chicken in this recipe to speed things up. Then you only have to heat it through. This is a recipe that was shared with me by a missionary companion years ago. Her family called it "Slick Rock Chicken" for fun.

Salmon Cakes

Who knew something so good could be made from your food storage!

1 (14 oz) can salmon, bones removed
2 eggs
1 cup bread crumbs
¼ cup reconstituted powdered milk
2 Tbsp oil
Chopped celery
Chopped onion
Salt and pepper to taste

Dill Sauce:
¼ cup mayonnaise
¼ sour cream (plain yogurt)
1 ½ tsp lemon juice
¾ tsp dry dill
½ tsp sugar
⅛ tsp pepper

Mix all ingredients for salmon cakes like you do meatloaf. Add more milk as needed to make the mixture moist enough to hold together. Use dried or frozen eggs as well as vegetables, if needed. Shape into 2-inch patties. Line cookie sheet with foil and spray with oil. Bake at 375° F for 15–20 minutes. Flip over and bake an additional 5 minutes. You can also cook these in a frying pan or on an electric griddle. They are done much faster this way. Serve with dill sauce. Leftover salmon cakes freeze well so don't hesitate to double the batch.

Grilled Salmon

When you count what is in your freezer as part of your food storage, fancy meals are a snap to pull together no matter what is happening in your life.

Frozen salmon, thawed
Dried, minced onion
Dehydrated green pepper

1–2 tsp oil
Dried basil, oregano
Salt and pepper

Rehydrate onion and green pepper. Choose the amounts based on the size of salmon you are cooking. Place the salmon on a large piece of foil. Top with onions, peppers, herbs, salt and pepper. Drizzle a little oil over the top. Wrap tightly in the foil. Grill over medium heat for 20–25 minutes, turning once or place on a baking sheet and bake in the oven at 350° F for 20–25 minutes. Fish is done when it flakes easily with a fork. Serve with the dill sauce from the Salmon Cakes recipe.

Baked Chicken Strips

Kids and adults alike can't resist this healthy version of a fun restaurant meal.

Frozen chicken breast, partially thawed
Melted butter

1 sleeve saltine crackers, crushed
Mrs. Dash or lemon pepper seasoning

Crush crackers by placing them in a ziplock bag and rolling over them with a rolling pin. Dump out onto a plate. Sprinkle some Mrs. Dash seasoning over the cracker crumbs and mix well. Cut the partially thawed chicken into strips. Line a baking sheet with foil. Dip chicken strips in melted butter and then in the cracker crumbs, turning to coat. Place on baking sheet. Drizzle any leftover butter over the strips. Bake at 350° F for 20–25 minutes, or until the chicken juices run clear. Be sure and have BBQ sauce available for dipping.

Chicken Bistro Twist
This looks fancy and tastes even better!

Soft garlic breadstick dough
1 cup chicken, cooked and chopped
⅓ cup dehydrated peppers
1 Tbsp dried basil
1 tsp dried, minced garlic

¼ cup chopped black olives
¼ cup mayonnaise
¼ cup Parmesan cheese
½ cup shredded cheese

Check out the bread section for the garlic breadstick dough recipe and make a double batch. After the first rise, punch it down and divide in half. While it is rising, rehydrate peppers and garlic. Make a chicken salad filling out of all the ingredients. On an oiled surface, roll each piece into a 14x10-inch rectangle. Spread half of the filling down each loaf. Cut 1-inch wide strips using kitchen scissors down either side of the dough, cutting from the outside edge of the dough into the edge of the filling. Braid the loaf by folding top strips together across the filling and continue alternating strips until you reach the bottom. (This will look similar to a Danish braid.) Spray the tops of each loaf with oil and sprinkle with Parmesan cheese and Italian seasoning or some of the bread dipping herb mix found in the bread section of this book. Bake at 350° F for 25–30 minutes. If browning too quickly, cover loosely with foil before baking the final 5 minutes. Let stand for 10 minutes before slicing. **To freeze:** Remove from oven after 25 minutes of cooking. Allow to cool. Wrap in a few layers of plastic wrap and freeze. **To use frozen loaf:** Thaw and wrap in foil. Place on a baking sheet and bake at 350° F for 10–15 minutes or until heated through.

Rice Haystacks
This is an easy recipe to do for a crowd. Heat the gravy in a crockpot so it stays warm for the entire crew.

Rice, cooked
Vegetables, chopped
Cream of chicken soup

Pineapple chunks
Cheddar cheese, grated
Chow mein noodles

Make gravy by heating the soup using only half a can of water per can of soup. Season with lemon pepper. You can also add chicken chunks if you'd like. Put rice on your plate, top with chopped carrots, celery, olives, etc. Cover with gravy. Top with pineapple, cheese, and chow mein noodles.

Pepperoni Pizza Twists
A fancy version of pepperoni pizza

Soft garlic breadstick dough
8 oz tomato sauce
Pepperoni slices, chopped
Black olives, chopped
Shredded cheese

½ tsp dried oregano
½ tsp dried basil
¼ tsp garlic powder
¼ tsp onion powder

Make a double batch of the soft garlic breadstick recipe found in the bread section. After the first rise, punch it down and divide in half. On an oiled surface, roll each piece into a 14x10-inch rectangle. Mix seasonings with tomato sauce and spread a thin layer on each rectangle. Top each with a thin layer of chopped pepperoni, olives, and cheese. Slice each rectangle in half the long way giving you 4 (14x5-inch) rectangles. Roll each piece up jelly-roll style, starting from a long side; seal seams and ends. Place one loaf seam side down on a greased baking sheet. Place 2nd loaf seam side down next to the first loaf. Twist loaves together three times and seal ends. Repeat this step with the remaining two loaves on the same baking sheet. Spray the tops of each loaf with oil and sprinkle with Parmesan cheese and Italian seasoning or some of the bread dipping herb mix found in the bread section of this book. Bake at 350° F for 25–30 minutes. If browning too quickly, cover loosely with foil before baking the final 5 minutes. Let stand for 10 minutes before slicing. Serve with pizza sauce for dipping if desired. **To freeze:** Remove from oven after 25 minutes of cooking. Allow to cool. Wrap in a few layers of plastic wrap and freeze. **To use frozen loaf:** Thaw and wrap in foil. Place on a baking sheet and bake at 350° F for 10–15 minutes or until heated through.

For a quicker version: On an oiled surface, roll each piece into a 14x10-inch rectangle. Mix seasonings with tomato sauce and spread a thin layer down the center of each rectangle. Add pepperoni slices, olives, and cheese on top of the sauce. You can substitute any pizza toppings you like. Cut 1-inch wide strips using kitchen scissors down either side of the dough, cutting from the outside edge of the dough into the edge of the filling. Braid the loaf by folding top strips together across the filling and continue alternating strips until you reach the bottom. (This will look similar to a Danish braid.) Bake as above.

Pizza Pinwheels

Just another twist on one of my kids favorite meals. It takes all the same ingredients as pizza, but if we were living off our food storage, it would feel like something new. These also work great in school lunches in place of a sandwich.

Soft garlic breadstick dough
Pepperoni slices, chopped
Black olives, chopped
Shredded cheese
8 oz tomato sauce

½ tsp dried oregano
½ tsp dried basil
¼ tsp garlic powder
¼ tsp onion powder

Make a batch of the soft garlic breadstick recipe found in the bread section or use your favorite pizza dough recipe. After the first rise, punch it down and roll out on an oiled surface into a 14x10-inch rectangle. Top with a thin layer of chopped pepperoni, olives, and cheese or any other pizza toppings you like. Roll up jelly roll style, starting from the long side. Do not roll too tightly or the centers of your rolls will pop up as they rise. Use a sharp knife to mark off 1-inch sections. You can either use a serrated knife to very carefully saw through the roll to make individual rolls or slide a piece of dental floss under the roll and bring the ends up crossing them as you do so. Pull the ends in opposite directions until the floss cuts through the dough forming individual rolls. They resemble cinnamon rolls when finished. Place in greased baking pans. Do not pack the rolls in the pan. They need to have space in between in order to allow room for them to rise. These rolls will rise out not up. Cover with a towel and allow to rise until double in size. After rising they should be touching each other and the sides of the pan. Bake at 400° F for 12–15 minutes or until golden brown. Mix seasonings with tomato sauce and dip the finished pinwheels in this.

Stuffed Burgers

This is always well received when we serve it to guests.

2 lbs hamburger, thawed
1 box chicken flavored stuffing mix
1 Tbsp dried, minced onion
2 cans cream of mushroom soup
1 (4 oz) can mushrooms
Salt and pepper to taste

Mix stuffing according to package directions. Form hamburger into 8 patties. Place a spoonful of stuffing in the center of each patty. Fold patties in half, pinching to seal edges. Shape them into ovals and place in a greased 9x13-inch pan. Sprinkle onions across top. Cover with soup and mushrooms. Cover pan with foil and bake at 350° F for 30–45 minutes or until meat is cooked through. Serve with potatoes or rice.

Panquecas

This is actually a Brazilian dish, but Americans seem to love it as well.

Shells:
2 cups reconstituted powdered milk
1 cup all-purpose flour
3 eggs
Pinch of salt
Filling:
½ cup chopped onion
1 tsp minced garlic
1 Tbsp oil
1 lb hamburger
Carrots, diced
Potatoes, diced
Worcestershire sauce
Salt

Shells: Mix all ingredients together and cook like very thin pancakes or crepes. Filling: Sauté onion and garlic in oil. Add uncooked hamburger, carrots, and potatoes. Cover and cook until meat is done and vegetables are tender. (Use dehydrated or frozen vegetables if needed.) Season with Worcestershire sauce and salt. To serve, place a small amount of filling in each shell and roll like enchiladas. These must be eaten with a fork. You cannot pick them up.

Sandwich Fillings

Tuna Salad
We often serve this on Saturday for lunch with a bowl of tomato soup.

1 can tuna, drained
2–3 Tbsp mayonnaise

Dill pickles, chopped
Carrots and black olives, chopped (optional)

Shred tuna pieces with a fork. Combine all ingredients in a bowl and mix well. Use as many pickles, carrots and black olives as you like. Serve on crackers, bread, buns or roll in tortillas. This is delicious grilled inside a cheese sandwich.

Salmon Salad
A great way to use up leftover grilled salmon.

1 can salmon, drained
2–3 Tbsp mayonnaise

Crushed dill weed to taste
Carrots and black olives, chopped (optional)

Remove bones and skin from salmon, if needed. Shred salmon pieces with a fork. Combine all ingredients in a bowl and mix well. Use carrots and black olives if you wish. I often use plain yogurt in place of half of the mayonnaise. Serve on crackers, bread, buns or roll in tortillas. This is delicious grilled inside a cheese sandwich.

BBQ Chicken Filling
It can't get any easier than this!

1 can chicken breast, drained

BBQ sauce to taste

Shred chicken pieces with a fork. Combine BBQ sauce with shredded chicken and heat through. Serve on crackers, bread, buns or roll in tortillas. You can substitute canned turkey for the chicken.

Chicken Salad

This turns into a fancy luncheon if you serve it on homemade crescent rolls.

1 can chicken breast, drained
¼ cup mayonnaise
Chopped onion to taste
Chopped celery to taste
Mrs. Dash original blend to taste
Salt and pepper to taste

Shred chicken pieces with a fork. Combine all ingredients in a bowl and mix well. Use rehydrated minced onion and rehydrated celery if no fresh vegetables are available. I have used ranch dressing or plain yogurt in place of half of the mayonnaise. I also add some minced garlic sometimes. You can substitute canned turkey for the chicken and use plain yogurt in place of ½ of the mayonnaise. Serve on crackers, bread, buns or roll in tortillas. To fancy this up a bit, you can add Craisins and sliced almonds.

BBQ Pulled Pork

We make a huge batch of this to serve at my husband's summer work BBQ. It is always a big hit!

1 pork picnic roast
1–2 jars BBQ sauce

Place pork roast in a crockpot and cook on low for 12–15 hours. I usually put the roast in just before going to bed. Test the pork by stabbing it with a fork and twisting. If the meat shreds easily, it is ready. Remove from the crockpot and place on a baking sheet. Using two forks, pull the pork apart and separate out all the visible fat and bone pieces. It pulls apart more easily when it is still warm. Pour BBQ sauce over the pulled pork and mix to combine. Use enough BBQ sauce to coat all the meat and give it a good flavor. Serve on hamburger buns—see recipe in bread section. Freeze any leftover meat for another meal. You can also freeze the meat with the BBQ sauce mixed in for a fast meal another time.

Easy Sloppy Joes

I watch for the cans of sloppy joe sauce to go on sale and then stock up so I can always have what I need for this simple favorite.

1 can sloppy joe sauce   1 lb hamburger, browned

Combine and heat. Serve on hamburger buns—see recipe in bread section. Freeze any leftover meat for another meal.

Sloppy Joes From Scratch

Here's an easy alternative if you don't have sloppy joe sauce on hand.

½ cup ketchup   2 Tbsp dried, minced onion
3 Tbsp sugar   1 lb hamburger, browned
1 Tbsp Worcestershire sauce

Combine in a crockpot and cook on low for 2 hours or heat in the microwave. Serve on hamburger buns.

Chinese-Style Dishes

Orange Chicken
This is a dinner that is requested often at our house.

2 chicken breasts, cubed
1 egg, beaten
1 Tbsp water
cornstarch
2 Tbsp margarine

1 cup brown sugar, packed
1–2 Tbsp soy sauce
1 cup orange juice
½ cup apple cider vinegar
2–3 Tbsp cornstarch

Place chicken in large bowl, mix egg and water (use dried or frozen egg, if needed) and pour over chicken. Pour cornstarch in bowl and mix until chicken is coated. Brown chicken in margarine and place in serving dish. Combine brown sugar, soy sauce, orange juice and vinegar in a saucepan and heat to boiling. Mix cornstarch and cold water. Stir into saucepan and cook until sauce is thickened. Adjust the amount of cornstarch used to make the sauce as thick as you like. Pour over chicken and serve with rice. You can quicken this recipe and lower the calories by skipping the steps of coating the chicken. Just brown the chicken in a frying pan and pour the sauce over to serve. I've also made a large batch of the sauce and substituted Ultra Gel for the cornstarch. (Check out the Preserving Your Harvest Section for more information on Ultra Gel.) When you do this, it freezes well. I can then just toss some chicken in the crockpot and top it with the sauce during the last 10 minutes of cooking time for a quick dinner.

Lemon Sauce for Chicken
Try eating this with chopsticks for a fun family experience.

1 ½ cups water
½ cup bottled lemon juice
3 ½ Tbsp brown sugar, packed
3 Tbsp cornstarch

3 Tbsp honey
2–3 tsp soy sauce
2 tsp chicken bouillon
½ tsp ginger

Prepare the chicken as you do for the Orange Chicken recipe above. Combine sauce ingredients in a saucepan and heat to boiling, stirring constantly. Boil for 2 minutes until sauce is thickened. Pour over chicken and serve with rice. I've also made a large batch of the sauce and substituted Ultra Gel for the cornstarch so I can store the sauce in the freezer.

Fried Rice

I don't share specific amounts in this recipe since I make it using leftovers and the amounts are different every time.

Cooked rice, cooled
Frozen peas and carrots
2–3 Tbsp dried, minced onion
Chopped, precooked, ham
Scrambled eggs
Salt and pepper to taste

Rehydrate onions in warm water until soft. Place 2–3 Tbsp oil in a skillet. Add frozen peas and carrots. (These come in a combination package so the carrots are cut into pea size pieces. You can always use dehydrated vegetables if desired.) Add ham and onion pieces and fry until heated through. Add rice and scrambled eggs. (You can create a hole in the center of the pan and scramble the eggs right as you are cooking everything else. I often save some scrambled eggs from breakfast to add to my pan.) Salt and pepper to taste. You can also add a little soy sauce or teriyaki sauce if desired.

Stir Fry Noodles

My daughter especially loves these. She had them when we went out for Chinese and asked if I could figure out making some at home.

1 pkg frozen stir fry vegetables
1 pkg Japanese style noodles or Ramen noodles, cooked
1 cup cold water
1 tsp chicken bouillon
1 tsp sugar
1 Tbsp soy sauce
2–3 tsp cornstarch

Cook noodles according to package directions, drain and set aside. Fry vegetables in a small amount of oil until tender. Mix remaining ingredients in a small bowl. Pour over vegetables and cook until thickened. Add noodles and stir to combine. Instead of adding noodles, you can serve the vegetables over rice.

Pasta Dishes

Fettuccine

Cream cheese stores a long time in the refrigerator. It can easily be part of the meals you plan for a 3-month supply.

1 ½ cups reconstituted powdered milk
8 oz cream cheese
Garlic powder
Onion powder
Salt and pepper
8 oz noodles, cooked

Combine milk and cream cheese in a saucepan. Cook over medium heat, stirring constantly until well blended and hot. Season with garlic, onion, salt and pepper. Serve over noodles. You can add cooked carrots, asparagus, fresh tomatoes, etc. I often drain my homemade yogurt to use it as a cream cheese substitute—check out the powdered milk section to see how to do this.

Alfredo Pasta

A quick and easy side dish for dinner or an entire meal at lunch time.

1 ½ cups reconstituted powdered milk
2 Tbsp margarine
2 pkts Alfredo sauce mix
8 oz pasta
Dry carrots or peas, optional

Follow directions on the back of sauce packet. Boil noodles and dry vegetables if desired. You just add your dry vegetables to your noodle water. Mix and serve.

Spaghetti

This is probably a storable meal that we all have the ingredients on hand to make.

8 oz spaghetti noodles
1 (26 oz) can spaghetti sauce
1 (15 oz) can diced tomatoes
1 (15oz) can tomato sauce
½ cup dried carrots
Oregano, garlic, basil to taste

Cook pasta until tender. Combine sauce ingredients and simmer until carrots are tender. You can also reconstitute the carrots separately and then just stir them into the warm sauce.

Hays' Special/Stove Top Lasagna

The story goes that my Grandpa Pack had a missionary companion on his first mission named Elder Hays. Whenever it was his turn to cook, he made this dish. It has been known as Hays' Special in our family ever since. You may know it as goulash.

2 cups elbow macaroni
1 lb hamburger, browned
1 (15 oz) can tomato sauce

Cheddar cheese, grated
Salt, onion powder, oregano to taste

Cook pasta until tender. Stir in remaining ingredients and heat through. You can stir in some cottage cheese to make Stove Top Lasagna

Pasta Primavera

Everything can be done in the time it takes the pasta to cook for a quick dinner any night.

1 can cream of mushroom soup
¾ cup reconstituted powdered milk
¼ cup dehydrated carrots
2 cups frozen broccoli florets

¼ cup grated Parmesan cheese
½ tsp dried, minced garlic
⅛ tsp pepper
3 cups cooked spaghetti

Combine everything but the spaghetti in a large saucepan. Bring to a boil and turn the heat off. Allow to sit for 15–20 minutes until vegetables are tender. Stir in pasta and heat through.

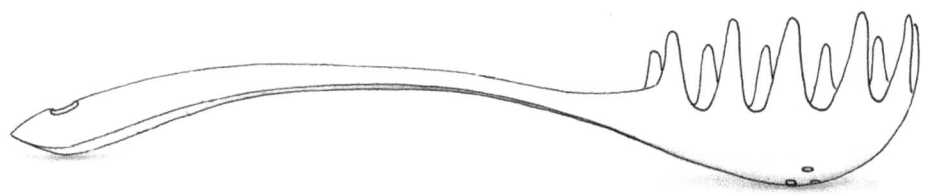

Pizza Pasta
Another take on a kid's favorite meal.

4 cups spiral noodles, uncooked
1 (26 oz) can spaghetti sauce
20 pepperoni slices, quartered
½ can black olives, sliced

1 cup grated cheese
Chopped green pepper, optional
Sausage, optional
Oregano, garlic, basil to taste

Cook pasta until tender. Mix all other ingredients with the pasta and heat through. Sprinkle some additional grated cheese on top just before serving.

Mediterranean Chicken
This is a dish I craved more than once when I was pregnant. My husband was sweet to make it for me while I hung out on the couch.

2 chicken breasts, cubed
2 (15 oz) cans diced tomatoes
½ can water
2 chicken bouillon cubes

¼ cup dried, minced onion
Sliced black olives
Garlic, oregano, parsley, thyme to taste
8 oz noodles

Cook chicken in a small amount of oil. Meanwhile, mix all other ingredients. Add chicken. Thicken with a flour and water mixture if desired. Serve over noodles. I love to make a big pot of this sauce in the crockpot. It freezes very well and makes for a quick meal another time.

Beef Stroganoff
Simple comfort food that every family loves.

12 oz pasta, cooked
1 lb hamburger or beef chunks, cooked
1 can cream of mushroom soup
1 soup can reconstituted powdered milk
1 cup sour cream (plain yogurt)

1 Tbsp dried chives
1 tsp pepper
2 tsp garlic powder
Salt to taste

Stir all ingredients together in a pan. Heat through and pour over noodles.

Pasta with Sour Cream Sauce

I have two brothers who served missions in Germany. They say this sauce tastes very similar to the German cuisine they grew to love.

7 ½ cups egg noodles (1 lb)
1 can cream of chicken soup
1 can cream of mushroom soup
1 cup reconstituted powdered milk
1 cup sour cream (plain yogurt)

1 tsp onion powder
1 tsp parsley
1 tsp garlic powder
2 cups diced chicken, cooked
1 cup cheddar cheese

Cook noodles. Meanwhile, stir all remaining ingredients together in a pan. Heat through and pour over noodles.

Saucy Tarragon Chicken

I have to remind my kids not to lick their plates clean when I serve this dish. They love the sauce so much.

5 cups egg noodles
2 chicken breasts, cooked and cubed
¾ tsp dried tarragon
¾ tsp lemon pepper
1 (4 oz) can mushrooms

2 tsp dried, minced garlic
2 cups water
2 tsp chicken bouillon
3 Tbsp all-purpose flour
1 cup sour cream (plain yogurt)

Cook noodles. Meanwhile, stir all remaining ingredients together in a pan except for the sour cream. Cook and stir until thickened. Stir in sour cream and serve over noodles.

Chicken and Veggie Pasta

By storing what you need for this dish in the freezer, dinner can be on the table in less than 20 minutes.

12 oz angel hair pasta
2 chicken breasts, cooked and cubed
½ cup frozen carrots
10 oz frozen broccoli
2 cloves minced garlic

2 Tbsp oil
1 cup water
1 tsp chicken bouillon
1 tsp basil
¼ cup Parmesan cheese

Cook noodles. Meanwhile, cook carrots, broccoli, and garlic in the oil until crisp tender. Stir in chicken and add remaining ingredients. Top pasta with the vegetable mixture before serving.

Tuna Noodle Supreme

Every family needs a good tuna casserole recipe. This one is our favorite!

2 cups small shell pasta
¼ cup dehydrated green peppers
2–3 Tbsp dried, minced onion
2 cups plain yogurt
½ cup mayonnaise

¼ cup Parmesan cheese
1 tsp Dijon mustard
2 cups frozen, chopped broccoli
1 (5 oz) can tuna, drained
Salt and pepper to taste

Cook noodles, dehydrated green peppers, and dried, minced onion in boiling water until noodles are tender. Drain. Meanwhile, stir all remaining ingredients together in a large glass bowl or casserole dish. Mix noodles with the sauce, cover and heat in the microwave until warmed through.

Soups and Stews

Creamy Chicken and Rice Soup

You can freeze this soup. It looks like it has separated when it thaws out, but it heats up wonderfully.

6 cups water
3 chicken breasts, cooked and cubed
¼– ½ cup dry carrots
½ cup rice, uncooked
1 Tbsp dried, minced onions

3 Tbsp chicken bouillon
1 ½ tsp lemon pepper
2 Tbsp cornstarch
12 oz evaporated milk
¼ cup margarine, optional

Combine all ingredients except the cornstarch, milk, and butter. Boil for 20 minutes or until vegetables and rice are tender. Stir cornstarch into milk and add to pot. Boil another few minutes until thickened. Add butter if desired. I often use evaporated skim milk or you can use powdered milk to make an evaporated milk substitute. Check out the instructions in the powdered milk section.

Tortellini Soup

This is a "grown-up" soup at our house. It's one I make for just me sometimes and let the kids have chicken noodle.

2–3 cups chicken broth
1 large can diced tomatoes

1 pkg frozen Cheese Tortellini
¼ cup chopped, frozen spinach

Make broth using chicken bouillon and water. Combine all ingredients and cook until noodles are very tender. Add additional broth, as needed.

Lentil Soup

This is a simple soup we enjoy served with tortilla chips.

Beef broth
1 lb lentils, rinsed
½ cup dried, minced onion

1 lb bacon, cooked and crumbled
1 (15 oz) can diced tomatoes

Make enough beef broth using water and beef bouillon to cover the lentils. Add lentils and onion to broth and cook until done (about 30–40 minutes.) Add more beef broth, as desired. When lentils are tender, add tomatoes and bacon. I love the precooked real bacon bits available in the salad dressing aisle at most grocery stores. Just sprinkle in the amount you like.

Hobo Stew

After watching the American Doll movie, "Kit Kitteridge," my kids understood why this is referred to as Hobo Stew.

1 can carrots
1 can potatoes
1 can green peas
1 can corn

1 can green beans
1 can diced tomatoes
½ lb hamburger, browned
1–2 tsp beef bouillon

Dump 1 can each of carrots, potatoes, peas, corn, green beans, and tomatoes in a pan. Do not drain. Add hamburger and bouillon and season as desired. We like this with a little oregano, basil, onion, and garlic added or you can use Italian style diced tomatoes. You really can use whatever combination of vegetables you like.

Beef and Barley Soup

A simple bowl of soup on a cold day is always enjoyable.

1 lb hamburger, browned
2 cups cubed potatoes
3 carrots, diced
1 celery stalk, sliced
1 cup chopped onion
2 Tbsp chopped green peppers
1 Tbsp sugar
1 (14 oz) can diced tomatoes
3 ½ tsp salt
1 tsp Worcestershire sauce
½ cup pearl barley
Pepper to taste
1 ½–2 quarts water

Combine all ingredients in a slow cooker. You can easily use dehydrated vegetables in this soup. Just cut the amounts in half since dehydrated vegetables double in size. Cook on high 7–8 hours or until vegetables are tender. If cooking on the stove top, simmer for 45–60 minutes until everything is tender.

Split Pea Soup

This is similar to the soup my husband remembers his mom making when he was young.

6–8 cups chicken broth
1 cup dehydrated diced potatoes
¾ cup dried, minced onion
1 cup dehydrated carrots
1 lb split peas
1 lb sausage, cooked and crumbled

Make broth using chicken bouillon and water. Combine everything except sausage. Cook until done—the peas will lose their shape. Add cooked sausage just before serving. This makes an easy mix to keep in the pantry.

Breakfast Dishes

Stovetop Rice Pudding

This is a delicious breakfast or a simple dessert. It reheats wonderfully, so don't hesitate to make enough for the kids to have a tasty after-school snack.

1 cup rice
¼ cup sugar
2 cups water
12 oz evaporated milk

Cinnamon to taste
Raisins, if desired
1 tsp vanilla

Stir sugar and rice into water. Bring to a boil, cover, and simmer for 20–25 minutes or until water is absorbed and rice is tender. Stir in milk, return to a boil. Remove from heat and stir in cinnamon, raisins, and vanilla. You can use powdered milk to make an evaporated milk substitute. Check out the instructions in the powdered milk section.

Mountain Man Breakfast

This is always a favorite on camping trips. It brings back those fun memories when we eat it at home.

2 cups dehydrated hash browns
⅓ cup dried, minced onion
1 lb sausage, browned

6 eggs, scrambled
Salt and pepper

Soak hash browns and onion in hot water for 15–20 minutes or until soft. Drain. Brown hash browns and onion in a frying pan with a little oil. When hash browns are done, stir in sausage and eggs. Stir until eggs are cooked. Salt and pepper to taste. You can use frozen hash browns or peeled, diced potatoes in place of the dehydrated hash browns.

Apple Cinnamon Oatmeal

I usually combine the dry ingredients in a mix and store in a quart-size ziplock bag to speed up busy mornings. Store the apples in a separate ziplock inside the other bag so you can drop them in the water when you first put it on the stove.

2 ½ cups water
⅓ cup brown sugar, packed
1 tsp cinnamon
¼ tsp salt

½ cup chopped, dried apples
Raisins or Craisins, if desired
Chopped nuts, if desired
2 cups regular oats

Combine the dried fruit with the water in a saucepan. Bring to a boil and add the remaining ingredients. Cook for about 5 minutes until all the water is absorbed, stirring occasionally. You can use 1 peeled and chopped apple in place of the dried apples. You can also substitute other fruits such as peaches or berries. It is always delicious!

Granola

I love this recipe because it only bakes for 20 minutes instead of 2 hours like many granola recipes require. It is quick, versatile, and full of great fiber.

4 cups rolled oats
¾ cup wheat germ or additional oats
¾ cup oat bran or additional oats
2 cups any combination of chopped nuts, coconut, or sunflower seeds
¾ tsp salt
¼ cup brown sugar, packed

2 Tbsp maple syrup
6 Tbsp honey
½ cup vegetable oil
½ tsp cinnamon
½ tsp vanilla
1 cup dried raisins, cranberries, etc.

Line two large baking sheets with aluminum foil. In a large bowl, combine the oats, wheat germ, oat bran, and nuts. In a saucepan over medium heat, stir together the salt, brown sugar, maple syrup, honey, oil, cinnamon and vanilla. Bring to a boil then pour over the dry ingredients and stir to coat. Spread the mixture out evenly on the baking sheets. Bake at 325° F for 20 minutes, or until toasted. Stir once about halfway through. Cool, then stir in the raisins or Craisins before storing in an airtight container. This recipe is very versatile. I have used rolled wheat in place of some of the oatmeal and you can use any dried fruit that you like. I often wait to add the dried fruit until right as I am eating it so I can choose the fruit I am in the mood for at the moment.

Apple Muffin Breakfast Cake

I love to cook this on Saturday night when we have early morning church. It is delicious cooled and I feel like we've had a nice weekend breakfast and we can still make it to church on time.

1 white cake mix
1 cup water
1 cup dried apples, chopped
2 Tbsp oil

¼ cup applesauce
2 eggs
1 tsp cinnamon, optional
Brown sugar, sugar, cinnamon

Chop the dried apples to fill a 1 cup measuring cup. Once they are in the cup, add water to fill the cup and allow to soak while you mix the remaining ingredients. Mix all remaining ingredients except the brown sugar topping in a mixing bowl. Mix just until moist. Stir in the apples. Pour into a greased 9x13-inch pan and sprinkle with a little brown sugar, cinnamon and sugar. Bake at 350° F for 30–35 minutes. Or bake as muffins for 20–22 minutes. **No egg version:** Substitute ½ cup white bean puree for the eggs and bake as muffins for best results.

Potato Pancakes/Latkes

Quick and easy—we love them for breakfast or dinner.

3 cups dehydrated hash browns
¼ cup dried, minced onion
¼ cup flour

Salt and pepper to taste
¼ tsp garlic powder

Place hash browns and onions in a pan. Cover with water so the water comes above the potatoes 2–3 inches. Bring to a boil, cover, and remove from the heat. Allow to sit for 15–20 minutes or until potatoes are tender. Drain off any extra water. Place potatoes in a bowl and mix in flour and seasonings. Shape into patties and fry in a frying pan with about ¼-inch of oil in the bottom. Flip when potatoes begin turning brown on the edge and cook until done. Drain on a paper towel. Enjoy! Leftovers freeze well. Reheat in the oven to keep them crispy.

Surprise Pancakes

When we sit down to the table for breakfast, the kids always try to guess the "secret" ingredient. It makes for a fun and healthy breakfast.

Pancake mix
Fruit puree or yogurt

Cinnamon or pumpkin pie spice

Use your favorite pancake mix. Before adding the water, pour in some fruit puree or yogurt. Add the water you need to make the right consistency. Sprinkle in a little spice. To help you know how much, we use about 3 cups of Krusteaz mix and I pour in ½–¾ cup fruit puree. Cook on a hot griddle.

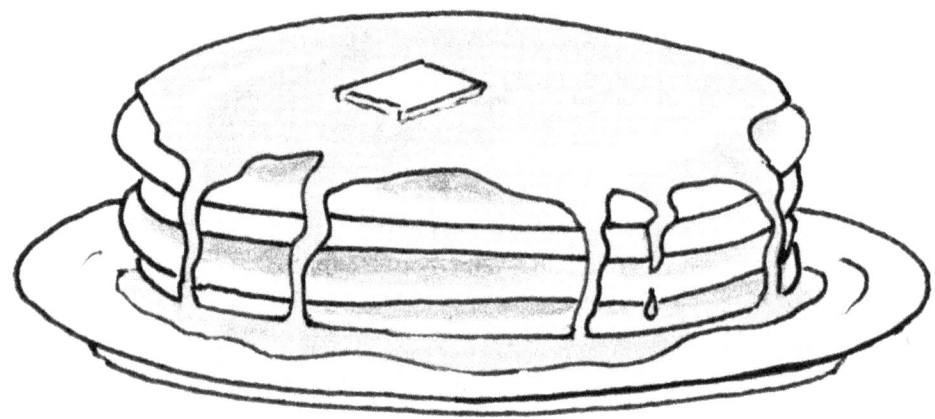

Hash Browns

Start the potatoes soaking before you hop in the shower and then fry them up when you are finished.

3 cups dehydrated hash browns

Salt and pepper to taste

Place hash browns in a pan. Cover with water so the water comes above the potatoes 2–3 inches. Bring to a boil, cover, and remove from the heat. Allow to sit for 15–20 minutes or until potatoes are tender. Drain off any extra water. Fry in a frying pan with about ¼-inch of oil in the bottom. Flip when potatoes begin turning brown on the edge and cook until done. Drain on a paper towel. Enjoy!

Salads and Side Dishes

No dinner is complete without a side dish or two. To really store what you eat on a regular basis, you need to think beyond the main dish. Side dishes can be as simple as a can of vegetables or a jar of fruit. Think about the way you eat already and plan your side dishes with that in mind. Here are a few of our favorite options that go beyond just opening a can or jar.

Confetti Salad

This salad is best chilled so plan ahead. Cooked rice and lentils freeze well so you can even have some in the freezer to speed up preparation.

1 cup lentils, cooked
2 cups rice, cooked
1 ½ cups Italian salad dressing
Tomatoes, chopped
Green peppers, chopped

Cucumbers, chopped
Celery, chopped
Green onions, chopped
Radishes, chopped

Mix the lentils and rice together. Add Italian dressing. Chill. Before serving, add chopped vegetables. When we don't have fresh vegetables available, I use dehydrated carrots, onions, celery, and peppers. Just rehydrate the vegetables before adding.

Creamy Fruit Cups

The young kids squeal with delight when they see these on the table as part of dinner. The older kids and adults enjoy them to.

1 (3 oz) box instant vanilla pudding
1 cup plain yogurt

1 large can fruit cocktail
1 can pineapple chunks

Drain the fruit and reserve the juice. Combine fruit, plain yogurt, and dry pudding mix. Mix in enough fruit juice to make the creamy consistency you desire. Chill and serve in individual size containers.

Fluffy Fruit Salad

This is another family favorite. It always disappears at potlucks as well so others must love it too.

1–2 cups precooked rice
1 cup plain yogurt, drained
8 oz frozen whipped topping

1 small box jello, any flavor
Fruit, drained (fruit cocktail, pineapple, mandarin oranges, etc.)

Drain the plain yogurt so it is the consistency of thick sour cream. Measure after draining. Look in the section on using powdered milk for the instructions on how to do this. Combine plain yogurt and thawed frozen whipped topping. Mix in fruit and rice. Sprinkle jello powder over salad and mix well. Chill.

Frog Eye Salad

This is an easy salad to make for a large group. It is fun at a casual BBQ,, but can also be served at a fancier brunch or reception.

½ cup acini di pepe noodles
1 large can fruit cocktail
1 can pineapple chunks

1 (3 oz) box instant vanilla pudding
Frozen whipped topping

Cook and drain pasta. Run cold water over pasta until it is cool. Drain fruit, reserving the juice. Stir pasta, fruit and dry pudding powder together. Add enough juice back to mixture to keep it moist. Stir in enough thawed whipped topping to coat fruit. Chill to thicken.

Macaroni Salad

This is the classic pasta salad my mom always made when I was growing up. Throw a simple summer dinner together with this salad and some hoagie sandwiches or sloppy joes.

8 oz elbow macaroni	Frozen peas, thawed
Carrots, grated	Cheddar cheese, grated
Black olives, sliced	Salad dressing (mayo type)
Dill pickles, diced	Lemon pepper, salt, onion powder, and garlic to taste

Cook pasta until tender. Drain and rinse in cold water. Mix vegetables and cheese with pasta. To make dressing, place about ½ cup salad dressing in a bowl. Add a little dill pickle juice to thin it and the seasonings. Stir to combine. Stir dressing into salad and adjust seasonings as needed before serving. You can use dehydrated carrots, just rehydrate them first. There are no amounts for this recipe because I never measure. I just mix it until it looks and tastes good.

Seafood Pasta Salad

I came up with this salad after having a similar one at a local restaurant. I have had many requests for the recipe.

8 oz rotini pasta	Mayonnaise
Canned tuna, salmon, or shrimp	Plain yogurt
Black olives, sliced	Dill, onion powder, garlic powder, salt, and pepper to taste
Cucumbers, diced, if available	
Celery, chopped, if available	

Cook pasta until tender. Drain and rinse in cold water. Mix vegetables with pasta. To make dressing, stir equal amounts of mayonnaise and plain yogurt with the seasonings. Stir dressing into salad and serve. I often use imitation crab meat in this salad also since it freezes so well and I can have it on hand. There are no amounts for this recipe because I never measure. I just mix it until it looks and tastes good.

Green Pea and Crisp Corn Salad

We love this colorful salad with, or without, the pasta. The mayonnaise and plain yogurt combination makes for a creamy dressing with half of the fat.

8 oz small shell pasta
Frozen peas, thawed
Frozen corn, thawed
Black olives, sliced
Real bacon bits

Shredded cheddar cheese, if available
Mayonnaise
Plain yogurt
Onion powder, garlic powder,
salt, and pepper to taste

Cook pasta until tender. Drain and rinse in cold water. Mix vegetables, olives, bacon bits, and cheese with pasta. To make dressing, stir equal amounts of mayonnaise and plain yogurt with the seasonings. Stir dressing into salad and serve. There are no amounts for this recipe because I never measure. I just mix it until it looks and tastes good. This salad is delicious without the pasta also.

Angel Hair Pasta

Simple pasta is always a quick side dish that will be enjoyed by adults and kids alike.

12 oz angel hair pasta, cooked
1 cup water
1 tsp dried, minced garlic

1 tsp chicken bouillon
1 tsp dried basil
¼ cup Parmesan cheese

Place water, garlic, bouillon and basil in skillet. Simmer until garlic is tender. Add cooked pasta and heat through. Add Parmesan cheese and toss. This is delicious with frozen broccoli, carrots, and chicken pieces added. Just precook everything, toss with pasta and enjoy a full meal instead of just a side dish.

Simply Delicious Potatoes

These pair nicely with any grilled meat. Because they cook in the microwave, they can be done in 10–15 minutes and won't heat up the kitchen on a hot summer day.

5–6 potatoes, peeled and sliced
¼ cup dried, minced onion
6 Tbsp margarine, optional
⅓ cup cheddar cheese, grated

2 tsp parsley flakes
1 Tbsp Worcestershire sauce
1 cup chicken broth
Salt and pepper to taste

Place potatoes and onion in a glass dish. Dot with margarine. Sprinkle cheese, parsley, Worcestershire sauce, salt and pepper over the potatoes. Add broth that you make using 1 cup water and 1 tsp chicken bouillon. Cover and cook in the microwave until potatoes are tender. You can use dehydrated potato slices in place of the potatoes. Just rehydrate them first.

Potato Wedges

Potatoes keep when stored in a cool, dry box for quite a few months. Don't hesitate to store them as part of your 3-month supply.

Potatoes, peeled and cut into wedges
Oil

Seasoned salt

Combine a small amount of seasoned salt and about 4–6 Tbsp of oil in a bowl. Toss potatoes in oil until well coated. Bake on a baking sheet at 425° F until potatoes are tender. If you don't have potatoes, you can use dehydrated potato slices. Just rehydrate first. They aren't really wedges, but they are still delicious.

Make Ahead Mashed Potatoes

These are nice to have in the freezer ready to go for a busy night. They are also great for a holiday dinner. You can just reheat in the crockpot on low for 5–6 hours.

5 lbs potatoes, peeled and diced
8 oz cream cheese (plain yogurt)
1 cup sour cream (plain yogurt)
½ cup reconstituted powdered milk
2 tsp onion powder
Salt and pepper to taste

Cook potatoes in boiling water until tender. Drain and mash. Mix in remaining ingredients only using enough milk to achieve the consistency you desire. Serve immediately or store in the fridge or freezer for later. Just package in ziplock bags or meal size containers. We also like to add grated cheese, chives, and bacon bits sometimes to dress them up.

Rice

Rice is such an easy staple to store. Many people shy away from cooking conventional rice and use the minute rice instead. You can see by these instructions that cooking conventional rice is quite easy to do and it is much less expensive per serving.

1 cup rice   2 cups water

Place rice and water in a saucepan. Sprinkle in just a little salt. Cover and bring to a boil over high heat. Once it begins to boil, turn the burner down to low and simmer for 15–20 minutes until the rice is soft and all the water is absorbed. To check to see if the water is absorbed, poke a fork in the center and slide some rice aside enough to see the bottom of the pan. If there is still a small amount of water, cover and allow it to cook a few minutes longer. When it is done, fluff with a fork and enjoy!

Storable Snacks

Anyone with children knows that as soon as you clean up from one meal the kids are telling you they are hungry again. You can't consider yourself prepared with food storage until you have taken some time to think about what snacks you could serve using your food storage.

Consider what you are serving for snacks on a regular basis. Are they items that will store for at least 3 months? If so, just buy more of them and find places to stash them. I always stock up on pretzels, crackers, granola bars, and cold cereal when they are on sale. I've also worked to collect recipes over the years for snack items that call for ingredients that I can store at home. A few of these call for eggs. You can use powdered eggs or frozen eggs if you are out of refrigerated eggs at the moment. Hopefully you'll find some in my collection that your family will enjoy and you can add them to your meal plan.

Coconut Chex Mix
This is a gooey snack that everyone enjoys!

1 (15 oz) box Honey Grahams
1 (15 oz) box Corn Chex
1–2 cups slivered almonds
1 (10 oz) bag coconut

1½ cups butter
¾ cup light corn syrup
¾ cup sugar

Combine cereal, almonds, and coconut in a large bowl. I usually use the store brand cereal to cut the cost. Boil butter, corn syrup, and sugar for two minutes. Pour over cereal and mix well.

Frozen Banana Snacks
Frozen bananas always hit the spot on a hot summer day and they have many more vitamins than a popsicle.

½ cup chocolate chips
1 tsp shortening

Sliced bananas
Chopped nuts, granola, coconut, etc.

Melt chocolate and shortening in the microwave. Dip bananas in chocolate and roll in desired coating. Place on a baking sheet and freeze at least 1 hour before serving or before placing in an airtight container and freezing up to 1 month. Sometimes we cut the bananas in half and place a popsicle stick in the cut end. Dip and freeze as above for a fun banana popsicle.

Frozen Pudding Pops
My kids love to use butterscotch or chocolate pudding for these, but you can choose your favorite flavor.

1 small box instant pudding

2 cups reconstituted powdered milk

Mix milk. Stir pudding mix into milk. Pour into popsicle molds or Dixie cups and freeze. If using Dixie cups, you will need to insert a popsicle stick before freezing.

Microwave Caramel Chex

The microwave makes this oh-so simple. Sometimes we have game nights and invite a few families over. We often make this quick and easy treat.

1 cup brown sugar, packed
½ cup butter
¼ light corn syrup

½ tsp salt
½ tsp baking soda
10 cups Corn Chex

Measure cereal into a large brown paper grocery bag. Combine brown sugar, butter, corn syrup, and salt in a glass bowl. Bring to a boil and cook for 2 minutes in the microwave. Remove and stir in baking soda. Pour caramel mixture over cereal and shake and stir until coated. Roll down the top of bag to close. Place bag in microwave and microwave for 90 seconds. (Each microwave is a little different so you may need to adjust cooking time.) Lay bag on table and tear open the side of the bag to allow the mixture to cool. Don't hesitate to double the recipe. If you do, you will need to shake the bag after cooking for 90 seconds and then return to the microwave for an additional 90 seconds. Try a mix of different cereals, popcorn, and nuts for a sweet snack mix.

Chocolate Oatmeal Bars

Who can resist an oatmeal cookie bar with chocolate on top? You can feel better serving these knowing they are lower in fat and cholesterol.

½ cup butter or margarine, softened
½ cup white bean puree
1 cup brown sugar, packed
1 cup white sugar
2 tsp vanilla

2 cups all-purpose flour
2 cups quick cooking oats
½ cup vegetable oil
1 cup chocolate chips
1 tsp shortening

Cream butter, beans, and sugar. Add vanilla. Add the flour and the oats. Mix well. Add the oil and mix until it pulls together. Press into a greased jelly roll pan. Bake at 375° F for 10–15 minutes or until lightly browned only around the edge. Allow to cool for a few minutes. Melt chocolate chips in the microwave with the shortening. Spread melted chocolate onto bars. You can sprinkle 1 cup of chopped walnuts or pecans on the top if desired. Cut into bars and serve.

Chocolate Chip Cookies

We package these up individually in snack size baggies and freeze them for the kids to take in their lunch to school.

⅔ cup shortening
⅔ cup butter
1 cup sugar
1 cup brown sugar, packed
2 eggs
2 tsp vanilla

3 cups all-purpose flour
1 tsp baking soda
1 tsp salt
2 cups chocolate chips
Chopped nuts, coconut, oatmeal (optional)

Cream together shortening and butter. Add sugar, brown sugar, eggs and vanilla. Blend in flour, baking soda, and salt. Stir in chocolate chips and optional ingredients if desired. I often bake half the batch just with chocolate chips and then add a handful of each of the optional ingredients to the remaining dough. Drop dough by rounded tablespoonfuls, 2 inches apart, onto baking sheet. Bake at 375° F for 8–10 minutes or until lightly brown. Do not over bake. Makes about 5 dozen. You can freeze dough balls for later. Cookies can also be frozen after baking. If freezing dough balls, place close together on a baking sheet and freeze. Once frozen, transfer to a ziplock bag and store in the freezer. To bake frozen dough balls, take out the number you need and place 2 inches apart on a baking sheet. Allow to thaw about 10 minutes, just until sticky. Bake as above.

Tortilla Roll-ups

I love quick to make snacks that I always have the ingredients to make. This is simple enough that the kids often do it by themselves.

Cream cheese
Chopped onions, peppers, black olives, ham, etc.

Flour tortillas

Mix chopped items with cream cheese. Spread on tortilla and roll. Cut each roll into bite size pieces. Be creative with what you mix with the cream cheese. Try this with jam and cream cheese for a sweet treat. We love to mix green onions or chives with cream cheese and then we dip the rolls in salsa.

Cheese Ball

Cream cheese stores for quite a few months in the refrigerator so you can always have some on hand to make a cheese ball. This tastes great on homemade crackers.

8 oz cream cheese, softened
2 Tbsp chopped onions
1 tsp minced garlic

½ cup chopped black olives
1 cup shredded cheddar cheese
Chopped walnuts, optional

Mix everything together with the cream cheese except for the nuts. Shape into a ball and roll in chopped nuts if desired. Chill. Serve with crackers. We prefer this with fresh onions, but you can use dehydrated if that is all you have. It is also good with chopped ham. Play with the amounts or seasonings as you desire. You can also heat this in the microwave and serve it warm as a cracker dip.

Pineapple Cheese Ball

If you love the combination of sweet and salty, you'll love this fun cracker spread.

8 oz cream cheese, softened
1 (8 oz) can crushed pineapple
1 Tbsp dehydrated bell peppers

1 Tbsp dried, minced onion
Chopped walnuts or almonds, optional

Rehydrate the peppers and the onions in a small amount of warm water. After they are soft, drain off any excess water. Drain the crushed pineapple until it is quite dry. Mix everything together with the cream cheese except for the nuts. Shape into a ball and roll in chopped nuts if desired. Chill. Serve with crackers.

No-Bake Cereal Bars

These make a great, protein packed breakfast when you need one on the run.

¼ cup brown sugar, packed
¼ cup light corn syrup
⅓ cup chunky peanut butter

2 cups Rice Krispies
½ cup chopped, dried fruit

Bring brown sugar and corn syrup to a boil, stirring constantly. Remove from heat and add peanut butter. Stir in cereal and fruit. Press into an 8-inch square pan. Cut into squares when cool.

Homemade Crackers

These taste amazingly good and they are simple to make. You can have lots of fun trying different mix-ins.

Cracker Mix
2 ½ cups whole wheat flour   2 tsp salt
3 cups all-purpose flour

Mix everything together and store in an airtight container.

To make crackers, combine:
1 cup + 1 Tbsp cracker mix   ⅓ cup water
2 Tbsp oil

Choose the mix-ins you desire: Here are a few ideas or be creative and come up with your own.
½ cup finely shredded cheese, any flavor
½ tsp garlic powder, ¼ tsp basil, 1 Tbsp Parmesan cheese
½ tsp onion powder, 1 tsp poppy seeds, 2 Tbsp ground flax seed

Combine the cracker ingredients and the mix-ins that you choose. Knead together just until mixed. Cover the dough with a cloth and allow to rest for 15–60 minutes. This step is important to make the dough easier to roll out. Roll out the dough between two pieces of plastic wrap until it is a very thin rectangle. Place on a baking sheet. Cut into small squares or diamond shapes using a pizza cutter. Prick each cracker with a fork and sprinkle with a little salt. Bake at 425° F for about 6 minutes. Flip the crackers over and bake for an additional 3–4 minutes. The baking time may be different depending on how thin you rolled your dough out. Remove from the baking sheet and allow to cool on a wire rack. Store in an airtight container. I usually make more than one kind if I am doing it. We have enjoyed all of the combinations listed above.

Honey Graham Crackers

A healthy alternative to store-bought crackers or cookies. My kids devour them whenever I mix up a batch.

1 cup butter or shortening
1 cup brown sugar, packed
½ cup honey
1 Tbsp vanilla
4 ½ cups whole wheat flour
1 cup ground flax seed, wheat germ, or oat bran or additional wheat flour
2 cups all-purpose flour
2 tsp baking powder
1 tsp baking soda
½ tsp salt
3 Tbsp dry milk powder
1 cup water
2 tsp cinnamon, optional

Cream together the butter and brown sugar. You can use a combination of butter and shortening or just one or the other. Add the honey and vanilla. Mix until combined. Add the dry ingredients. Use a combination of ground flax seed, wheat germ, or oat bran, if desired. Begin mixing and add the water gradually until it pulls together into a stiffer cookie dough consistency. Divide dough into 5–6 balls. Wrap all but one in plastic wrap and flatten into a disk. Refrigerate or freeze for later. Roll the remaining ball out between two sheets of plastic wrap. You want it to be very thin, much like pie crust. Peel off the top layer of plastic wrap and cut the dough using mini cookie cutters or use a pizza cutter to cut into rectangles. Prick the rectangles with a fork, if desired, for appearance. Place crackers on a greased baking sheet and bake at 350° F for 5–7 minutes until they are just turning brown along the edge. Remove to a wire rack to cool. You can roll them a little thicker and cut with a larger cookie cutter. Bake for 7–8 minutes and use as a sugar cookie substitute. The kids love to frost these and they have no idea they are eating a much more healthy treat. You can store any leftovers in an airtight container or freeze for later. For a dairy free version, you can substitute powdered soy or rice milk for the dry milk powder or you can omit it all together and use liquid soy or rice milk in place of the water. You may have to adjust the amount of liquid slightly to make a stiff cookie dough. For a honey free version, you can substitute brown sugar for the honey and adjust the water amount as needed.

Chewy Granola Bars

These cost far less than the ones from the store and you get about 24 bars. They store for 2–3 months in snack size baggies so don't hesitate to make a few batches when you are in the mood. They disappear quickly at my house with five kids and they are nut-free so they make a perfect snack to share at school.

½ cup brown sugar, packed
½ cup honey
¼ cup butter

2 cups regular oatmeal
2 cups Rice Krispies
½–¾ cup chopped dried fruit, ground flax seed, coconut, M&M's Minis, etc.

Combine brown sugar, honey, and butter in a medium-size saucepan. Bring to a boil over medium heat. Boil until it reaches soft-ball stage which means when you drop a little in a bowl of ice water it holds together in a little ball. This usually takes about 2–3 minutes. Cool. (It is a little tricky—if you cook the mixture too long they are crunchy and not cooking it long enough means they don't hold together. Just have a bowl of ice water ready.) Meanwhile, combine oatmeal, Rice Krispies, and whatever fun items you are adding in a large bowl. Stir brown sugar mixture into oatmeal mixture. Spread in a 9x13-inch pan. You can press a few chocolate chips into the top if desired. It is also fun to add some chocolate chips to the oatmeal mixture sometimes. They melt and give you a chocolate granola bar. Refrigerate 1 hour or until completely cooled. Cut into bars. Be creative – the oatmeal mixture just needs to be a little less than 5 cups of yummy things. I often do a combination of a few things. I make a few different varieties and then store the bars in individual snack baggies in the pantry. The kids are free to grab one whenever. The ground flax seed makes them extra healthy and the kids love them!

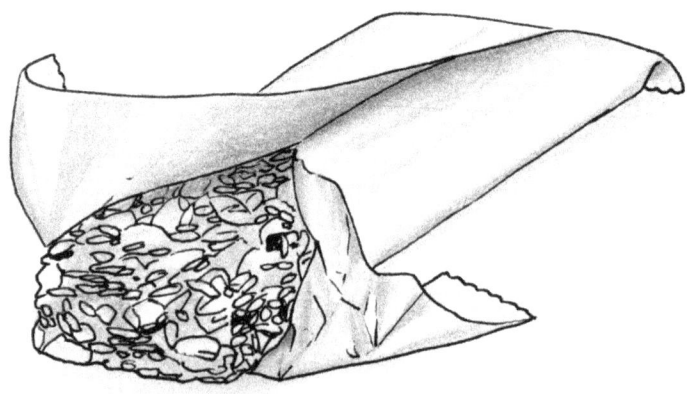

No-bake Granola Bars

Here is another fun recipe for granola bars. The peanut butter helps them stick together and adds a lot of protein.

2 ½ cups Rice Krispies cereal
2 cups quick-cooking oats
½ cup raisins
½ cup brown sugar, packed

½ cup light corn syrup
½ cup peanut butter
1 teaspoon vanilla extract
½ cup milk chocolate chips

Combine first 3 ingredients in a large bowl; set aside. Bring brown sugar and syrup to a boil in a small saucepan, stirring constantly. Remove from heat. Stir in peanut butter and vanilla until blended. Pour peanut butter mixture over cereal mixture, stirring until coated; let stand 10 minutes. Stir in chocolate chips. Press mixture into a 9x13-inch pan. Allow to cool. Cut into bars. The peanut butter helps these hold together without being as tricky as the Chewy Granola Bar recipe. If you have peanut allergies in the family, you can substitute almond, soy, or sunflower butter for the peanut butter with great results.

Homemade Kettle Corn

Popcorn stores for a very long time. It is inexpensive and makes a great snack. This is so fast and easy to put together.

¼ cup oil
¼ cup brown sugar, packed

½ cup popcorn seed
Salt

Heat oil in bottom of a large, covered pan. We use a special Whirly-pop pan made for doing popcorn on the stove, but you can use a regular pan. Drop in 3 popcorn kernels. When the kernels pop, the oil is ready. Quickly add the brown sugar and popcorn seed. Replace the lid. If using a Whirley-pop pan, twist the handle until all popcorn is popped. If using a regular pan, shake the pan back and forth on the burner until all kernels are popped. Pour popcorn into a large bowl and add a little salt. Mix the popcorn with your hands as it cools so it doesn't stick together. You can use white sugar in place of the brown sugar. It gives it more of a popcorn ball flavor instead of a caramel flavor.

Harvest Snack Mix

If you love sweet and salty mixes, you'll love this combination! It is always a hit at harvest parties.

1 batch homemade kettle corn
Golden Grahams cereal
Pretzel sticks

Candy corn
Reese's Pieces candies
Salted mixed nuts

Mix everything together, choosing the amounts that look right for the amount of kettle corn. Enjoy!

Funnel Cakes

Give your family a "fair" experience without having to go to the fair. We don't make these very often, but we devour them when we do.

2 eggs, beaten
1 ½ cups reconstituted powdered milk
2 cups all-purpose flour

1 tsp baking powder
½ tsp salt
2 cups cooking oil (for frying)

Combine milk and eggs. Stir in dry ingredients. Drip through a funnel into hot oil, swirling the funnel a little as you go. Fry until lightly browned, turning once with tongs. Remove to a paper towel covered plate. Sprinkle with powdered sugar. I use an electric frying pan with the temperature set at 350° F to help control the temperature of the oil.

Orange Julius

Always a great idea on a hot day!

1 tray ice cubes
6 oz frozen orange juice concentrate
½ cup sugar

2 cups reconstituted powdered milk
1 tsp vanilla

Combine all ingredients in a blender. Blend and serve.

Peanut Butter Yogurt Dip

Amazingly delicious! Serve with pretzels, cheese crackers, apples, celery, or bananas. This is also good spread on a tortilla.

¾ cup homemade yogurt
2–3 Tbsp powdered sugar
1 tsp vanilla

½ cup peanut butter
½ tsp cinnamon

Drain the yogurt until it is the consistency of store-bought yogurt and then measure out ¾ cup. (Check out the section on using powdered milk for the directions for draining the yogurt.) Combine all ingredients in a bowl and mix well.

Brownie Marshmallow Bars

These are rich enough you'll feel like you are eating a candy bar. My kids love to freeze some to put in their school lunches. I love that I can snitch just one from the freezer and don't have to be tempted all day with a full pan of them.

1 pkg brownie mix (9x13-inch pan size)
1 (10 oz) pkg mini marshmallows
2 cups chocolate chips

1 cup peanut butter
1 Tbsp shortening
1 ½ cups Rice Krispies

Mix brownies according to directions. (You can also make the Black Bean Brownies found in the Cooking with Dry Beans section.) Bake at 350° F for 28–30 minutes. Top with marshmallows; bake an additional 3 minutes. While brownies cool a bit, combine chocolate chips, peanut butter and shortening in a saucepan. Cook and stir over low heat until smooth. Add Rice Krispies. Allow to cool a few minutes. Spread over marshmallow layer. Refrigerate 1–2 hours or until firm. Cut into squares. To freeze, wrap each square in foil and place in a ziplock bag. Just grab as many as you need. They thaw quickly.

Storable Desserts

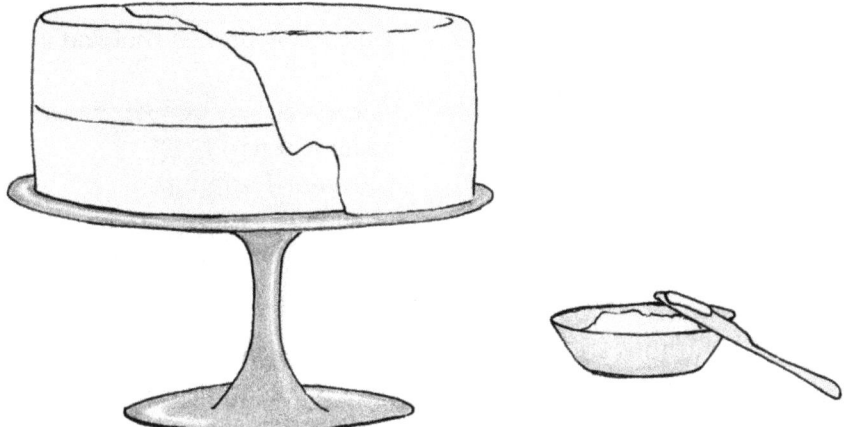

A cookbook isn't complete without a section on desserts. Desserts are often the quick thing to make because we always seem to have things on hand to make a treat. I've included recipes here that do not require any eggs. The butter or margarine can easily be frozen and so you can always have plenty on hand for when your sweet tooth acts up, unexpected company is coming, or you need to take something in to school. You will find other simple and delicious dessert or treat recipes scattered throughout this book. As you think about storing ingredients to make your own favorite desserts, remember that you can always use powdered eggs or frozen eggs with great success.

Any "Old Fruit" Cake

I love that I can use any variety of fruit in this cake. It tastes great every time!

2 cups whole wheat flour
2 cups all-purpose flour
4 tsp baking soda
1 tsp salt
2 cups sugar
2 tsp cinnamon
1 tsp nutmeg
½ tsp cloves

1 quart any bottled fruit and its juice
¼ cup oil
¾ cup mashed white or pinto beans (or additional oil)

Caramel Topping:
½ cup margarine
1 cup brown sugar, packed
½ cup evaporated milk
1 tsp vanilla

Combine dry ingredients in a large mixing bowl. Puree fruit in blender and add to dry ingredients. Add oil and mashed beans. If batter seems too runny, you can add up to ½ cup more flour. You can stir in chopped nuts, raisins, or coconut if desired before baking. Pour into a greased 9x13-inch pan and bake at 350° F for 40–45 minutes or bake as muffins for 15–20 minutes or until it tests done with a toothpick. To make topping, mix margarine, brown sugar, and milk together and boil until thick, stirring constantly. Add 1 tsp vanilla when done. You can stir in powdered sugar to gain a frosting consistency if desired. We love to serve this cake as muffins with caramel topping drizzled over the top and a dollop of whipped topping or vanilla ice cream. It actually is quite a fancy dessert served this way.

Apple Crisp

The topping for this crisp is very versatile and can be used as a crumble topping on any pie. It stores well in the refrigerator for up to 6 months so I often double or triple the batch to have some on hand for a quick dessert another time.

3 medium apples, peeled and sliced
½ cup all-purpose flour
¾ cup brown sugar, packed
½ cup butter or margarine
¾ cup quick oats

Place apples in an 8-inch square pan. Mix brown sugar and flour together. Cut butter into mixture. Stir in oats. Spread over apples. Bake at 350° F for 35–40 minutes. You can use dehydrated apples very easily in this recipe. Just place 2 cups dry apples in a saucepan and cover with water. Bring to a boil and turn off the burner. Let sit for 10–15 minutes or until tender. Drain and use in recipe.

Chocolate Crinkles

The original recipe for these cookies came from my grandmother. She always had a cookie can filled when we came to visit. I've played with this recipe to make it more healthy and to have it taste great without any eggs.

2 ½ cups all-purpose flour
2 cups sugar
6 Tbsp cocoa
½ tsp salt
2 tsp baking powder
1 tsp baking soda

¾ cup + 2 Tbsp thick black bean puree
2 tsp vanilla
2 Tbsp oil
1 Tbsp white vinegar
¼–½ cup water

Combine dry ingredients. Puree black beans with just a little bit of water to make a thick paste. Add to dry ingredients. Add the remaining ingredients. Add just enough water to make a sticky dough. (The amount of water you will add will depend on how thick your bean puree was.) Form into balls and roll in powdered sugar. Drop onto greased cookie sheet. Bake at 350° F 8–10 minutes. Allow cookies to cool for a couple of minutes on baking sheet before removing to a wire rack. Makes about 4 dozen cookies.

Applesauce Oatmeal Cookies

These cookies are high in protein, low in fat, and taste wonderful.

¼ cup butter
½ cup sugar
1 cup brown sugar, packed
1 ½ cups all-purpose flour
1 ¾ cups quick oats
1 tsp baking powder
1 tsp baking soda
1 tsp salt

1 tsp cinnamon
½ tsp nutmeg
½ cup mashed navy beans
¾ cup applesauce
Optional:
1 cup chocolate chips
1 cup raisins
1 cup chopped walnuts

Cream together the butter and sugars. Add remaining ingredients. You can use ¾ c. wheat flour and ¾ c. white flour. Mix or stir together. Stir in optional ingredients if desired. Drop by spoonfuls onto a greased baking sheet. Bake at 375° F for 8–10 minutes. Allow cookies to cool for a couple of minutes on the baking sheet before removing to a wire rack. Makes about 3 dozen cookies. You can freeze the cookies once they are baked.

Coconut Bread
Sweet and delicious!

¼ cup butter or margarine
1 cup sugar
2 cups all-purpose flour
¼ tsp salt
1 tsp baking powder
¼ tsp baking soda

1 cup reconstituted powdered milk
1 tsp vanilla
1 Tbsp white vinegar
¾ cup flaked coconut
Cinnamon and sugar

Cream butter and sugar. Add remaining ingredients except the coconut and cinnamon and sugar. Mix until combined. Fold in the coconut. Pour into a greased loaf pan. Sprinkle with cinnamon and sugar. Bake at 350° F for 50–55 minutes or until a toothpick comes out clean. Cool for 10–15 minutes and then remove from pan to a wire rack to cool.

Magic Fruit Dumplings
A wonderful, old-fashioned, easy, and very versatile recipe. The crust just "magically" appears on top.

½ cup margarine
1 cup + 2 Tbsp all-purpose flour
¼ tsp salt
1 cup sugar
1 tsp baking powder

1 cup reconstituted powdered milk
1 tsp vanilla
1 quart fruit, any kind
Cinnamon and sugar

Melt margarine in 8x12-inch pan. Mix together flour, salt, sugar, baking powder, milk and vanilla. Pour over margarine and stir lightly. Cut up the fruit into the size pieces you'd like and pour into pan, include all the juice. Distribute evenly. Bake at 325° F for 25 minutes. The crust just magically appears on top. Sprinkle crust with cinnamon and sugar. Continue cooking for an additional 20–30 minutes until crust on top is lightly browned. Serve warm with a scoop of vanilla ice cream or whipped topping.

Banana Cookies

My daughter usually requests traditional chocolate chip cookies. The day I developed this recipe and had them ready for an after school snack, she declared them "the best cookie I had ever made!"

½ cup butter
½ cup sugar
½ cup brown sugar, packed
1 ¼ cups mashed banana
1 tsp vanilla
2 ½ cups all-purpose flour

1 tsp baking powder
1 tsp baking soda
½ tsp salt
½ tsp cinnamon
1 cup chocolate chips

Cream together the butter and sugars. Add bananas and vanilla. Add remaining ingredients. You can use half wheat flour and half white flour. Mix or stir together. Drop by spoonfuls onto greased baking sheet. Bake at 350° F 8–10 minutes. Allow cookies to cool for a couple of minutes on a baking sheet before removing to a wire rack. Makes about 3 dozen cookies. You can freeze the cookies once they are baked.

Crazy Cake

This is the recipe that inspired me to experiment with egg-free recipes. My mom has had this recipe for years and it is the best "from scratch" chocolate cake! You can easily make your own cake mix with this recipe and just store it in a ziplock bag. Use a sharpie pen to write the wet ingredients on the bag for quick mixing another time. We love this cake served with a generous spoonful of chocolate pudding topped with a dollop of whipped topping in place of frosting.

3 cups all-purpose flour
1 ½ cups sugar
1 tsp salt
2 tsp baking soda
3–4 Tbsp cocoa

2 tsp vanilla
2 Tbsp white vinegar
⅔ cup oil
2 cups cold water

Mix all ingredients together. Bake in a 9x13-inch pan at 350° F for 30–35 minutes.

Danish Dessert

Growing up, this was the dessert everyone requested for their birthdays. It takes a little bit of work, but my mom was always willing to do it for us.

Crust:
½ cup margarine
¼ cup sugar
½ cup chopped nuts, optional
1 cup all-purpose flour

Topping:
2 envelopes Dream Whip, whipped
1 (8 oz) pkg cream cheese, softened
½ cup powdered sugar

Fruit Topping:
1 pkg Danish Dessert mix, cooked
1 small pkg frozen berries

To make crust, mix together like pie crust. Push into the bottom of a 9x13-inch pan. Bake at 350° F until light brown (about 10 minutes.) For topping, mix until creamy and spread over cooled crust. Allow to cool in fridge until firm. Cook fruit topping and allow to cool. Spread over white mixture and chill until set. You can find Dream Whip and Danish Dessert mix near the jello in most grocery stores. You can also substitute the Pie Glaze recipe found in the Ultra Gel section of this book for the fruit topping.

Instant Pumpkin Pudding

Layer this over a no-bake cheesecake for a delicious pumpkin dessert.

1 small box instant vanilla pudding
1 ½ cups reconstituted powdered milk

2 cups pumpkin puree
½–1 tsp pumpkin pie spice

Mix together with a wire whisk and allow to set. For a richer pudding, you can use evaporated milk in place of the reconstituted powdered milk.

Pumpkin Oatmeal Cookies
What a fun taste of fall!

4 cups all-purpose flour
2 cups quick oats
½ cup sugar
2 cups brown sugar, packed
2 tsp baking soda
2 tsp pumpkin pie spice
1 tsp salt

2 ½ cups pumpkin
1 tsp vanilla
¼ cup vegetable oil
½ cup white bean puree
2 cups chocolate chips

Mix dry ingredients together in a bowl. You can use 2 c. wheat flour and 2 c. white flour. Add wet ingredients. Mix or stir together. Drop by spoonfuls onto greased baking sheet. Bake at 350° F 15–20 minutes or until firm and lightly browned. Makes about 5 dozen cookies. Unbaked dough can be frozen. Thaw in refrigerator and bake as directed. You can also freeze the cookies once they are baked. For a different version, instead of adding chocolate chips, frost cooled cookies with **Maple Buttercream Frosting**:

2 Tbsp butter, softened
¼ cup maple or pancake syrup
1 ½ cups powdered sugar

Using a hand beater, beat butter and syrup until blended. Gradually beat in powdered sugar until smooth. Add a little milk if needed to achieve the right consistency.

Chewy Caramel Corn
This was a Sunday night tradition at my home growing up.

½ cup butter or margarine
1 cup light corn syrup

1 lb brown sugar
2–3 Tbsp reconstituted powdered milk

Melt butter and stir in corn syrup and brown sugar. Boil for 3 minutes. Add milk. Pour over 6–8 quarts of popped popcorn. Mix and eat.

Peanut Butter Chocolate Chip Cookies

You can turn these into peanut butter and jelly thumbprint cookies by leaving out the chocolate chips. Make a thumbprint in the cookie before baking and fill it with just a little jam. Bake as directed.

1 cup shortening
1 ¼ cups peanut butter
1 cup sugar
1 cup brown sugar, packed
2 tsp vanilla
1 tsp salt
2 tsp baking soda
3 cups all-purpose flour
1 cup quick oats
6 Tbsp water
2 Tbsp oil
2 cups chocolate chips

Cream shortening, peanut butter, and sugars. Add vanilla. Add dry ingredients and mix well. Add water and oil and mix until the dough pulls together and is the consistency for cookies. Stir in chocolate chips. Drop by spoonfuls onto a greased baking sheet. Flatten slightly with your hand. Bake at 350° F for 8–10 minutes. Do not over bake. Take out when the cookies still appear doughy but the edges are just beginning to brown. Allow to cool on the baking sheet for a few minutes before removing to a wire rack. Makes about 5 dozen cookies. Unbaked dough can be frozen. Thaw in refrigerator and bake as directed. You can also freeze the cookies once they are baked.

Hockey Pucks

These are fun on a Christmas platter.

1 box Ritz crackers or Maria cookies
1 pkg vanilla almond bark
1 pkg chocolate almond bark
1 small jar peanut butter
1 small jar Nutella

Spread Nutella on 36 crackers. Spread peanut butter on another 36 crackers. Top each cracker with another cracker, creating a sandwich. Melt the almond bark in two separate containers. Dip the Nutella crackers in the vanilla almond bark and the peanut butter crackers in the chocolate almond bark. Be sure to completely cover them in candy coating. Place on waxed paper to harden. Decorate with drizzles of leftover almond bark. The Maria cookies are available in the Hispanic aisle of our local grocery stores.

Jello Marble Pie

A cool, refreshing dessert for a hot day or any day.

1 pkg vanilla wafers
1 ⅓ cups boiling water
2 small pkgs jello, any two flavors
1 cup cold water
Ice cubes
12 oz frozen whipped topping, thawed

Place one layer of vanilla wafers in bottom of 9-inch pie pan. You can also use a graham cracker crust. Stir ⅔ cup boiling water into each pkg of jello in separate bowls until dissolved. Mix cold water and ice cubes to make 2 ½ cups. Stir half of the ice water into each bowl until gelatin is slightly thickened. Remove any remaining ice. Stir ½ of cool whip into each bowl. Refrigerate 20–30 minutes or until mixtures are very thick and will mound. Spoon both mixtures into crust, plopping a spoonful of each kind next to each other so you have a good mix of color. Swirl with a knife to marbleize. Refrigerate 4 hours or until firm.

No Bake Chocolate Cookies

Everyone loves no-bake cookies. It's easy to keep the ingredients on-hand to whip up these fun treats.

2 cups sugar
½ cup reconstituted powdered milk
⅓ cup cocoa
½ cup margarine
3 cups oatmeal
½ tsp vanilla
1 spoonful peanut butter

Boil sugar, milk, cocoa, and margarine hard for 2 minutes. Remove from heat and add remaining ingredients. Place by spoonfuls onto waxed paper to cool and harden.

Popcorn Balls

These will bring back memories of your youth and Halloween parties. At least in our area, these are still a fun treat at that time of year.

6 quarts popped popcorn
1 small box jello, any flavor

1 cup sugar
1 cup light corn syrup

Combine jello, sugar, and corn syrup in a saucepan. Cook until everything is dissolved. Pour over popcorn and mix well. Let cool for about 5 minutes and then form into balls.

Popcorn Cake

Substitute M&M's for the gumdrops and peanuts for a different version of this tasty dessert.

4 quarts popped popcorn
½ cup butter
16 oz marshmallows

2 cups gumdrops
1 cup peanuts

Melt butter and marshmallows. Mix in nuts and gumdrops. Pour over popcorn and mix well. Put in buttered tube pan. Let cool, dump out and serve. You can also form into popcorn balls.

Rice Krispie Candies

Purchase Rice Krispies when they are on sale so you can stock up. They store for more than a year in their original packaging and give you the option of making this tasty treat anytime.

1 cup sugar
1 cup light corn syrup

1 cup peanut butter
6 cups Rice Krispies

Heat sugar and corn syrup until dissolved. Remove from heat and add peanut butter and Rice Krispies. Pour into 9x13-inch pan and pat down. You can melt chocolate over the top to make it even more delicious.

Peanut Brittle

This is a favorite at Christmas time around our house.

1 cup sugar
1 cup light corn syrup
½ cup water
¼ tsp salt

1 lb butter (do not use margarine)
1 ½ lbs raw peanuts
1 heaping tsp baking soda

Combine sugar, corn syrup, water, salt, and butter in a saucepan. Cook until candy reaches approximately 280° F. Add peanuts and cook until approximately 305° F stirring constantly. Remove from heat and add baking soda. Pour out on a buttered cookie sheet to cool. Break into pieces and serve.

English Toffee

It doesn't seem like Christmas until I've made a batch of this candy to share.

2 ½ cups sugar
1 lb butter (do not use margarine)
½ cup water
⅓ lb slivered almonds

¼ cup light corn syrup
1 lb milk chocolate, grated
Walnuts, chopped

Grate chocolate and set aside with the chopped nuts. Combine the remaining ingredients in a saucepan. Cook until candy reaches 300° F stirring constantly. It will turn to a light brown color. Pour onto a cookie sheet. Sprinkle grated chocolate over the hot candy and spread out as it melts. Sprinkle with chopped nuts. Let cool completely. Break into pieces and serve. Many times I melt 1 cup of milk chocolate chips with 1 tsp of shortening in the microwave to spread over the candy instead of grating a large piece of chocolate.

Peanut Butter Balls

These are one of my husband's favorites, but no one else can resist them either.

1 cup peanut butter
6 Tbsp butter
2 cups powdered sugar

2 cups milk chocolate chips
2 tsp shortening

Mix peanut butter, butter, and powdered sugar together until creamy. Form into small balls and place on waxed paper. Melt chocolate chips with the shortening in the microwave for 1–2 minutes on high, stirring every 20–30 seconds. Dip peanut butter balls into the chocolate and return to the waxed paper to harden. Melt additional chocolate, if needed.

Turtle Delights

This is a favorite holiday treat. We also love to share them for Valentine's Day.

60 caramels (14 oz)
2 Tbsp water
2 Tbsp butter

2 cups coarsely chopped pecans
2 cups milk chocolate chips
2 tsp shortening

Combine the caramels, water, and butter in a microwave safe bowl. Heat for 3–3½ minutes on high, stirring every 30 seconds. Stir in the pecans. Chill in the fridge until you can form the mixture into balls. Once chilled, drop by tablespoons onto a waxed paper covered baking sheet. Slip back into the fridge for a few minutes if they seem to spread too much. Melt chocolate chips with the shortening in the microwave for 1–2 minutes on high, stirring every 20–30 seconds. Dip caramel pieces into the chocolate and return to the waxed paper to harden. Melt additional chocolate, if needed.

Pie Crust

This crust recipe freezes very well. Double or triple the batch and freeze in individual crust sizes. It will keep for 6 months or more in the freezer.

2 cups all-purpose flour
½ tsp salt

1 cup shortening
Ice water

Cut the shortening into the flour and salt mixture with a fork until the pieces of shortening are between the size of quarters and nickels (no smaller.) Add ice water a tablespoon at a time. Toss the moistened area with a fork until it begins to pull together into a ball. Set it aside and add more ice water to the dry parts, tossing as you go. When all the dough is moistened, but not sticky, separate into two parts. Shape into disks about 4 inches across and wrap in plastic wrap. (You can freeze the dough at this point to use later. Thaw and roll out when it is still cold.) Refrigerate the dough for at least 10 minutes, but 2–3 hours is best. (The trick to a crispy crust is larger pieces of fat that are cold so they can create pockets of steam in the crust when it bakes.) Roll out between two pieces of plastic wrap to fit the pan. If baking empty, place a piece of foil over the crust and fill with a hand full of dry beans. This will keep bubbles from forming in the crust. Bake at 400° F for 8–10 minutes until lightly browned. If filling crust, use a precooked filling that is already thickened to speed up the baking process. Top with crust, cut a few vent holes, and bake at 400° F for 30–35 minutes or until golden brown. Check after 25 minutes and cover edges with foil if crust is browning too quickly.

Raspberry Cream Pie

You can substitute any kind of berry for the raspberries in this delicious pie.

1 single crust pie shell, baked
1 small box instant vanilla pudding
1 ½ cups reconstituted powdered milk
1 box frozen raspberries in juice
Sugar, to taste

Cinnamon, to taste
Nutmeg, to taste
Lemon juice, to taste
Cornstarch
Frozen whipped topping, thawed

Mix pudding and milk and pour into pie shell. Combine raspberries, sugar, cinnamon, nutmeg, and lemon juice in a small saucepan. Add enough cornstarch to thicken. Heat until thick. Allow topping to cool. Pour over pudding layer. Top with whipped topping just before serving. You could also use Ultra Gel to thicken instead of cornstarch.

Fruit Pandowdy

You may remember the old song about shoo-fly pie and apple pandowdy. Isn't "pandowdy" just a fun word to say? This is a very fast way to make a pie.

Pie Crust dough for a single crust   1 quart fruit pie filling, any flavor

Pour pie filling into a greased 9-inch pie pan or 7x11-inch rectangular pan. Roll out chilled pie crust dough between two pieces of plastic wrap until it is thin and uniform. Remove the top piece of plastic wrap and use a pizza cutter to cut the dough into 1 ½-inch squares. (With a pandowdy, it doesn't have to be exact.) Place the squares on top of the filling in a haphazard pattern, being sure to cover all the filling, but don't overlap the dough very much. Spray the dough with a little water, using a spray bottle and sprinkle cinnamon and sugar on top, if desired. Bake at 400° F for 30 minutes or until lightly browned. Scoop into serving bowls and top with vanilla ice cream or whipped topping for a delicious and easy dessert.

Cream Pie

Stir in coconut or bananas to add bulk and fun flavor to this pie.

1 single crust pie shell, baked   1 ½ cups reconstituted powdered milk
1 small box instant pudding, any flavor   8 oz frozen whipped topping, thawed

Allow pie crust to cool. Mix pudding with milk using a wire whisk. Allow the pudding to set up. Fold in the whipped topping and spoon into pie crust. Chill until serving. We love bananas with chocolate pudding and coconut with vanilla pudding.

Cooking with Whole Wheat

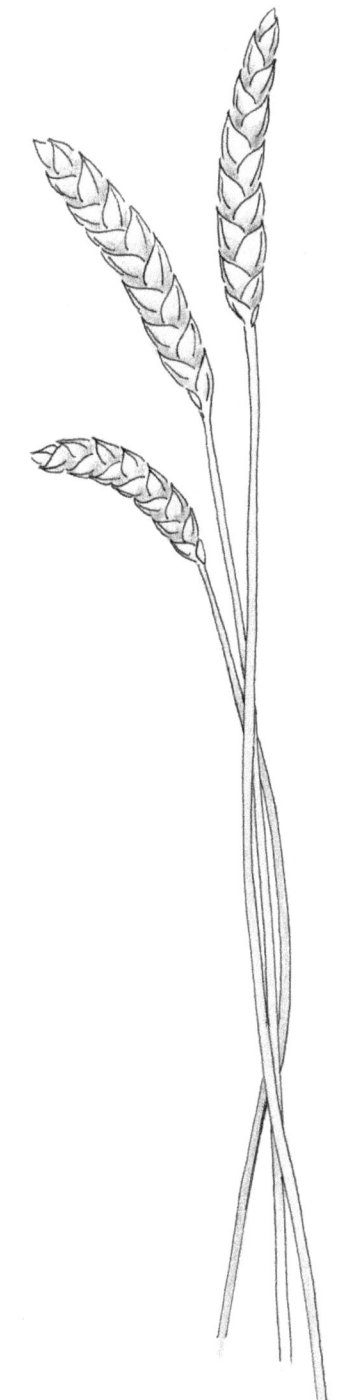

Wheat is the bulk of what most people store. It stores for over 30 years when dry-packed and provides many options for cooking and baking. We all know that we are to be eating more whole grains for better health. Using wheat on a regular basis can help you do this. Substituting wheat berries for white rice or pasta in some of your recipes could help you work toward getting more whole grains. Also making your muffins and cookies with half wheat and half white flour can also increase your whole grains.

This section focuses on sharing some basic information about wheat. The recipes are intended to inspire you to try some new things with wheat. To really benefit most from storing wheat, you need to have a wheat grinder. There are still a few things you can do without a grinder. Hopefully, these ideas will motivate you to do something with all the wheat you have.

Hard White vs. Hard Red Wheat – The main difference is in the color. Everything I have read suggests that nutritionally they are the same. The red wheat has a stronger flavor and a darker color. The white wheat is lighter and acts more like white flour in your recipes. It is easier to convert your family to using it since the taste is sweeter and more like what they are used to. I prefer the hard white wheat now that I have tried both. They both store for 30+ years when packaged in a #10 can or bucket with oxygen absorbers.

Soft Wheat – Used for quick breads, pastries, cookies, etc. It has a lower protein content than the hard wheat. Some people who bake more quick breads instead of yeast breads choose to store soft wheat. I have excellent results in my quick breads and muffins by using half whole wheat flour (ground from hard white wheat) and half all-purpose flour so I haven't worried about storing soft wheat. I do store all-purpose white flour to give me the chance to do half and half in my recipes.

Wheat Berries or Kernels – A wheat berry is actually the unprocessed wheat seed, also known as the kernel. Wheat berries contain the whole grain—endosperm, bran and germ—and that's what makes them so healthy. They contain all of the fiber, vitamins, minerals, and nutrients that are removed during the refinement process used to make standard white flour.

12 cups wheat berries will grind into about 20 cups of flour

1 cup whole wheat flour = 15 grams of fiber

Choosing a Wheat Grinder – Everyone ends up with their own opinion when it comes to a wheat grinder. I'm not going to tell you the perfect model, I'm going to share with you a few things to consider when you are purchasing. You will want some way to grind wheat even during a power outage. Some electric models have a hand crank option so this solves the no power problem. I've found that these combination grinders are quite expensive. We've chosen to store a simple hand grinder for those "what if" times and then a basic electric grinder I use all the time. Cost is definitely a factor to think about when choosing a grinder.

My first grinder spit flour all over the place so it was a mess to grind wheat. I found that if I draped an old towel over the unit when I was grinding, it would at least contain the mess. I had purchased this grinder at a thrift store for $8 and was so excited just to have a grinder that I put up with the mess until we could afford a better model. My thrift store model was also very loud.

When we researched grinders, I was looking for one that would not make a mess and would be much quieter than my old model. I also wanted the versatility to grind other grains if I needed to. The internet is a great resource for determining just which model you will like. Choose the one you want and then budget for it. I ended up choosing the Nutrimill Grain Mill. It took us some time to save for the one we wanted, but we have been very happy.

For making cracked wheat for use in breads and as a hot cereal, you can just purchase an inexpensive coffee grinder. It will give you the coarser grind you are looking for.

Substituting Whole Wheat Flour for White Flour – Whole wheat flour usually can be substituted for part or all of the all-purpose flour in most recipes. For example, if the recipe calls for two cups flour, try one cup of all-purpose and one cup of whole wheat flour. When I substitute half and half like this, I don't have to play with the moisture amounts. When completely substituting whole wheat for white, use ⅞ cup whole wheat for one cup of white flour. Whole wheat flour absorbs more moisture than all-purpose white flour. In my experimenting, it seems that hard red wheat flour absorbs more moisture than hard white wheat flour. As you play with some of your recipes, you may need to adjust the amount of water or milk by a few tablespoons when using wheat flour instead of white.

To make it convenient for me to substitute whole wheat flour, I grind a 5-gallon bucket all at once. If I have the flour ground, I use it. I've heard that fresh ground wheat is better for you, but I have not been able to find any specific research telling me why. I figure even if a few of the vitamins break down slightly over time, I am still better off than if I were to use white flour all the time because of convenience. With all the baking I do, we go through a bucket in 6–8 weeks.

Cooking Wheat Berries

On the Stovetop – Combine 1 c. wheat berries and 2 ½ c. water in a saucepan. Cover, bring to a boil, lower heat to simmer on lowest setting. (Just as you would for cooking rice.) Cook until grains are soft—about 1 to 1 ½ hours. You might have to add water to prevent scorching. Just check on it periodically. Cooked wheat berries freeze very well so don't be afraid to cook a large batch.

Crockpot Instructions – Combine 5 cups wheat berries and 10 cups water. Turn on low and leave overnight. My friend's family would eat this for breakfast with a little sugar and milk added. They called them footballs. You can freeze any extra to use in recipes another time.

Thermos Instructions – Put 5 cups wheat berries in a thermos with 10 cups boiling water and leave on the counter overnight. In the morning, you'll have 15 cups of wheat berries. Freeze any you don't use.

How to Test Wheat Berries for Doneness – Test for doneness by removing a grain and tasting. It will be chewy with a soft center. Whole wheat berries stay chewier than rice. You can substitute them for almost all the recipes that require rice. Try to remember that wheat berries take longer to cook and need a little more liquid than rice. For more flavor, try cooking the berries in chicken broth or vegetable juices.

Stretching Your Hamburger with Wheat Berries – Cook wheat berries and allow to cool. If desired, grind with a meat grinder. This will give them the appearance and texture of ground beef. Combine equal parts ground wheat berries and hamburger in your frying pan. The hamburger with the highest fat content will give the wheat berries more of a meaty flavor. Cook together to season your wheat and use in recipes calling for hamburger. You can do this same thing with ground turkey or sausage. Ground wheat berries store very well in the freezer. I keep some on hand and add them to meat whenever I am cooking up a big batch. Once the meat is cooked, I freeze the wheat/meat combination to make dinner prep go quickly another night. It makes a healthier meal and stretches our food budget as well.

Freezing Wheat Berries – Wheat berries freeze very well once they are cooked. Be sure to cook up a large batch and freeze for later use. I just put the cooked wheat berries in freezer ziplock bags marked with the date. They last for 1 year in the freezer.

A Word of Caution – Whole wheat is very high in fiber compared to what most people are used to. Switching to whole wheat all at once can upset your digestive tract and make you uncomfortable. As with any major food change, add it to your diet gradually over time and you will adjust just fine.

Autumn Wheat Berry Salad
A unique, nutty tasting salad that is also healthy.

1 cup wheat berries
½ cup dried cranberries
½ cup pecan pieces, toasted
½ cup chopped green onions
⅓ cup Italian dressing

Cook wheat berries, drain and cool. Add remaining ingredients; mix lightly. Serve immediately or cover and refrigerate up to 4 days. You can rehydrate 1–2 Tbsp minced onions to replace the green onion.

Wheat Berry Fruit Salad
A take on the popular Frog Eye Salad. This version uses wheat berries instead of noodles.

½ cup wheat berries
1 large can fruit cocktail
1 can pineapple chunks
1 (3 oz) box vanilla pudding
1 (8 oz) frozen whipped topping, thawed
Additional fruit as desired (bananas, apples, etc.)

Cook and drain wheat berries. Run cold water over wheat berries until cool. Drain fruit, reserving the juice. Stir wheat berries, fruit and dry pudding powder together. Add enough juice back to the mixture to keep it moist. Stir in whipped topping and add additional fruit if desired. Chill.

Wheat Berry Chili
I often add wheat berries to chili whenever I make it, but it is also delicious with just wheat berries.

Make your favorite chili recipe and substitute cooked wheat berries for your beans. You'll be surprised at how good it tastes. Leftovers freeze very well.

Wheat Berry Pilaf

Use as a side dish for dinner and enjoy a high-fiber, low-fat alternative to other options.

2 cups wheat berries
5 cups water
5 tsp chicken or beef bouillon
3–4 Tbsp dried, minced onion
2 Tbsp dehydrated celery

2 Tbsp dehydrated green pepper
2 Tbsp dehydrated carrots
1 bay leaf
½ tsp thyme
1–2 tsp parsley

Combine all ingredients in a large saucepan. Cover, bring to a boil, lower heat to simmer on lowest setting. Cook until grains are soft. About 1 to 1 ½ hours. You might have to add water to prevent scorching. Just check on it periodically. This freezes very well so don't be afraid to cook a large batch.

Overnight Whole Wheat Pancakes

Many of you may be familiar with a blender wheat pancake recipe. I have had better success when I soak my wheat overnight. Feel free to try this recipe without soaking the wheat first. Maybe you have a more powerful blender than I do.

2–3 cups water
1 cup whole wheat berries
¼ cup powdered milk
1 ½ cups warm water
1 egg
2 Tbsp oil

2 Tbsp sugar
½ tsp salt
1 Tbsp baking powder
1 tsp vanilla
Dash of cinnamon

Soak wheat berries in 2–3 cups of water for 8–12 hours. Drain. Combine soaked wheat berries, milk powder and warm water in a blender. Blend on high for 3 minutes. Add the remaining ingredients to blender and blend for an additional 2 minutes. Cook on hot griddle. If you don't blend long enough, your wheat grains will remain crunchy. VARIATION: Add ¾ cup cooked pumpkin, applesauce, mashed squash or sweet potatoes in place of ¾ cup of the water. Add additional cinnamon or pumpkin pie spice to taste. Add a little more water to adjust the moisture level as needed to make the batter the right consistency.

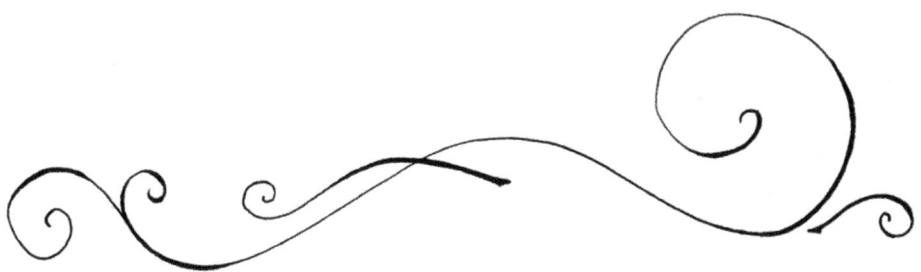

Whole Wheat Brownie Mix
A fun, healthy alternative to a store-bought mix.

4 cups sugar
3 cups whole wheat flour
1 cup baking cocoa
2 tsp baking powder
2 tsp salt

Additional Ingredients (for each batch):
¼ cup shortening
2 eggs
1 tsp vanilla
½ cup chopped walnuts, optional

Combine the dry ingredients in a ziplock bag or other container. Yield: 4 batches. To prepare brownies: Combine 2 ½ cups mix, shortening, eggs, and vanilla. Batter will be stiff. Stir in nuts if desired. Spread in a greased 8-inch square pan. Bake at 350° F for 20–25 minutes or until a toothpick comes out clean.

Whole Wheat Sugar Cookies
A scrumptious cookie with just a touch of spice.

1 cup brown sugar, packed
½ cup butter, softened
1 egg
2 Tbsp reconstituted powdered milk
¼ tsp almond extract, optional
1 tsp vanilla extract
2 ¾ cups whole wheat flour

1 tsp baking powder
½ tsp baking soda
¼ tsp salt
½ tsp ground nutmeg
1 Tbsp fresh or 1 tsp dried grated orange peel

Cream together sugar and butter. Add egg, milk, extracts and mix well. Add remaining ingredients and mix until well blended. Shape dough into balls. Roll in granulated sugar. Place about 2 inches apart on a cookie sheet coated with cooking spray. Flatten cookie slightly. Bake at 375° F for 8–10 minutes or until golden brown. Cool on pan for 2 minutes and transfer to a wire rack. Makes about 3 dozen.

Whole Wheat Muffins

I love good friends who share my passion for being prepared. This great recipe was passed to me by one of those special friends.

2 cups whole wheat flour
1 cup brown sugar, packed
1 tsp baking soda
3 Tbsp dry milk powder
¼ tsp salt

1 cup water
½ cup melted margarine or oil
1 tsp vanilla
1 egg
Dried fruit or chocolate chips, if desired

Mix dry ingredients together in a bowl. Add liquid ingredients and stir until moistened. Spoon into greased muffin tins. Bake at 350° F for 15 min.

Whole Wheat Baking Powder Biscuits

Enjoy a hot biscuit with dinner tonight and give yourself a pat on the back for being provident today.

2 cups sifted whole wheat flour
1 tsp salt
4 tsp baking powder

6 Tbsp shortening
⅓–1 cup reconstituted powdered milk

Sift dry ingredients together. Cut in shortening with 2 knives or pastry blender. Mix in just enough milk to make a soft dough—not too wet. Turn out on a lightly floured surface. Pat out to ½-inch thickness. Cut with floured cutter. Or you can make drop biscuits by just dropping a biscuit sized portion onto the cookie sheet, no cutting required. Bake on greased cookie sheet at 400° F for 15–20 minutes. Makes about 8–10 biscuits.

Bread Making

There is nothing that says "home" more than the smell of freshly baked bread. Baking bread can be fun and it makes the house smell soooo nice! With just a few tips, a good mixer, and a little practice you can become a great bread maker!

There are two basic methods for making bread dough. Some recipes ask you to dissolve the yeast and sugar in a small amount of warm water and then add this to your dry ingredients along with additional warm liquid. The other method suggests that you combine your dry ingredients, including your yeast and add your warm wet ingredients all at once. Really all that dissolving your yeast ahead of time does is prove that your yeast is working. I suggest you follow this advice if the yeast you are using has been stored for a very long time and you are questioning its effectiveness. Otherwise, I always add my yeast right along with my dry ingredients and skip the extra step and dirty dishes.

I store my unopened yeast in the freezer to lengthen its shelf-life and once opening it, I store it in the fridge. I prefer to use SAF instant yeast. It is the least expensive way to purchase yeast in my area and I have always had success when using it. Many recipes call for 1 package of yeast, this is equal to about 1 Tbsp of yeast. Bread will rise if you use less yeast. It will just take it a lot longer to double in size. If you are in a period of needing to ration your yeast, keep this in mind.

To be able to make one loaf of bread a day for a year, you will need to store approximately 300 lbs of wheat and 8 (1 lb) packages of SAF instant yeast. I also like to keep some white bread flour on hand so I can have the option of making half wheat and half white bread or all white bread every now and then. You can use all-purpose flour in your bread, but it is not as high in protein as bread flour so the texture of the bread will not be as nice. The other kind of flour you will want to store is gluten flour (sometimes called vital wheat gluten.) Gluten is the protein portion of the wheat, and by adding additional gluten flour to your bread, you will get a loaf that has a more desirable texture.

We store our wheat in #10 cans that have been sealed with oxygen packets. I also have my gluten flour stored this way. I do not open these cans on a regular basis since they have long shelf-lives. They are stored in hard to reach places since we don't need to access them regularly. I keep 100 lbs of wheat at the house in buckets. This is the wheat I rotate on a regular basis. When I am getting low, I look for a good deal and purchase another 100 lbs. I also store my all-purpose flour and bread flour just in buckets without the oxygen absorbers. We rotate through it quickly enough that I don't go to the extra expense or time to seal it for long-term storage.

Tips for Better and Faster Bread Baking

- Once you have found a favorite recipe, make some mixes of the dry ingredients to store in your pantry, but only include half of the flour. Store them in a ziplock bag and use a sharpie pen to write the wet ingredients that you need to add, knowing that you will also be adding additional flour. Make 3–4 of these mixes when you have all of your ingredients out to quicken your work next time.

- Create a baking center in your kitchen where all your ingredients, spices, and measuring cups are kept in one place. I have a cupboard above my mixer for this. Then I am not having to circle my kitchen multiple times to finish the recipe.

- Tape copies of your favorite recipes that you find yourself using often to the inside door of your baking cupboard. This saves you the time of looking up the recipe when you are ready to bake bread.

- Grind a bucket full of wheat when you have your grinder out. I use a 5-gallon bucket full of wheat flour in 2–3 months and it has never gone rancid for me. Because it is all ground, I find myself using wheat flour more often in cookies and muffins also.

- Loosen the flour in your bucket or bin by turning over the top layer with your measuring cup before measuring out your flour. This will help make sure you do not pack your measuring cup too tightly with flour and end up with a heavier bread.

- Add gluten flour to any bread recipe. Add 1–2 Tbsp for each cup of flour called for in the recipe. For example: if the recipe calls for 4 cups of flour, add 4 Tbsp or ¼ cup of gluten flour if you are using whole wheat flour or bread flour. If you are using all-purpose flour, you will want to add about 2 Tbsp per cup of flour in your recipe. Remember you are trading gluten flour for some of the flour in the recipe so reduce your overall amount of flour by the amount of gluten flour that you add.

- Don't hesitate to try adding white vinegar to your bread recipes. (½ Tbsp per loaf of bread.) Vinegar is a dough enhancer and aids in the reaction of the yeast. It also acts as a preservative so your bread will not mold as quickly.

- Let your dough rise in the oven. Turn your oven to 150° F to get it warm. Turn the oven off once it reaches this temperature. Cover your dough with a cloth and place the oven safe bowl in the oven to do its first rise. It usually takes about 20 minutes instead of an hour or more. This trick cuts the total bread making time to about 1 ½ hours.

- Most bread recipes can be made with half wheat and half white flour without changing their texture. When you add whole wheat flour, increase the water or milk by a couple of tablespoons since wheat flour absorbs more moisture than white flour.

- You can freeze bread dough to use later. Make a large batch of dough and when it comes time to add the liquids, use room temperature water instead of hot. (This makes the yeast grow at a slower rate so it doesn't rise too much in the freezer and pop your ziplock bag open.) Divide into the size portions you would like. Spray the inside of your ziplock bags with a little cooking spray and then place your dough inside and freeze. You can also shape into loaves or rolls first and then freeze. I place the loaves in loaf pans and the rolls on a baking sheet and cover with plastic wrap or foil. Once they are frozen, transfer to ziplock bags and store for 1–2 months. They do rise a little as they freeze and putting them in pans helps them keep the shape I want. When you are shaping your dough before freezing, remember to make your loaves and rolls small since they will rise as they thaw. To use frozen dough: Allow to thaw at room temperature and rise until double. (This takes about 3 hours.) If you did not shape the dough before freezing, shape as you wish and allow to rise again. Bake as the original recipe suggests. Sometimes I speed this process up a bit by using a warm oven as described above. (This method for freezing dough has only been tested with SAF instant yeast.)

- You can make dough ahead of time and store in the refrigerator until later in the day. This slows down the rising process. I've also made dough the night before and left it in the fridge so I could make maple bars or cinnamon rolls quickly in the morning. When doing this, I use room temperature water as described above to mix the dough. Spray the top of the dough with cooking spray and then cover the bowl with a towel and slip it into the fridge. (This method has only been tested with SAF instant yeast.)

Basic Instructions That Work with All Recipes:

Mix all dry ingredients only adding half of the flour in your mixer bowl.

Add wet ingredients and begin mixing using the dough hook following the suggested speed in your mixer instruction book for bread. (Water should be about 115°–120° F to allow the yeast to rise.)

Gradually add additional flour until dough cleans the sides of the bowl. The exact amount of flour you will add will depend on the humidity in the air and whether you are using all whole wheat flour. Be patient as you add the flour. Only add ¼–½ cup at a time and watch to see if the dough pulls together and leaves the sides of the bowl basically clean. Remember that when making bread by hand, you are to knead the dough for 6–8 minutes. The mixer doesn't necessarily do it any faster, it just does the work for you. The mistake that often makes bread too heavy is adding too much flour.

Once the dough is pulling together and leaving the sides of the bowl clean, stop adding flour and just allow the mixer to knead the dough until smooth, elastic, and resistant. (About 2–3 minutes.)

Lightly oil top of dough (or spray with cooking spray), cover with a cloth and let rise until double in size. You can speed this step up by turning your oven to 150° F. Once it is hot, turn the oven off and set your bowl of dough into the oven. (If your mixer has a plastic bowl, you will want to transfer the dough to an oven safe bowl first.) On the counter, it usually takes an hour or more to let your dough rise. In the oven, it is double in size in about 20 minutes.

Punch dough down and remove from bowl. (You can allow the dough to rise multiple times. Sometimes you just can't get to it when it's ready. Maybe the turkey is still in the oven or the baby needs to be fed or the phone rings. You know you have days like this. Just keep punching it down each time it is double in size. Letting it rise a few times actually makes for a fluffier, lighter texture.)

Shape into loaves or rolls on an oiled countertop and place in greased pans.

Cover with a cloth and let rise until almost double, about 20 minutes.

Bake according to specific recipe instructions. Bread is done when it is golden brown and sounds hollow when you tap it.

Take bread out of pans when done and cool on a cooling rack. Spread melted butter over the tops of the bread if you want a soft crust.

Making Bread by Hand

Follow the basic instructions as above. You are just going to do the work the mixer usually would. It will take a few times of trying bread to determine just how much flour to add. It is better to add a little less flour than a little too much. Many women who bake bread all the time for their families find that they can do a larger batch by hand than they can do in a mixer so they prefer doing it by hand all the time. Don't let not having a mixer be an excuse not to bake bread!

Basic Bread Dough

If you only want to learn one recipe, this is the one to learn—it is so versatile!

3 + cups bread flour
3 Tbsp gluten flour
3 Tbsp dry milk powder
2 Tbsp sugar

1 tsp salt
1 Tbsp yeast
2 Tbsp oil
1 ¼ cups hot water

Mix according to basic bread making instructions (page 126). I always do ½ white and ½ wheat flour. Cover and allow to rise until double in size. Shape and bake as desired.

Dinner Rolls: Once dough has completed the first rise, shape into rolls. Let rise for 20 minutes. Bake at 375° F for 15 min. or until golden brown. Triple the recipe to make 4 dozen rolls and fill an entire baking sheet. Freeze any extra to pull out later. To reheat: Wrap thawed rolls in foil and bake at 350° F for 10–15 minutes.

Hamburger Buns: After the first rise, roll out and cut 7 buns, using a wide mouth canning ring as your "cookie cutter." Place on greased baking sheet so they are 2 to 3 inches apart. Allow to rise for about 20 minutes. Bake at 375° F for 15 min. or until golden brown. Cool slightly, then split them in half horizontally to fill.

Hot Dog Buns: After the first rise, shape into thick breadsticks the length of hot dogs. Place on greased baking sheet so they are touching along the long sides. Allow to rise for about 20 minutes. Bake at 375° F for 15 minutes or until golden brown. Cool slightly, then split them in half horizontally to fill.

Pizza Dough: After the first rise, roll or push out on pizza pans and add toppings. Bake pizza at 425° F for 10–12 minutes or until crust is lightly browned.

Breadsticks: After the first rise, shape into breadsticks. Place on a greased baking sheet. Allow to rise 15–20 minutes and bake at 425° F for 10–12 minutes or until breadsticks are lightly browned. Brush with butter while hot to soften the crust.

Pita Bread: After the first rise, divide the dough into 10–12 pieces. Roll out each piece into a flat circle that is 5–6 inches across and about ¼ inch thick. Place on a greased baking sheet. Bake at 500° F on the bottom rack of the oven. Bake for 2–4 minutes on the first side until the bread puffs up. Flip over, flatten with a spatula, and bake an additional 30 seconds to 1 minute until golden brown. Flatten with the spatula again and place on a plate. Cover with a kitchen towel to keep it soft while you cook the remaining pitas. Leftovers can be frozen.

Bread Bowls: Triple the batch to get 6–8 bread bowls. After the first rise, shape into 6–8 large rolls. Place a few inches apart on a greased baking sheet. Remember that the rolls will double in size. They will grow up and out a little so allow space for this to happen. I can usually fit 4 larger or 6 smaller bread bowls on a jelly roll pan. Allow to rise until nearly double in size. Cut an "X" shape in the top of each roll with a sharp knife, just barely scoring the top of the dough. Bake at 375° F for 20–25 minutes or until golden brown. Hollow out and enjoy filled with cream soup.

Maple Bars: Add an additional 2 Tbsp sugar and 1 tsp cinnamon to the above recipe. After the first rise, roll dough out to about ½-inch thickness and cut with a pizza cutter into rectangles. Place on a greased baking sheet. Allow to rise for about 20 minutes. Bake at 375° F for 10–15 minutes or until lightly browned. Frost with maple icing and enjoy! I always triple the batch and freeze any extra before frosting. Pull them out of the freezer at night and frost in the morning for a quick breakfast treat or serve for a fun after school snack.

Maple Icing: Mix with a hand mixer 3 cups powdered sugar, 2 Tbsp margarine or butter, 1 tsp maple flavoring and just a bit of milk (1–2 tsp).

Cinnamon Twists: Add an additional 2 Tbsp sugar and 1 tsp cinnamon to the above recipe. After the first rise, roll dough out to about ¼-inch thickness. Spray dough with vegetable cooking spray. Make a mix of ¼ c. brown sugar, ¼ c. white sugar and ½ tsp cinnamon. Spread this on the dough. Cut with a pizza cutter into strips about ½-inch wide by 12-inches long. Fold each strip in half and twist to resemble the pink breast cancer ribbon. Place on a greased baking sheet. Allow to rise for about 20 minutes. Bake at 375° F for 10–15 minutes or until lightly browned. Drizzle with powdered sugar icing when cooled, if desired.

Whole Wheat Bread

Gluten flour and vinegar make a huge difference in the texture of whole wheat bread. This loaf stays soft and pliable far longer than loaves without these key ingredients.

6 ½–7 cups whole wheat flour
½ cup gluten flour
2 Tbsp yeast
2 tsp salt

1 Tbsp white vinegar
⅓ cup oil
⅓ cup honey
2 ¼ cups hot water

Mix according to basic bread making instructions (page 126). Hint: Measure your oil first and then use the same measuring cup for your honey and the honey will slip right out. Bake at 350° F for 30–35 minutes or until golden brown. Turn loaves out onto cooling rack. Makes 2 loaves.

Fabulous Homemade Bread

This is my favorite recipe that we use on a regular basis. It also makes amazing French toast.

1 cup quick oats or flax meal
3 cups whole wheat flour
3–4 cups white bread flour (or additional whole wheat flour)
6 Tbsp gluten flour
2 tsp salt

⅓ cup brown sugar, packed
1 ½ Tbsp yeast
¼ cup dry milk powder
1 Tbsp white vinegar
⅓ cup oil
3 ½ cups hot water

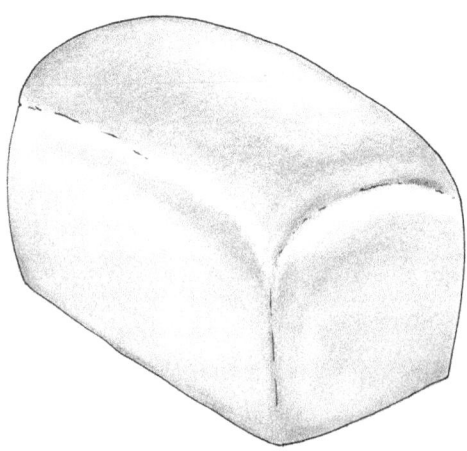

Mix according to basic bread making instructions (page 126). Bake at 350° F for 30–35 minutes or until golden brown. Turn loaves out onto cooling rack. With the oatmeal and all whole wheat flour, each loaf has about 50 grams of fiber. With the flax meal, each loaf has about 60 grams of fiber. Makes 2 loaves.

Honey Butter

Who can resist honey butter on homemade bread?

½ cup butter, softened   ⅓ cup honey

Beat butter and honey together until creamy. Serve at room temperature. Store in the refrigerator.

Focaccia Bread

A delicious bread to pair with a simple soup or cut into sticks and add to a buffet.

1 ½ cups whole wheat flour
1 ½–2 cups white bread flour
¼ cup gluten flour
1 tsp salt
1 tsp sugar
1 tsp garlic powder
1 tsp dried oregano
1 tsp dried thyme
1 tsp dried basil
1 pinch black pepper
1 Tbsp yeast
¼ cup dry milk powder
1 Tbsp oil
1 ¼ cups hot water
1 cup mozzarella cheese
1 Tbsp Parmesan cheese

Mix according to basic bread making instructions (page 126). Once dough has completed the first rise, place on greased baking sheet. Push out into a ½ inch thick rectangle. You do not let it rise a second time. Spray top of loaf with oil and sprinkle with additional dry herbs if desired. (I like to sprinkle some rosemary on top along with some of the Bread Dipping Herb Mix—recipe follows.) Bake at 400° F for 10 minutes. Sprinkle with mozzarella and Parmesan cheeses. Bake an additional 5 minutes or until golden brown. Makes 1 loaf.

Bread in a Bag

This is a fun family activity since it is great for kids to do. Clean-up is a breeze.

2 cups white bread flour
1 cup whole wheat flour (or more white)
3 Tbsp dry milk powder
3 Tbsp sugar
1 tsp salt
1 Tbsp yeast
3 Tbsp oil
1 cup hot water

Combine 1 cup flour, yeast, sugar, dry milk, and salt in a 1 gallon, heavy duty freezer ziplock bag. Squeeze upper part of bag to force out air. Seal bag. Shake and work bag to mix ingredients. Add water and oil to bag. Reseal bag and mix by working bag with fingers. Add whole wheat flour and reseal bag. Mix thoroughly. Gradually add enough remaining flour to make a stiff dough that pulls away from the bag. On a floured surface, knead dough 2–4 minutes until smooth and elastic. Cover dough and let rest for 10 minutes. Shape into a loaf and bake in a loaf pan or on a cookie sheet. Spray dough with oil and cover for 20 minutes or until double in size. Bake at 375° F for 25 minutes or until done. It works well as rolls also. If baking as rolls, bake for 15–20 minutes or until golden brown. Remove from pan and cool on a wire rack.

Basic Pizza Dough

Making pizza is a great thing to do on a Friday night with family or friends. Have everyone supply their favorite toppings and you can make a large batch of dough.

2 ½–3 cups bread flour
1 tsp salt
1 Tbsp yeast
1 tsp sugar
2 tbsp oil
1 cup warm water

Mix according to basic bread making instructions (page 126). Once dough has completed the first rise, roll or push out on pizza pans and add toppings. Bake pizza at 425° F until crust is lightly browned. You can also form this dough into bread sticks. Bake at 425° F for about 10 minutes. We really prefer to prebake the crust a bit before adding toppings. We like lots of sauce on our pizza and the crust tends to be a little soggy if we put the toppings on the dough before baking. We bake the crust for 5–8 minutes, until it is just beginning to turn light brown and then add toppings and return it to the oven for 3–5 minutes or until done. Makes 1 large crust.

Cheesy Garlic Breadsticks

Here is another one of my experiments that we are glad for. It is irresistible!

1 recipe for pizza dough
⅓ cup mayonnaise
⅓ cup Parmesan cheese
½–1 tsp minced garlic
1 cup grated cheddar cheese
Additional grated cheese

Bake pizza crust just long enough that it is lightly brown. Mix mayonnaise, Parmesan cheese, garlic and grated cheese together. Spread onto warm crust, be sure to distribute evenly. Sprinkle a little more grated cheese on top. Bake at 425° F for 5–7 minutes or until cheese is melted. Cut in strips with a pizza cutter. Dip in pizza sauce. This is also delicious made with the soft garlic breadstick dough.

Making Bread Crumbs

Many casseroles are topped with bread crumbs. It is also delicious to use bread crumbs in coatings for chicken or fish. You can purchase bread crumbs from the store, but it is far more economical to make your own.

I usually use the heels of the bread since my children are picky about eating them. When we finish a loaf of bread the heels always seem to remain in the bag. I break these heels up into small pieces and place them on a plate or baking sheet depending on how much I am doing. Allow the plate to sit out on the counter over night so that the bread can dry out. Once dry, I place the bread pieces in a ziplock bag and roll over them a few times with a rolling pin. Store the crumbs in an airtight bag or container until ready to use.

I also like to keep some seasoned bread crumbs in the pantry so I can coat fish or chicken quickly. Just sprinkle in a little onion and garlic powder. Lemon pepper or Mrs. Dash is always good also. Next time you want to coat some meat for dinner you are ready to go.

Soft Garlic Breadstick/Pizza Dough

My son is famous at school for taking these for snack when he has the assignment. We are asked to bring them to all of the parties.

2 ½–3 cups bread flour
¼ cup gluten flour
3 Tbsp grated Parmesan cheese
¼ cup dry milk powder
2 Tbsp sugar
1 Tbsp garlic powder

1 ½ tsp salt
½ tsp dried basil
1 Tbsp yeast
2 Tbsp vegetable oil
1 ¼ cups hot water

Mix according to basic bread making instructions (page 126). Once dough has completed the first rise, shape into breadsticks or roll out as pizza dough. Put on greased pans and let rise slightly. For breadsticks, bake at 425° F for 10–12 minutes or until golden brown. Brush with melted butter. For pizza, bake for 8–10 minutes or just until dough is beginning to turn light brown. Put toppings on and then bake an additional 5–10 minutes or until cheese bubbles. Makes 10–12 breadsticks or 1 large pizza crust.

Homemade Soft Pretzels: Use the above recipe or any other basic bread recipe. When finished with the first rise, shape into very thin, long snakes and then twist into pretzels. (Look online for a tutorial on just how to do this if you are a visual person.) Place on greased baking sheets and allow to rise about 20 minutes. Bake as breadsticks above if you like the soft crust. If you are in the mood for the more chewy texture of store-bought soft pretzels then boil 2 cups water with 2 Tbsp baking soda. After shaping, dip each pretzel in the boiling water and remove with a slotted spoon to a greased baking sheet. Allow to rise about 20 minutes and bake as above.

Crusty French Bread

This is delicious plain, but it is really good if you spray the loaf with oil just before baking and sprinkle some of the bread dipping herb mix on top.

3 ½–4 cups bread flour
¼ cup gluten flour
1 Tbsp sugar
2 tsp salt

1 Tbsp yeast
1 Tbsp oil
1 ½ cups hot water

Mix according to basic bread making instructions (page 126). Once dough has completed the first rise, divide in half. Shape into 1 long loaf or 2 shorter loaves. Put on a greased baking sheet, cover and let rise until almost double. Make 4–5 shallow diagonal cuts across the top of each loaf for decoration. Bake at 400° F for 20–30 minutes. For a crispier crust, spray with water just before baking. For Christmas one year, my husband gave me a French bread baking pan. I didn't even know they existed. It keeps the crust crispy and it helps the loaves keep their shape instead of being flat and wide like they sometimes turn out when I use a baking sheet. I love it!

Bread Dipping Herb Mix

Here is my creation that mirrors the bread dipping oil you are served at Italian restaurants. Simply delicious!

1 tsp dried basil
1 tsp dried thyme
1 tsp dried parsley
1 Tbsp dry minced garlic
1 tsp dried oregano

1 tsp ground black pepper
½ tsp salt
½ tsp chopped, dried rosemary
¼ tsp crushed red pepper flakes

Combine all ingredients and store in a ziplock bag. To serve: Combine a small amount of the spices and a little olive oil in a shallow dish. This herb mix is also delicious over roasted or steamed mixed vegetables. If you are like me, you'll find a million uses for it so you might as well make a large batch. It will store forever. It is fun to give as a gift with a fresh baked loaf of French bread.

Casserole Bread

This bread gets its name because you bake it in a casserole dish to give it a unique shape. It is very versatile and goes well with soup, casseroles, or meat dishes.

5–5 ½ cups bread flour
¼ cup gluten flour
2 Tbsp sugar
1 ½ tsp salt
½ tsp pepper

2 Tbsp yeast
2 Tbsp oil
2 cups hot water
¾ cup shredded cheddar cheese
2 Tbsp dried, minced onion, rehydrated

Mix according to basic bread making instructions (page 126). Stir in cheese and onions with the wet ingredients. Shape into a ball. Put in a greased 2-quart round baking dish. (You can also cook as two small loaves.) Cover and let rise until almost double. Bake at 350° F for 40–45 minutes. (If baking two loaves cook for only 25–30 minutes.) Sprinkle with a little more cheese if desired just as you pull the bread from the oven.

Pumpkin Yeast Rolls/Braid

This is a favorite on the Thanksgiving table. It has a fun hint of orange color.

4 cups whole wheat flour
½ cup gluten flour
¼ cup dry milk powder
6 Tbsp sugar
3 Tbsp yeast

½ Tbsp salt
¼ cup oil
¾ cup hot water
3 cups mashed pumpkin or squash
2+ cups white bread flour

Mix according to basic bread making instructions (page 126). Heat pumpkin or squash to 120–125° F and add with your wet ingredients. After the first rise, shape into rolls and place on a greased cookie sheet. Spray with oil and cover and let rise until almost double. Bake at 375° F for 15 minutes or until golden brown. Spread butter over the top of hot rolls. Serve immediately or cool on wire rack. When cool, wrap and freeze for later. To reheat: thaw on counter and then wrap in foil. Place in 350° F oven for 15 minutes or until warm. Makes about 4 dozen dinner rolls and fills one cookie sheet. This is also pretty done as a braided loaf. This recipe will actually make 2 loaves. Divide the dough into 6 pieces and roll them out into thick snakes. Pinch 3 together at one end and braid. Tuck ends under and place loaf in greased pan. Repeat with remaining 3 snakes. Bake at 375° F for 25–30 minutes or until golden brown.

One Hour Hot Rolls

This is a great recipe to use for cinnamon rolls since it can be done so quickly. I increase the sugar to ½ cup when making cinnamon rolls.

4–5 ½ cups bread flour
¼ cup gluten flour
¼ cup sugar
1 tsp salt
2 Tbsp yeast

½ cup dry milk powder
1 egg
3 Tbsp oil
2 cups hot water

Mix according to basic bread making instructions (page 126). Form into rolls. Place in a greased 9x13-inch pan. Bake at 350° F for 15 minutes. You do not need to let this dough rise. I have found that the rolls are a little lighter if you do. If you skip the rising time, you can have hot rolls on the table in 45 min. to1 hour!

English Muffin Bread

I love to make this bread when my mixer is not available. It does not require any kneading so it is easier to do by hand. It makes delicious toast with butter and strawberry freezer jam.

5 ½–6 cups bread flour
2 Tbsp yeast
1 Tbsp sugar
2 tsp salt

¼ tsp baking soda
6 Tbsp dry milk powder
2 ½ cups hot water
Cornmeal

Combine the dry ingredients, only using 3 cups of flour. Add hot water and beat well. Stir in enough additional flour to make a stiff batter. Grease two loaf pans and sprinkle with cornmeal. Pour batter into pans, dividing it evenly. Sprinkle tops with cornmeal. Allow to rise until nearly double (about 45 min.) Bake at 400° F for 25 minutes or until lightly browned. Remove from pans and cool on a wire rack.

Züpfa or Braided Swiss Bread

This recipe has been passed down in my father's family for generations. We make it every year for Christmas, but it is delicious all year long! Tradition dictates that you make this bread using only white flour.

18 cups white bread flour
1 cup sugar
5 tsp salt
½ heaping cup dry milk powder
2 Tbsp yeast

4 ½ cups hot water
2 Tbsp shortening, melted
½ lb butter, melted
6 eggs, beaten
Beaten egg and colored sugar

You will need to cut this recipe in half to fit in most mixers. Mix according to basic bread making instructions (page 126). Once dough has completed the first rise, divide into 6 equal parts. Divide each part into 3 equal strips. Braid strips and seal ends to form 6 loaves. Put in well greased pans. Let rise once more. Brush with beaten egg and sprinkle with colored sugar. Bake at 350° F for 25–30 minutes.

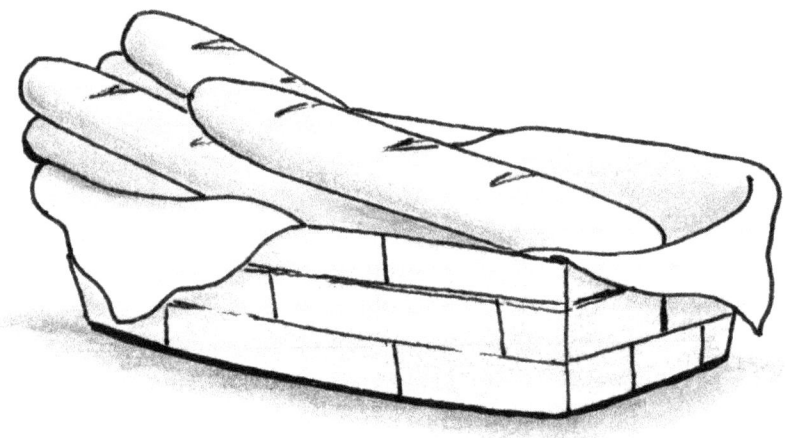

Freezer Cinnamon Rolls

Fresh, homemade cinnamon rolls can be enjoyed anytime since you can make them ahead and have them in the freezer.

4 ½–5 cups white bread flour
¼ cup gluten flour
½ cup sugar
½ tsp salt
1 Tbsp yeast
3 Tbsp dry milk powder
½ cup butter, melted
2 eggs, beaten
1 ¼ cups hot water
1 tsp vanilla

Filling:
½ cup butter, melted
1 cup brown sugar, packed
4–5 tsp cinnamon or to taste
¾ cup chopped nuts, optional

Frosting:
2 oz cream cheese, softened
¼ cup butter, softened
1 cup powdered sugar
½ tsp vanilla

Mix according to basic bread making instructions (page 126). After completing the kneading process in your mixer, allow to rise for 10 minutes. Roll dough out into a 15x24-inch rectangle. Combine the filling ingredients to form a thick paste and spread over dough. (Chopped apples are delicious in place of the nuts.) Roll up jelly roll style, starting from the long side. Do not roll too tightly or the centers of your rolls will pop up as they rise. Use a sharp knife to mark off 1 ½-inch sections. You can either use a serrated knife to very carefully saw through the roll to make individual rolls or slide a piece of dental floss under the roll and bring the ends up crossing them as you do so. Pull the ends in opposite directions until the floss cuts through the dough forming individual rolls. Place in greased baking pans. Do not pack the rolls in the pan. They need to have space in between in order to allow room for them to rise. Remember cinnamon rolls rise out not up. **To bake immediately:** Cover with a towel and allow to rise until double in size. After rising they should be touching each other and the sides of the pan. Bake at 350° F for 20–25 minutes or until golden brown. Spread with frosting after cooling slightly and enjoy! **To bake in a day or two:** Cover with plastic wrap and refrigerate. They will slowly rise in the fridge. When ready to bake, remove from the fridge and allow to rise a little more, if needed. Then bake and frost as above. **To freeze:** Cover with heavy duty foil and freeze immediately. They can be frozen for up to 1 month. The night before baking, remove from the freezer and sit on your counter for 10–12 hours to thaw and rise. Then bake and frost as above. **To make frosting:** Cream butter and cream cheese until smooth. Add powdered sugar and vanilla. If needed, you can also add just a touch of milk to get the consistency you like. You can make the frosting ahead and refrigerate until ready to use.

Freezer Crescent Rolls

I had a special friend share this recipe with me. She tells me this recipe is perfect for Sunday dinner since you can pull the rolls from the freezer before leaving for church and they will be ready to pop into the oven right when you get home.

2 ½ cups hot water
6 Tbsp dry milk powder
1 cup butter
6 eggs
1 cup sugar

1 ½ tsp salt
2 Tbsp yeast
8 cups white bread flour
2 cups hot water

Use a whisk to mix the powdered milk with the water. Add the butter and allow it to melt. Heat the mixture in the microwave or on the stove top if needed to get the butter to melt. Set aside and allow to cool slightly. You want it to get down to 115° F. In another large bowl, beat the eggs until foamy. Add sugar and salt to the eggs and beat until dissolved. Add the cooled milk mixture to the egg mixture. Stir in yeast and flour. The dough will be very sticky. Cover and let rise 4–5 hours. Turn out on well-floured board and divide in 4 pieces. (You will add quite a bit of flour.) Roll out into 4 circles and brush melted butter across each one. Use a pizza cutter to slice each circle into 12–16 pieces. Roll 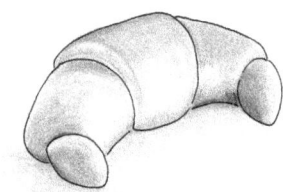 each triangle up from the wide end forming a crescent. **To bake immediately:** Place on greased baking sheets, allow to rise and bake at 375° F for 10–15 minutes or until golden brown. **To freeze:** Place rolls on baking sheets after shaping. Freeze immediately. When they are solid, put them in ziplock bags and keep them for 1–2 months in the freezer. **To use frozen rolls:** Take the appropriate number of rolls out of the bag and place on greased cookie sheets. Cover and let rise in a warm place until doubled (about 3+ hours.) Bake as directed above.

Breakfast Danish

I developed this recipe at the request of one of my sons. Feel free to experiment with other fillings. We also love it with a cinnamon and sugar filling.

4 ½ cups white bread flour
¼ cup gluten flour
½ cup sugar
½ tsp salt
1 Tbsp yeast
3 Tbsp dry milk powder
½ cup butter
2 eggs, beaten
1 ¼ cups cool water
1 tsp vanilla

Filling:
6 oz cream cheese, softened
3 Tbsp sugar
4 tsp cornstarch
1 egg
¾ tsp vanilla
½ cup berry jam
Glaze: Mix together until smooth
½ cup powdered sugar
½ tsp vanilla
1–2 Tbsp reconstituted powdered milk

Combine dry ingredients in mixer bowl. Cut butter into small pieces and fold into dry ingredients. Add eggs, water, and vanilla. Mix using your dough hook just until dough ball is formed. Spray dough with oil and cover bowl. Refrigerate for 2 hours or overnight. While dough is chilling, make the filling. Mix cream cheese, sugar, cornstarch, egg and vanilla until smooth. Refrigerate until ready to use. Remove dough from refrigerator. Oil your work surface and pat dough into a square. Add a little flour if dough is sticky. Roll out to 16x16-inch square. Fold dough in thirds like a business letter. Roll out into a 10x24-inch rectangle. Fold in thirds again. Roll out into a 20x20-inch square. Fold in thirds again. Roll out one final time into a 10x20-inch rectangle and fold in thirds again. Work quickly so dough stays chilled. Divide dough into two pieces. Roll out each piece into a 10x14-inch rectangle. Spread half of the cream filling down the center of each rectangle. Top with the berry jam. Cut 1-inch wide strips using kitchen scissors down either side of the dough, cutting from the outside edge of the dough into the edge of the filling. Braid the loaf by folding top strips together across the filling and continue alternating strips until you reach the bottom. **To bake immediately:** Place on baking sheet, cover with a towel, and allow to rise until double in size. Bake at 350° F for 25–30 minutes or until golden brown. Cover loosely with foil if it browns too quickly. Drizzle with glaze after cooling slightly, slice, and enjoy! **To bake in a day or two:** Place on baking sheet, cover with plastic wrap and refrigerate. It will slowly rise in the fridge. When ready to bake, remove from the fridge and allow to rise a little more if needed. Then bake and frost as above. **To freeze:** Cover with heavy duty foil or a few layers of plastic wrap and freeze immediately. Remove from the freezer 10–12 hours before baking. Thaw on counter and allow to rise. Then bake and frost as above. Makes 2 braids.

Angel Biscuits

These make great sausage, egg muffins or sandwich rolls. Feel free to cut them more the size of English muffins if you'd like.

5–5 ¼ cups all purpose flour
¼ cup sugar
1 tsp salt
2 tsp baking powder
1 tsp baking soda
1 Tbsp yeast

6 Tbsp dry milk powder
¾ cup shortening
4 Tbsp butter
2 Tbsp white vinegar
2 ¼ cups hot water

Mix dry ingredients, including the yeast, together in a large bowl. Use a hand mixer to mix in shortening and butter until mixture resembles coarse crumbs. Add vinegar and hot water. Mix until it forms a soft dough. Turn out on floured surface and knead a few times with your hands. Push or roll out to a thickness of about ½ inch. Cut with a biscuit cutter or glass cup. **To bake immediately:** Place biscuits on a greased baking sheet. Cover and let rise for about 30 minutes. Bake at 400° F for 8–10 minutes or until golden brown. Brush tops with the melted butter while still hot. Makes about 2 dozen biscuits. **To Freeze:** Place on baking sheet after cutting and freeze. Transfer to ziplock bag when frozen. **To use frozen biscuits:** Thaw and allow to rise about 3 hours or until double in size and then bake as directed. **To use a little at a time over the next week:** Store dough covered in the fridge. Pull out what you need and bake as above. It will keep in the fridge for 1–2 weeks, just punch it down if it rises too much.

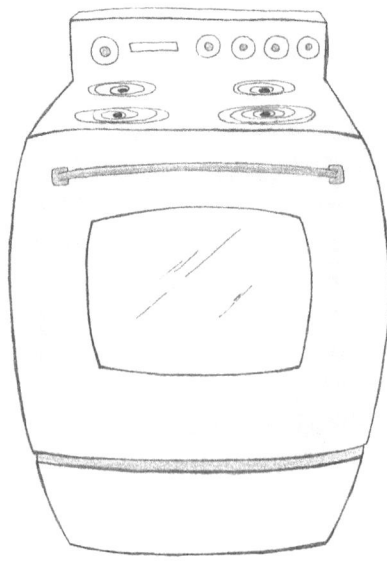

Pantry Mix Recipes

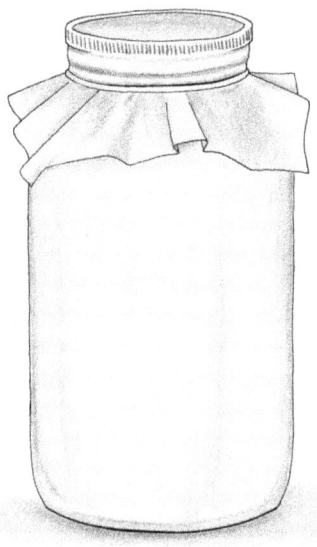

Mixes are a handy way to use your staples. They help you rotate through your stored items and they are much less expensive to make than buying premade mixes. This is one way I have found to make doing food storage easier for me.

Here are the recipes for the mixes I keep in my pantry. I always use powdered milk in my mixes and then add water when I actually make them. (I adjusted the recipes here to account for that.) I store them in ziplock bags and use a sharpie pen to list the ingredients I need to add on the bag to make things quicker. (I reuse my bags as many times as possible.) I make 4 mixes of each recipe at a time. I also keep pumpkin, zucchini, bananas, etc. frozen in the appropriate amounts so all I do is thaw them in the microwave and add them to the recipe. We make these without eggs all the time. No one can ever tell the difference! And you never have to worry about how many eggs you have. Plus the vinegar acts as a preservative so any leftovers will stay good on your counter for a week or more.

Use these recipes as a guide. If you have a favorite muffin or cookie recipe, just make it into a mix. It isn't hard to do. You'll be eating what you like and using your food storage at the same time. Now even my 8-year-old can bake a completely homemade breakfast or fun treat!

Corn Bread

Our family loves this for breakfast! Split pieces in half horizontally, butter and then pour peach nectar over for a great breakfast. We make our own nectar by blending peaches until smooth.

1 cup all-purpose flour
1 cup yellow corn meal
3 ½ tsp baking powder
1 tsp salt
3 Tbsp sugar
3 Tbsp dry milk powder

Add:
1 egg
1 cup water
¼ cup oil

Mix dry ingredients together in a ziplock bag. **To make:** Pour mix into a bowl and add wet ingredients. Mix or stir together. Pour into greased 8x8-inch pan. Bake at 425° F 20–25 minutes. **No egg version:** Add ½ tsp baking soda, 1 Tbsp white vinegar and ¼ cup cooked, mashed navy or pinto beans in place of the egg. Reduce the oil to 2 Tbsp. If you double the no egg version, cook in two 8x8-inch pans instead of one 9x13-inch.

Basic Muffin Mix

This recipe is very versatile. I sprinkle cinnamon and sugar on top. You can stir in berries or chopped fruit. Sometimes I make Surprise Muffins by filling muffin cups half full and then hiding a spoonful of jam before filling the rest of the way with muffin batter. Just use your imagination.

1 ½ cups all-purpose flour
½ cup sugar
2 tsp baking powder
¼ tsp baking soda
¼ tsp salt
2 ½ Tbsp dry milk powder

Add:
1 tsp vanilla
1 egg
2 Tbsp oil
¾ cup water

Mix dry ingredients together in a ziplock bag. You can use ¾ c. wheat flour and ¾ c. white flour. **To make:** Pour mix into a bowl and add wet ingredients. Mix or stir together. Pour into greased or paper lined muffin tins. Bake at 400° F 20–22 minutes. **No Egg Version:** Add 1 Tbsp white vinegar and ¼ cup applesauce in place of the egg.

Pumpkin Muffin Mix

My husband called his mom early on a Saturday morning during my first pregnancy to get this recipe. He even had to run to the store to get a muffin pan.

1 ½ cups all-purpose flour
¾ cup sugar
2 tsp baking powder
½ tsp salt
½ tsp cinnamon
¼ tsp nutmeg
1 ½ Tbsp dry milk powder

Add:
½ cup water
½ cup pumpkin puree
2 Tbsp oil
1 egg

Mix dry ingredients together in a ziplock bag. You can use ¾ c. wheat flour and ¾ c. white flour. **To make:** Pour mix into a bowl and add wet ingredients. Mix or stir together. Pour into greased or paper lined muffin tins. Bake at 375° F 15–20 minutes. I've used applesauce, mashed sweet potatoes, and butternut squash in place of the pumpkin and had great results every time. **No Egg Version:** Add ½ tsp baking soda, 1 Tbsp white vinegar and ¼ cup cooked, mashed navy or pinto beans in place of the egg. You can also add ¼ cup additional mashed fruit instead of the beans.

Banana Muffin Mix

Muffins are great for breakfast, but they can also be enjoyed as a snack. They freeze well so I always make a double batch.

1 ½ cups all-purpose flour
¾ cup sugar
1 tsp baking powder
1 tsp baking soda
½ tsp salt
1 tsp cinnamon
¼ tsp nutmeg

Add:
3 large bananas, mashed
1 tsp vanilla
1 egg
2 Tbsp oil

Mix dry ingredients together in a ziplock bag. You can use ¾ c. wheat flour and ¾ c. white flour. **To make:** Pour mix into a bowl and add wet ingredients. Mix or stir together. Pour into greased or paper lined muffin tins. Bake at 350° F 20–25 minutes. **No Egg Version:** Add ¼ cup cooked, mashed navy beans in place of the egg. You can also add ¼ cup additional mashed fruit instead of the beans.

Zucchini Bread/Cookies

I love having the choice to make bread, muffins, or cookies with this mix.

3 cups all-purpose flour
2 cups sugar
1 tsp salt
1 tsp baking soda
1 tsp baking powder
1 Tbsp cinnamon

Add:
3 eggs
1 Tbsp vanilla
½ cup vegetable oil
½ cup applesauce
3 cups zucchini, grated
1 cup chopped nuts, optional

Mix dry ingredients together in a ziplock bag. You can use 1 ½ c. wheat flour and 1 ½ c. white flour. **To make:** Pour mix into a bowl and add wet ingredients. Mix or stir together. Pour into greased or paper lined muffin tins and bake at 350° F for 15–20 min. or pour into 2 well greased loaf pans and bake at 350° F for about 1 hour. **No Egg Version:** For wet ingredients, add 1 Tbsp vanilla, 2 Tbsp white vinegar, 1 cup cooked, mashed navy or pinto beans, 2 Tbsp oil, 3 cups grated zucchini, 1 tsp baking soda, and ¾ cup water . You will want to cook the no egg version as muffins to achieve the right consistency. **For Cookies:** Use the same dry mix. Add 1 cup of flour, ⅓ cup oil, 2 cups grated zucchini, 1 Tbsp vanilla, 2 eggs (or 2 Tbsp white vinegar and ⅔ cup cooked, mashed navy or pinto beans in place of the eggs) and 1 cup chocolate chips. Be patient as you mix the dough. It looks like it is going to be too dry, but as you continue to mix, the moisture from the zucchini pulls it all together. Drop by tablespoons onto a greased baking sheet. Bake at 350° F for 10–12 minutes.

Instant Oatmeal Mix

To make it easy for the kids, I taped the instructions to the top of the ice cream bucket that we store this in.

13 cups quick cooking oats
⅔ cup dry milk powder
1 cup brown sugar, packed
1 Tbsp cinnamon

Mix dry ingredients together in a ziplock bag or ice cream bucket. **To make 1 serving:** Mix ½ cup of oatmeal with ½–⅓ cup water. Add any dried fruit you would like. Microwave on high for 1 minute.

Gourmet Oatmeal

I often make my mixes without any of the fun additions and then I can add what I am in the mood for the day of. You can also cook this in a crockpot overnight. Spray the crockpot with cooking spray and then add the ingredients. Cook it on low all night and wake up to a delicious breakfast.

3 ½ cups water
1½ cups steel-cut oats
1 tsp cinnamon
¼ tsp salt
⅓ cup brown sugar, packed
½ cup chopped, dried apples
Raisins, Craisins, coconut,
chopped almonds—be creative!

Combine all ingredients in a saucepan. Bring to a boil then turn down the heat. Cover and simmer for 20–25 minutes until all the water is absorbed, stirring occasionally. You can use 1 peeled and chopped apple in place of the dried apples. You can also substitute other fruits such as peaches or berries. It is always delicious!

Mint Hot Cocoa Mix

When it is time to rotate some of my instant powdered milk that we store for drinking, I mix up a batch of this. It is great in the cold winter months or on a summer camping trip. You can leave the crushed candy canes out and still have a delicious hot cocoa mix. Try some of the flavored creamers that are available to make a different flavor.

11 cups instant dry milk powder
24 oz Nestle Quick chocolate drink mix
5–6 cups powdered sugar
16 oz non-dairy creamer
12 large candy canes, crushed

To crush the candy canes, break them into small pieces and place them in a ziplock freezer bag. Place this bag in another ziplock freezer bag for added strength. Take the bag out to the garage floor or patio. Hit the bag repeatedly with a rubber mallet. (The kids love this job!) Combine all ingredients and store in ziplock bags or another airtight container. Add 3–4 spoonfuls of hot cocoa mix to one cup hot water.

Mint Hot Cocoa Mix Shortcut

The hot cocoa mix available from the LDS cannery is delicious! You can mix it up in hot water and then chill it for a delicious chocolate milk that any kid would love. It also makes it fast to mix up my favorite–Mint Hot Cocoa Mix. Just mix 12 crushed candy canes with one #10 can of cannery hot cocoa mix and enjoy.

Spiced Orange Drink Mix

This is great on a cold morning and gives you lots of vitamin C to boost your immune system and fight against those winter colds.

2 cups Tang orange drink mix
⅓ cup sweetened lemonade drink mix
1 ⅓ cups sugar

1 tsp cinnamon
½ tsp cloves

Combine all ingredients. Store in an airtight container. Add 1–2 tsp of Spiced Orange Drink Mix to one cup of hot water.

Oatmeal Waffles

A great, healthy alternative for breakfast that everyone loves. Sometimes we serve these for dinner.

1 ½ cups whole wheat or white flour
1 cup quick cooking oats
1 Tbsp baking powder
¼ tsp salt
½ teaspoon cinnamon
2 Tbsp brown sugar, packed
¼ cup dry milk powder

Add:
2 eggs, slightly beaten
1 ½ cups water
6 Tbsp oil

Mix dry ingredients together in a ziplock bag. **To make:** Pour mix into a bowl and add wet ingredients. Mix together and let sit 5 minutes. Bake in waffle iron. If batter is too thick just add more water. **No egg version:** Add ¼ cup applesauce in place of the eggs.

Pancake Mix

A very convenient mix to have on hand that uses your staples.

6 cups all-purpose flour
6 cups whole wheat flour
¾ cup sugar
¼ cup baking powder
2 Tbsp baking soda

1 Tbsp salt
2 ¼ cups dry milk powder
1 ½ cups dry whole egg powder
Add:
Oil and water

Mix all of the dry ingredients together and store in an airtight container. **To make:** Place the amount of mix you want in a bowl and add 1–2 Tbsp oil and enough water to make it the right consistency. Stir until combined. Allow to sit for 20–30 minutes to allow the leavening agents to be most effective. You will see little bubbles forming in the batter. Cook on a hot griddle. If you mix up more batter then you need, it will stay good in the refrigerator for 3–4 days. Store it covered and pull it out another morning for a quick breakfast. **No Egg Version:** Omit the dry whole egg powder from the recipe above and just make the mix without it. These taste fine, they just don't seem to be as fluffy so we prefer them with the eggs. To add a little fluffiness, add 1 Tbsp vinegar with the water when you are mixing the batter. It will react with the baking soda to help with the leavening.

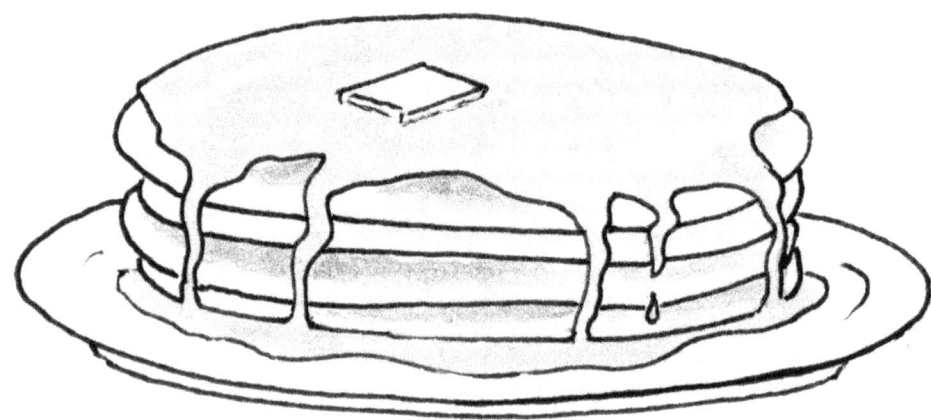

Hearty Whole Grain Pancake Mix

Add a handful of dry or frozen berries when mixing for an extra tasty meal!

9 cups whole wheat flour
4 cups corn meal
1 cup sugar
3 Tbsp baking powder
4 tsp baking soda

1 tsp salt
1 ½ cups dry milk powder

Add:
water

Mix all of the dry ingredients together and store in an airtight container. **To make:** Place the amount of mix you want in a bowl and add enough water to make it the right consistency. Stir until combined. Allow to sit for 5–10 minutes and then cook on a hot griddle.

Biscuit Mix

Everyone needs access to a good biscuit mix. This one is simple and delicious.

12 cups flour
2 Tbsp salt
4 Tbsp baking powder

2 cups shortening
1 ½ cup dry milk powder

Use a hand mixer to blend the ingredients. The shortening just disappears into the mix. We like it using 6 cups whole wheat flour and 6 cups white flour. Use as a substitute in any recipe that calls for Bisquick. **To make biscuits:** Combine 3 cups mix with 1 cup water. (Dough will be a little sticky.) Drop onto greased cookie sheet and bake at 400° F for 10–12 minutes. Or, roll out to ½-inch thickness using more biscuit mix on the counter instead of flour so you keep your ratio of fat to flour like you need for a fluffy biscuit. Bake as directed. **To make cheddar garlic biscuits:** Stir in 1 ½ cups grated cheddar cheese and 1 ½ tsp garlic powder to the above biscuit dough. Shape and bake as above. Brush with additional melted butter and sprinkle with more garlic powder before serving, if desired. **To make pancakes:** Combine 2 cups of mix with 1 cup of water and 2 eggs. If you do not have eggs available, you can substitute ½ cup of mashed bananas, applesauce, or pumpkin. It's great with a little cinnamon sprinkled in as well.

Rice Pilaf

This is great served as a side with any Mexican or meat dish. It is also delicious using brown rice. Just increase the water to 2 ½ cups. It will take approx. 40–45 minutes for brown rice to be done. It freezes well.

1 cup white rice
2 tsp chicken bouillon
1 tsp dried, minced garlic
1–2 Tbsp dehydrated bell pepper
2–3 Tbsp dried, minced onion
1–2 Tbsp wild rice, optional

Add:
2 cups water

Mix dry ingredients together in a ziplock bag. **To make:** Combine all ingredients in a sauce pan. Cover and bring to a boil. Turn down to low and simmer until rice is done and water is absorbed (approx. 20 minutes.)

Chicken Noodle Soup

Great for lunch or a simple dinner.

1 cup egg noodles or broken spaghetti
2 Tbsp chicken bouillon
¼ cup dehydrated carrots
¼ cup dehydrated celery
2–3 Tbsp dried, minced onion

Add:
6 cups water
1 (12 oz) can chicken breast
Pepper or lemon pepper to taste

Mix dry ingredients together in a ziplock bag. **To make:** Combine all ingredients in a sauce pan. Include the juices that are in the chicken can. Cover and bring to a boil. Turn down to low and simmer until noodles are soft and vegetables are tender (approx. 20 minutes.) This is also great to do in the crockpot. Cook on high for 2–3 hours.

French Lentil Rice Soup

This is a very hearty soup that takes seconds to prepare since you have the mix already made. I often give this as a baby gift so the new mom can have an easy dinner at the end of a frazzling day.

1 cup lentils, any color
2 Tbsp chicken bouillon
½ cup dehydrated carrots
¼ cup dehydrated celery
3 Tbsp dried, minced onion
3 Tbsp white rice
2 tsp dried, minced garlic
1 tsp dried thyme
½ tsp salt
⅛ tsp pepper

Add:
6 cups water
Sour cream or plain yogurt

Mix dry ingredients together in a ziplock bag. **To make:** Combine mix with 6 cups of water in a crockpot. Cover and cook on low for 8 hours or on high for 4–5 hours. Add more water, if needed. Before serving, use a hand immersion blender to puree some of the soup. Serve in bowls garnished with a dollop of sour cream or plain yogurt.

Cooking with Dry Beans

Dry beans require you to think a little bit ahead, but don't let that stop you from using them. They are very high in fiber and a great source of protein. Many people put beans and rice together since beans are an incomplete protein and require you to eat them with some grain in order to have all the amino acids required for nutrition. Nutritionists used to think you needed to eat the beans and grain during the same meal, but they now realize you just need to have them sometime during the same day which makes beans much more versatile.

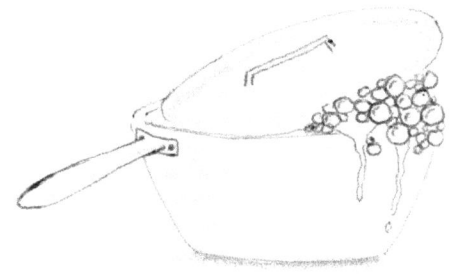

Dry beans are a lot less expensive to use than canned beans and they are much lower in sodium. Cooked beans freeze very well. When I cook beans, I do a large amount so I can have some in the freezer ready to use whenever I need them.

1 lb of dry beans = 2 cups which cooks into about 5–6 cups of beans

1 can of beans = 1½ cups beans + ¾ cup water

I always place beans in a large pot and cover them with water so the water is 2–3 inches above the beans. Bring the water to a boil and boil for 2–3 minutes. Remove from the heat. Cover and allow the beans to soak in the warm water for 4 hours. (You have to soak beans for a minimum of 4 hours to break down the gas producing protein so you will be able to digest them easier. Draining and rinsing also helps with this undesirable side effect.) Drain, rinse and cover with new water. Bring to a boil again and then turn down the heat and simmer beans for 30–45 minutes or until tender. A gentle simmer will keep the skins from bursting and allow the beans to hold their shape. Also, stir as little as possible to keep beans from turning to mush. Drain and rinse again after the beans are done and then use in any recipe. You can soak the beans overnight in cold water instead of doing the warm water soak. When you cook them after soaking in cold water, it will take 1½–2 hours to have them get soft. I just never seem to think about it a whole day ahead.

I usually do 2 or 3 pots of different kinds of beans at once since I have thought ahead enough to allow for soaking. When I plan to freeze my beans, I under cook them by 10–15 minutes. They seem to break down in the freezer and end up too soft if I have cooked them all the way. After rinsing them, I fill ziplock freezer bags and freeze them. When I need some for a recipe, I just microwave them long enough to break out what I need and return the rest to the freezer for another time. Place the amount you want for your recipe in a glass bowl with a small amount of water. Continue heating in the microwave until warm. If you are using them in a soup, you can put them in partially frozen and let them simmer until done.

Having beans in the freezer allows me to add beans to lots of recipes. I always stretch my taco meat with beans. I also add them with some rice to my chicken when making chicken enchiladas. We have found many different bean soups we love on cold winter nights. I just add the frozen beans 10–15 minutes before serving so they don't simmer too long and get too soft.

Troubleshooting

If you are short on time, you can speed up the cooking time for beans by cooking them in a pressure cooker. I have found this works well for beans that will be used in soup or to make refried beans. I tend to cook my beans a little too long when they are closed in the pressure cooker so they don't freeze well as whole beans. You can find instructions for pressure cooking beans online. I really have found myself cooking beans more the traditional way on the stovetop or crockpot so I can watch more closely and pull them off the heat when ready.

There are some food items that will keep the beans from softening and cooking correctly. For this reason, you will want to wait to add salt, sugar, vinegar, tomato, or anything else acidic until after beans are cooked. You can add onion or garlic while cooking if desired. Usually I just cook beans without seasoning them at all so they can be stored and used in any recipe.

Older beans will sometimes refuse to soften even after hours of cooking. Try adding ¼ tsp baking soda to the cooking water for every pound of beans you are cooking to help soften the stubborn beans.

Instead of freezing precooked beans, you can bottle them and preserve them for later use. You will need a large pressure cooker in order to do this. Because recommendations can change, check a current copy of the *Ball Blue Book of Preserving* or look online for an extension office website with current information and recipes.

Replacing fat and eggs in baked goods

I've discovered through experimenting, that mashed beans can replace the fat and the eggs in many baked goods. Plenty of diet books suggest replacing the fat in a recipe with mashed beans, but I've also learned that they work as an egg replacer as well. Make a bean puree by using a blender or hand immersion blender. Just add a little water and blend to make a thick, peanut butter-type consistency. Use this for the mashed beans or bean puree called for in the recipes throughout this book. Check out the section on Pantry Mixes for storable recipes using beans. You'll also find some delicious options in the Storable Desserts section. I freeze some bean puree in ¼ cup portions so it is very easy to thaw and use in recipes.

When you are ready to try using beans in a recipe, think about which color bean will hide best. It really doesn't matter what kind of bean you use, they all work equally well as a replacement for fat and eggs. White beans seem to hide well in any recipe so they are the ones I use most often. If the recipe calls for navy beans, really any white bean would be fine. Pinto or red beans are pretty interchangeable in recipes that have a brownish color after baking such as banana bread or pumpkin muffins. Black beans hide well in chocolate cakes and muffins. You get the idea.

When using in your own recipes, remember that 1 egg is equal to about ¼ cup of moisture in a recipe. So when the recipe calls for 2 eggs, I use about ½ cup bean puree to substitute for the eggs. As far as replacing the oil or fat, I've found that if you replace the entire amount of fat, the muffins or cakes don't usually brown as well and the texture is often too moist. Try making your recipe replacing all of the fat before deciding if you would really prefer it with a just a little oil. It is definitely a little healthier that way and you may decide it really doesn't matter for that particular recipe. I usually put about 2 Tbsp of oil in the recipes that I decide would be more appetizing with just a little more browning and then use beans for the remaining amount.

Beans work well in creating cake-type textures, so using beans in muffins and cake-like cookies doesn't seem to change the texture at all. No one has been able to tell that I have substituted beans in these items. On the other hand, it is difficult to achieve a chewy-chocolate-chip-cookie-type-texture. After much experimenting, I have finally figured out a chocolate chip cookie recipe that is delicious and chewy just like we expect them to be. They just *need* some fat to achieve this texture.

If you are not expecting this chewy texture, then you can still use beans in your chewy cookie recipes. Just don't expect your traditional ginger snap or snickerdoodle recipe to come out like it usually does. It will still have a great flavor, but it will be more cake-like and won't snap or be chewy. You will know you are serving your family a very healthy treat and you may find that you don't miss the chewy texture.

The other word of advice is to realize that you don't need to replace the oil and eggs cup for cup all the time. If you put too much bean puree in a recipe, it comes out very dense and often too moist. I wish I could tell you a fool-proof formula. Most of the time, I don't put more than about ¾ cup of bean puree in any single recipe. (If I double the batch, I won't use more than about 1 ½ cups.) I'll add additional water if needed to thin the batter instead of more beans. The items still rise like they should and they taste great. If you are willing to do some experimenting, I'm sure you'll come up with the amounts that will work to give you a healthier version of a family favorite that uses your food storage and tastes great!

Don't forget that now is your time to experiment. You aren't in a period of rationing your food to last as long as possible. So mash up some beans and choose a recipe to try. You will be surprised at how great it tastes!

Check out the Idaho Bean Commission website for many more great recipe ideas using beans.

Homemade Baked Beans

These always disappear at potlucks!

2 cups dry navy beans
½–1 cup real bacon bits
½ cup dehydrated onion
3 Tbsp molasses
2 tsp salt

¼ tsp black pepper
¼ tsp dry mustard
½ cup ketchup
1 Tbsp Worcestershire sauce
¼ cup brown sugar, packed

Soak and cook beans according to directions or substitute 5–6 cups of precooked or canned beans. Layer the beans, bacon, and onion in a 2 qt casserole dish. Combine the remaining ingredients in a saucepan and bring to a boil. Pour over beans. Pour in just enough water to cover the beans, if needed. Cover the casserole dish with a lid or foil. Bake at 325° F for 30–45 minutes or until heated through. You can heat in the microwave also. If you want the BBQ flavor to permeate the entire bean, you can cook for 1½–2 hours instead of just 30–45 minutes.

Homemade Refried Beans

These are a little bit of work, but they freeze well so make a large batch and enjoy them for many meals!

2 cups dry pinto beans
½ cup dried, minced onions
1–2 tsp dried, minced garlic

2 Tbsp oil or bacon grease
Cumin to taste
Chili powder to taste

Soak and cook beans according to directions or substitute 5–6 cups of precooked or canned beans that have been rinsed. Rehydrate the onions by soaking in warm water for 5–10 minutes. Place beans in a large frying pan. Mash beans using a potato masher. Add remaining ingredients and cook until heated through, stirring occasionally. Add additional water, if needed, to keep beans from getting too dry. Any leftovers can be frozen.

Restaurant Style Refried Beans

My daughter requests these often as part of her birthday dinner—she loves Mexican food!

1 can refried beans
2 tsp oil
Garlic powder to taste
Cumin to taste

Chili powder to taste
Water as needed
Grated cheese, optional

Empty can into frying pan. Add remaining ingredients and cook until heated through, stirring occasionally. Add water as needed to achieve desired consistency. Sprinkle with grated cheese, if ¾desired.

Quick and Easy Chili

Serve with cornbread for an easy meal.

½ lb hamburger
⅓ cup dried, minced onion
1 tsp dried, minced garlic
2 Tbsp dehydrated green pepper
1 (14 oz) can diced tomatoes

1 can condensed tomato soup
2 cups precooked red beans
2–3 tsp chili powder
½ tsp dried basil
¼ tsp black pepper

Combine all ingredients in a pan or slow cooker. Add water as needed to achieve desired consistency. Simmer for 15–20 minutes or until heated through and vegetables are tender. In a slow cooker, heat on low for 5–6 hours or on high for 2–3 hours.

Bean and Rice Burritos

This is another one of those dinner experiments that became a quick family favorite!

1 cup rice, cooked
1 cup cooked beans, any variety
1 Tbsp dried, minced onions, rehydrated

1 tsp chili powder or taco seasoning
2 Tbsp oil
Sour cream (or plain yogurt)

Fry rice and beans in oil. Add seasonings and roll in flour tortillas. Top with sour cream, lettuce, diced tomatoes and cheese if you have them.

Black Bean Soup

This works as a side dish for enchiladas or tacos, but it is also great on its own for a simple meal.

4 ½ cups cooked black beans
1 cup salsa
2 cups chicken broth

½–1 tsp ground cumin
1 tsp lime juice, optional
Sour cream and grated cheese

Puree ⅓ of the beans with salsa and chicken broth in a blender. Pour into a pan with the remaining ingredients. Heat through. Top each bowl with a little sour cream and cheese. Serve with tortilla chips. You can use 3 cans of black beans, rinsed. You can also use 2 tsp chicken bouillon and 2 cups of water in place of the broth. I also substitute plain yogurt for the sour cream.

Moist and Delicious Cornbread

Mix up a batch of honey butter to enjoy with this tasty dish.

2 cups all-purpose flour
2 cups corn meal
½ cup sugar
1 tsp baking soda
1 ½ tsp salt

2 cups plain yogurt
¾ cup white bean puree
2 Tbsp oil
2 Tbsp honey
¼ cup water

Combine the dry ingredients. Add the wet ingredients and mix just until moistened. Pour batter into a greased 9x13-inch pan and bake at 400° F for 20–25 minutes or until a toothpick comes out clean. You can cut the recipe in half and it fills an 8x8-inch pan. Bake for 15–20 minutes.

Mexican Rice

Hearty enough to be a meal all its own or use as a great side dish.

⅓ cup dried, minced onion
1 tsp garlic powder
1 cup rice
1 tsp chicken bouillon
1 cup water

8 oz tomato sauce
2 Tbsp bacon bits
1–1½ cups cooked kidney beans
1 can corn, drained
Salt and pepper to taste

Mix together onion, garlic, rice, bouillon, water, and tomato sauce. Bring to a boil, lower heat, cover and simmer 20–25 minutes or until rice is tender. Stir in bacon, beans, and corn. Heat through. You can use 1 can of kidney beans, rinsed. I love the precooked real bacon bits for this recipe. They make it convenient and easy.

Navy Bean Soup

I adapted this from a recipe in a magazine years ago. It is wonderful on a cold night.

2 cups dry navy or white beans
2 qts chicken broth
2 tsp dried parsley
2 bay leaves
¼ tsp pepper

½ cup dried carrots
⅓ cup dried celery, optional
4–5 Tbsp dried, minced onion
6 bacon strips, cooked and crumbled

Place beans in a soup kettle; add water to cover by 2 inches. Bring to a boil; boil for 2 minutes. Remove from the heat; cover and let stand 1 hour. Drain and rinse beans, discarding liquid. Combine remaining ingredients except the bacon in soup kettle. Bring to a boil. Reduce heat; cover and simmer for 1 ½ hours or until beans and vegetables are tender. Stir in the bacon. Discard the bay leaves before serving. Makes 8–10 servings. I use real bacon bits that come in a jar and can be found near the salad dressings or you can buy them in a ziplock bag at Costco. I also make this soup often with precooked beans from the freezer. Just adjust the amount of broth as needed. With precooked beans, this soup can be done and on the table in less than 30 minutes!

Hearty Bean Soup

A great soup to use up that leftover ham!

⅓ cup dry navy beans
⅓ cup dry great northern beans
⅓ cup dry pinto beans
⅓ cup dry kidney beans
4 Tbsp dried yellow split peas
4 Tbsp dried green split peas

½ cup dried carrots
½ cup dried celery, optional
2 Tbsp dried, minced onion
4 tsp chicken bouillon granules
½ tsp cumin
¼ tsp garlic powder
1 cup chopped ham

Cover beans with water and soak overnight or boil for 2 minutes and remove from heat then soak for 4 hours. Rinse. Combine remaining ingredients in a pot with 6–8 cups of water. Simmer for 30–45 minutes until beans are tender. This is a great soup to use precooked beans in to add the variety quickly. I also keep some precooked ham in the freezer all diced up to be able to add it quickly to this soup. If you have a ham bone left from serving a ham for dinner, you can simmer it in with the soup to add great flavor. Remove from the pan and then cut off any leftover ham to add back into the soup before serving.

Black Bean Brownies

Simple and delicious and very healthy for a brownie!

1 box brownie mix for 9x13-inch pan
1 (15 oz) can black beans

or 1 ½ cups black beans
¾ cup water

Open the can of black beans, rinse well. Put the beans back in the can. Add enough water to cover the beans and fill the can. Instead of canned beans, you can use 1 ½ cups cooked black beans and ¾ cup water . Pour beans and water in blender or food processor and puree. (I actually love using my little hand immersion blender in a deep bowl to make bean puree.) Stir together the bean puree and the brownie mix. Pour into a greased 9x13-inch pan and then bake according to package directions. The beans replace the oil and eggs in this recipe. You will be surprised by how delicious these healthy treats are!

Pinto Bean Fudge

You don't have to feel as guilty about having an extra piece of this fudge. It's full of fiber and protein.

1 cup warm cooked pinto beans
¾ cup melted butter or margarine
1 cup cocoa

1 Tbsp vanilla
8 cups powdered sugar
1 cup chopped walnuts or pecans (optional)

Puree beans. Add butter or margarine, cocoa, and vanilla. Gradually stir in powdered sugar. Mix in nuts if desired. Press into a greased 9x13-inch pan and chill until solid. Cut into squares and serve. It is also fun to cut the fudge with tiny cookie cutters in holiday shapes. We then dip the top of the shape in sprinkles to add a little color and a lot of fun to our holiday platters. Store in the refrigerator.

Chewy "Healthy" Chocolate Chip Cookies

You and your kids can eat all the dough they would like since there are no eggs! These cookies are lower in sugar, lower in fat, and lower in cholesterol. You can't get much healthier than that and still enjoy a cookie! This is the result of a year's worth of experiments. I'm so glad I didn't give up!

½ cup butter
½ cup white bean puree
⅔ cup sugar
1 cup brown sugar, packed
3 cups all-purpose flour

2 tsp baking soda
1 Tbsp vanilla
¼ cup vegetable oil
1 cup chocolate chips
Oatmeal, coconut, chopped nuts (optional)

Cream together butter, bean puree and sugars. Add flour, baking soda, and vanilla. It will look pretty dry at this point. Slowly add in the oil and mix until it has pulled together into cookie dough consistency. Stir in chocolate chips and any other optional ingredients you'd like. Roll into balls and place on greased baking sheets. Bake at 350° F for 8–10 minutes. Pull them out of the oven just as they are beginning to turn light brown in a couple of spots. They still look pretty doughy overall. Allow to rest on baking sheet for about 5 minutes to set and them move to a wire rack to cool. Makes 3 dozen.

Ultimate Chocolate Chocolate Chip Cookies

Experiment by adding different flavored chips. We've tried mint flavored chips and we've also added white chocolate chips and chopped nuts. We've loved every combination.

½ cup butter
½ cup white bean puree
1 cup sugar
½ cup brown sugar, packed
¼ cup vegetable oil
2 tsp vanilla

⅔ cup baking cocoa
2 tsp baking soda
2 ⅓ cups all-purpose flour
1 cup chocolate chips
Chopped nuts (optional)

Cream together butter, bean puree, sugars, vanilla, and oil. Add flour, baking soda, and cocoa. Stir in chocolate chips and any other optional ingredients you'd like. Roll into balls and place on greased baking sheets. Bake at 350° F for 8–10 minutes or just until set. They still look pretty doughy overall. Allow to rest on baking sheet for about 5 minutes to set and them move to a wire rack to cool. Makes 3–4 dozen.

Scotchies

This is adapted from a recipe I was given in Home Ec. when I was in junior high. This is a much healthier version. They make a simple butterscotch flavored brownie.

2 Tbsp oil
1 ½ cups brown sugar, packed
1 tsp vanilla
1 ½ cups all-purpose flour

1 tsp baking soda
1 tsp baking powder
¾ cup white bean puree
2–4 Tbsp water

Mix all of the ingredients together, adding just enough water to make it a thick brownie batter consistency. You can stir in chocolate or butterscotch chips if desired. Pour into a greased 9x13-inch pan and bake at 350° F for 25–28 minutes. Cut into bars and serve.

Using Powdered Milk

Gaining confidence in using powdered milk is necessary to allow you a lot more variety in the meals you can make using your food storage. I grew up in a large family and we only had one car for a lot of years. It was a challenge for my mom to make it grocery shopping very often. Her solution was to have us use powdered milk. We grew up drinking powdered milk—I should probably say *some* of us drank powdered milk. My mom didn't mind the taste, but most of the kids preferred drinking something other than milk. We learned it definitely tasted better chilled and my mom learned to buy the non-instant milk from the dairy instead of the instant milk from the grocery store. We all decided it was fine on our cold cereal and we baked with it all the time without my mom having to hear us complain.

From this experience, I knew baking with powdered milk would be easy and did not change the flavor or texture of any of the dishes we traditionally cooked. My husband has a picky milk taste. There was a period of his growing up years where they actually milked a goat to get milk. He learned pretty quickly that he preferred cow's milk. He was sure he would be able to taste a difference when I baked with the powdered milk. I started experimenting and not telling him and he couldn't tell the difference!

As far as drinking powdered milk goes, we haven't made that transition in our home. I have taste tested different brands and we've found the one we like best. In my opinion, it doesn't taste any different than skim milk. My husband thinks he can *maybe* taste a hint of powdered flavor. This is the brand that we store in case we would have to drink it. We prefer the "County Cream" brand of milk for drinking. It is available online and at some local retailers. For baking, I purchase the non-instant powdered milk from the LDS cannery.

I have enough instant "Country Cream" brand milk to give us 3 gallons a week for 3 months. You really need to determine which taste your family prefers before you decide what you are going to store. I know many families like the flavor of "Morning Moo" which is a milk substitute. It is made of whey and you cannot use it to make yogurt and cheese like you can with the other powdered milk, but it would be fine to store for drinking. Ask around and see if some of your friends would allow you to taste some of what they have before you make a decision on what you would like to store.

I store non-instant powdered milk for all my baking and yogurt and cheese making needs. It takes up half the space and I can find it for a better price than the instant milk. I actually bake with it and make yogurt on a regular basis. I figure that I use at least 3 gallons a week less of store-bought milk by baking with it. Because I spend less per gallon for the powdered milk, this adds up to significant savings over the course of the year. We cannot tell a difference in the taste of any dish that I make with powdered milk instead of using store-bought milk.

As you try to determine how much powdered milk you need to store, start thinking about how much you go through each week. If you regularly buy 5 gallons of milk each week, then you should store enough powdered milk to replace that amount. As you put together your meal plan, you will know just how many cups of milk you need to make the recipes you have included. Use this information to purchase the correct amount of powdered milk for your family. Add to it the amount of powdered milk you would need to make the number of gallons per week your family drinks. The amount of powdered milk needed will be unique to every family.

I store our powdered milk in sealed #10 cans. You could also store it in sealed buckets, if you'd prefer. You want to be sure you use oxygen absorbers in the containers to lengthen the time it will store. Since I do so much baking with powdered milk on a regular basis, I keep one bucket of powdered milk that I haven't gone through the work to seal. It is what I rotate through on a regular basis. When I am getting low, I purchase another 25 lb bag from the LDS cannery to refill my bucket. This means that I am not having to go through the time and money to replace my longer-term storage. When I am approaching the 20-year mark on the milk in my longer-term storage, I will open those containers and begin using them.

Instant vs. Non-Instant Powdered Milk

Non-instant milk powder requires that you use warm water to mix it. Instant powdered milk can be mixed in cold water which is nice, but it takes twice as much milk powder to make the same amount of milk. For this reason, you have to store twice as much to give you the same amount of milk. I actually store some of both.

Using Non-Instant Powdered Milk in Baking

(If you have instant milk powder, just double the amount of milk powder listed.)

> 3 Tbsp dry milk powder mixed with 1 cup water = 1 cup milk
>
> ¾ cup dry milk powder mixed with 1 quart water = 1 quart milk
>
> 6 Tbsp dry milk powder mixed with 1 cup water = 12 oz evaporated milk

Tips for Baking with Powdered Milk

- Set a rule for yourself that if you are cooking, you are going to use powdered milk. You will save money and gain knowledge as you move forward with this goal.

- Keep a container of powdered milk in your pantry for easy access.

- Use a sharpie pen to write the amounts needed to make 1 cup, 1 quart, etc. right on the lid or side of the container. I also store a tablespoon measuring spoon right in my container to make it easy.

- Mix your milk in your blender. After mixing, allow it to sit a few minutes. The foam will rise to the top and then you can slowly pour the milk out of the blender leaving the foam behind. You can also set the blender in the fridge overnight and the foam will be gone in the morning.

- Keep a quart or two of reconstituted milk in your fridge all the time so you can quickly grab it when a recipe calls for milk.

- When baking bread or muffins, if the recipe calls for 1 cup of milk just put in 3 Tbsp non-instant milk powder with your flour and other dry ingredients and add 1 cup of water when it is time for your wet ingredients. Adjust the amount of milk powder and water to match the recipe.

- When making your own mixes, include the milk powder with all your other dry ingredients and write the correct amount of water to add on the outside of the ziplock bag.

- Make a large batch of the White Sauce Mix recipe and change your habits so you use it when a recipe calls for a basic white sauce.

- If you don't have any milk mixed up, don't fall back into old habits and grab your gallon from the store. It is really quick and easy to use a whisk in a bowl of warm water to mix up just the amount you need. By using a whisk instead of the blender, you don't get the layer of foam on top.

- Store some Nestle Quick or the store brand of chocolate and strawberry flavoring powders to mix in milk. When your kids want this to drink, mix it with your powdered milk. They will never know.

- Make instant pudding with powdered milk. The flavoring in the pudding hides the powdered milk taste.

- Try chilling your hot cocoa. The cocoa mix I get from the LDS cannery is delicious chilled. The kids tell me it tastes just like the chocolate milk they get at school.

Substitutes for the Real Thing Using Powdered Milk

Buttermilk or Sour Milk

To make 1 cup buttermilk or sour milk, put 1 Tbsp white vinegar or lemon juice in the bottom of a 1 cup measuring cup. Fill it to the top with reconstituted powdered milk and then add to your recipe. If adding buttermilk to a cake or some other baked good, you can add 3 Tbsp non-instant dry milk powder to the dry ingredients and then 1 scant cup water and 1 Tbsp white vinegar or lemon juice with the wet ingredients.

Evaporated Milk

To make one 12 oz can evaporated skim milk, mix 6 Tbsp of non-instant dry milk powder with 1 cup hot tap water with a wire whisk or in your blender. If using the blender, allow the milk to sit just a minute or two for the foam to rise and then pour it slowly out of your blender, leaving the foam behind. If you would like evaporated whole milk instead of skim milk, you will need to add some fat. Mix the evaporated skim milk as described and then add 2 Tbsp vegetable oil. Whisk the oil vigorously to emulsify the fat and milk. It will separate as it stands so quickly add it to your recipe.

Sweetened Condensed Milk

Mix ½ cup water, 1 cup sugar and 1 Tbsp margarine or shortening together in a saucepan. Bring to a full boil, stirring occasionally. Remove from heat and allow to cool slightly. Pour into your blender and add 1 cup of non-instant dry milk powder. Blend until smooth. Store in the fridge for up to one year. If it begins to crystallize in the fridge, put it in the blender. This recipe makes about 2 cups. Use in all your baking and candy making. You can double the batch if you are making lots of holiday goodies. When your recipe calls for 1 can of sweetened condensed milk, it is equal to ½ cup + 2 Tbsp (10 Tbsp) of the homemade version.

Homemade Yogurt

Reconstitute powdered milk to make 1 quart. (Do not use the "Morning Moo" brand. It will not turn into yogurt.) Heat milk to 180° F stirring constantly, if heating on the stove. You can also heat the milk in the microwave. It takes me about 7 minutes in my microwave. Remove from heat and let cool until milk reaches 120–125° F. Set a timer for about 20 minutes so you don't forget about it. Use an instant read food thermometer to measure the temperature. Mix in ¼–½ cup of plain yogurt with active cultures. Stir with a wire whisk. Pour into a thermos and screw on the lid. Allow to incubate for 2 ½–8 hours on your counter. I've found that when I use plain yogurt from the store it takes 4+ hours to set up. If I use my homemade yogurt as a start, it is often done in 2 ½–3 hours. The longer you incubate the yogurt, the tangier it will be. You know it is done when you open your thermos and you see a small amount of clear, yellowish liquid (whey) on the top and thick white yogurt below. If you still see milk, it needs to incubate longer. Quickly close the thermos so you don't lose much heat and let it sit another hour or more before checking again. Refrigerate after incubating. It will thicken a little more as it cools.

If you have problems having success, it is one of two things. Either your thermometer is off or your thermos does not hold the temperature at 120° F. You can test your thermometer by putting it in boiling water. It should register 212° F. If your thermometer is on, then you can assume it is your thermos and you'll have to try with another one. There are other methods for incubating yogurt. A quick search online will lead you to some articles describing the other methods. The thermos method has always worked for me, it is the least costly, and it requires less steps so it is my method of choice.

Fruit Flavored Yogurt

Add chopped fresh fruit and sugar or sweetener to taste once the yogurt has chilled. I prefer using powdered sugar so I don't feel the sugar grains on my tongue. I often add freezer jam for a fruit on the bottom style yogurt. Do not stir too much or yogurt will get runny. If a thicker yogurt is desired, you can thicken it with ultra gel (available online) or 1 Tbsp unflavored gelatin. Mix gelatin with cold water and heat to dissolve. Cool and mix with yogurt.

Kid-Friendly Fruity Yogurt

Use flavored gelatin. This makes a bright colored, kid friendly yogurt. Mix a 3 oz box of jello with ½ cup of boiling water. Allow to cool and mix in 2–3 cups of yogurt. Pour into small containers and chill in the fridge until set.

Greek Style Yogurt

When mixing milk to make yogurt, put in double the amount of milk powder. This gives you more milk solids for the amount of water. It will give you a yogurt that is richer and higher in protein. Follow the remaining directions for making yogurt. When the yogurt is done, drain it as described below for the cream cheese or sour cream substitute. When it reaches the consistency you'd like, pour it into a container and mix with a wire whisk for a smooth texture. Flavor as desired.

Yogurt Smoothie

This yogurt makes great smoothies. Just put a few cups of yogurt in the blender. Add the frozen fruit and sweetener that you desire and blend. We love it with a frozen banana, a few frozen berries, and some powdered sugar to sweeten it. I also add some vanilla sometimes.

Cream Cheese, Sour Cream Substitute (Yogurt Cheese)

Line a colander with a clean piece of cheese cloth, white paper towel, or coffee filter. (If you use a paper towel with a pattern, you'll end up with colored cream cheese.) Set a bowl under the colander. Pour prepared yogurt into the paper towel. Allow the yogurt to drain in the fridge. After 30–60 minutes, it will be the consistency of sour cream. Leave it in the fridge overnight to make a cream cheese substitute. This can be used anywhere you would use cream cheese or sour cream. The liquid that drains off is the whey. You can use this in your bread or muffins in place of the water if you'd like. 1 cup yogurt = ½ cup yogurt cheese.

Cream Cheese Spread/Dip Options – Add any of the following to 1 cup of cream cheese substitute.

1 tsp vanilla

¼ cup jam, any flavor

Chopped, sundried tomatoes and herbs

Ranch dressing packet or any other flavor

1 tsp imitation butter seasoning such as Butter Buds

Use your imagination. If you like it with cream cheese, you'll like it with this totally fat-free substitute!

Ricotta or Cottage Cheese

2 cups warm water
¾ cup non-instant or 1 ½ cups instant dry milk powder
3 Tbsp lemon juice or white vinegar

If using non-instant milk, blend water and dry milk together and bring to a boil, stirring constantly. Remove from heat. (If using instant milk, bring water to a boil and remove from heat. Stir in milk with a wire whisk.) Drip lemon juice or vinegar around the edge of the pan and gently stir. Milk will immediately start to curdle, separating into curds and whey. If the liquid is still a milky color, add just a little more lemon juice or vinegar. Let rest one minute. Pour into a colander and rinse with hot then cold water. Drain until no whey remains. Makes about 1 ½ cups of curds. The dry cheese curds will work for ricotta cheese in most recipes. To turn it into cottage cheese add a little yogurt to cream it and stir to combine. You also may want to add a little salt. Instant milk gives you a softer curd. The non-instant milk creates curds that are more chewy, but they still work great in lasagna or other similar dishes. Our family enjoys this in baked recipes. We prefer the store-bought cottage cheese for eating plain or using in salads.

Parmesan Cheese

1 cup boiling water
1 cup non-instant or 2 cups instant dry milk powder
2–3 Tbsp lemon juice or white vinegar
1 tsp white cheddar cheese powder (available at specialty popcorn shops or online)

Follow the directions for making cottage cheese. Pour curds into a sturdy paper towel or piece of cheese cloth and squeeze dry. Spread on a cookie sheet and break up into very fine pieces with a fork. Dry for 10 minutes in a 150–170° F oven. Pour into a bowl and add white cheddar cheese powder. Add a little bit of salt and then use in place of Parmesan, or mix it with store-bought dried Parmesan cheese to stretch what you have. You can use this immediately, or refrigerate or freeze for up to 3 months. The flavor changes during aging. Makes about 1 cup of curds. I just store plenty of the store-bought Parmesan cheese since it has such a long shelf-life. If I ever run out though, I know how to make my own and I have the ingredients on hand so I can.

Medium Cheddar Cheese

3 cups hot water
½ cup vegetable oil
2 ¼ cups non-instant or 4 ½ cups instant dry milk powder
1 ¼ cups white vinegar
¼ tsp salt
3 Tbsp cheddar cheese powder (Use white or orange or a combination of both. Available at specialty popcorn shops or online. You can also use dry cheese sauce mix if that is all you can find.)

Blend water, oil, and milk powder and pour into a hot, greased saucepan. Add vinegar and stir. Curds will begin to form immediately. Remove from heat and rinse curds in warm water and then in cold. Let drain in a colander for 2–3 minutes. Add salt and cheese powder. Mix well. Use as a cheese spread for crackers or make grilled cheese sandwiches. You can also press into a container to shape it. Dump from container and wrap in plastic. Store in refrigerator or freezer. To grate, take from freezer and let stand for a few minutes to soften enough to grate. You can also crumble the thawed cheese over your recipe instead of grating. Use in all recipes calling for grated cheese. I store 3 months worth of the grated cheese I need in my freezer. I have used this homemade cheese in many casseroles and pasta dishes and it is very tasty. I keep the ingredients on hand so I can make it if my frozen supply runs out.

No-bake Yogurt Cheesecake

I serve this to guests often—no one can ever tell it is made from powdered milk!

2 cups yogurt cheese
⅓ + cup powdered sugar
2 tsp vanilla

8 oz frozen whipped topping
1 (9 in) graham cracker crust
Fruit topping of your choice

In a mixing bowl, beat together yogurt cheese, sugar, and vanilla. Fold in frozen whipped topping. Pour into crust and chill for at least 2 hours. Top with your favorite fruit topping. Instant pudding is also a fun topper.

Homemade Ice Cream

Making ice cream is a summer tradition in our family—now we can do it with our food storage.

4 cups plain yogurt
2 cups reconstituted powdered milk
1 ½ cups sugar

1 pinch salt
2 Tbsp vanilla
Fruit puree or pie filling (optional)

Combine all ingredients and mix well. Freeze in ice cream freezer according to manufacturer's instructions. You can add extra milk powder to the water when you are reconstituting the milk for a richer flavor. We also love adding maple flavoring instead of vanilla to make a maple nut flavor. This is a great basic recipe. You are only limited by your imagination on the flavors you can come up with.

Crustless Quiche

Quiche can be ready in a snap with this crustless version. Check out the Pantry Mix section to find a recipe for making your own biscuit mix.

3 eggs
1 ½ cups warm water
4 ½ Tbsp dry milk powder
¼ cup margarine, melted

½ cup biscuit mix
Dash pepper
Bacon, ham, onion, green pepper, etc.
¾ cup shredded cheese

Combine eggs, water, milk powder, margarine, biscuit mix, and pepper in your blender. Pour into a greased 9-inch pie plate. Top with your choice of fillings and cheese. Bake at 350° F for 30–35 minutes or until a knife inserted in the center comes out clean. Let stand for 10 minutes before serving

Chocolate Chews

These are a homemade version of a Tootsie Roll. Just four simple ingredients make for an afternoon of fun!

1 cup honey
1 cup dry milk powder

½ cup baking cocoa
1 tsp vanilla

Cook the honey until it reaches a temperature between 250° F and 255° F. You will need to use a candy thermometer to test the temperature. If you get it too hot, the candy will not be chewy. It will be hard. Once the honey reaches the right temperature, remove it from the heat. Mix the dry milk powder and the baking cocoa together. Add this mixture to the hot honey along with the vanilla. Stir until well combined. Pour out onto a greased surface and allow to cool for about 15 minutes or until it is cool enough to handle. Knead just a bit. Roll into long, thin snakes and then cut into individual size candies. Wrap in pieces of waxed paper. Makes about 50 small chews.

White Sauce Mix Recipes

So many recipes call for the basic white sauce ingredients of butter, milk and flour. I created this mix to help me rotate my powdered milk and to reduce the fat in our diet. Most recipes suggest that you melt butter in a pan, stir in flour and then add milk gradually. This mix skips the step of melting butter which means that not only is the milk fat free, you are also reducing the fat by not adding the butter. You are more than welcome to add butter to your cream soups. I just found it difficult to feel good about allowing an entire cube of butter to melt into my broccoli soup one day when I was making a huge batch. I thought I would try it without and we found that we liked it just as well. I have since experimented with this mix in many recipes. I especially go through it in the winter during soup season, but there are recipes to use it in year round so don't hesitate to make a large batch!

Dealing with a Dairy Allergy

Powdered soy milk and rice milk are available online. They should work just fine in this mix and then make it possible for those of you with dairy allergies in your family to be able to use this time-saving mix. Experiment by making just a small amount of the mix and then try it in some of these recipes to see how it works.

White Sauce Mix

Mix up a large batch—believe me, you'll find a million uses for it. It will become a great time saver.

3 cups non-instant dry milk powder 2 tsp salt
2 cups all-purpose flour

Mix together and store in an airtight container. Use in any recipe that calls for making a white sauce using milk, butter and flour. It is a completely fat free alternative and tastes great! It will store for up to 5 years on the pantry shelf.

Basic White Sauce

Many recipes ask for 1 cup of milk, some flour and a little butter. You can use this white sauce in any of those recipes.

5 Tbsp white sauce mix 1 cup hot water

Whisk white sauce mix with hot water in a saucepan. Cook over medium heat, stirring constantly until thick. Use in any recipe calling for 1 cup white sauce.

Sausage Gravy

Biscuits and gravy couldn't be more delicious!

1 scant cup white sauce mix Pork sausage, browned
3 cups hot water Pepper to taste

Whisk white sauce mix with hot water in frying pan. Cook over medium heat, stirring constantly until very thick. Stir in sausage and add pepper to taste. Enjoy over biscuits. Check out the pantry mix section of this book for a great biscuit mix. If you have precooked sausage in the freezer, biscuits and gravy can be done in less than 20 minutes!

Cream of Chicken Soup Substitute

This is lots less expensive than using a can of cream soup. You will be saving money and using your food storage—go ahead, feel extra provident today!

5 Tbsp white sauce mix
1 cup hot water

1 tsp chicken bouillon
Onion powder, garlic powder, parsley, and pepper to taste

Whisk all ingredients together in a sauce pan. Cook over medium heat, stirring constantly until very thick. Use in any casserole or recipe calling for 1 can cream of chicken soup. You can easily double the recipe as needed. To thin for using as chicken gravy, just add a little more water.

Nachos

A kid's favorite!

5 Tbsp white sauce mix
1 cup hot water
⅛ tsp pepper
1 tsp dried, minced onion reconstituted

1 tsp Worcestershire sauce
1 cup cheddar cheese, grated
½ cup Mozzarella cheese, grated

In a saucepan, whisk white sauce mix and water together and cook until smooth. As sauce begins to thicken, add remaining ingredients. Serve over tortilla chips. Top with chili, spiced hamburger, sliced black olives, salsa, etc. You can use pepper jack cheese for a more spicy sauce.

Pizza Carbonara

Try a unique flavor of pizza for dinner tonight. It is a fun one to make when you host a pizza party to give people the option of a new flavor.

Soft garlic breadstick dough
1 cup warm water
1 Tbsp dried, minced onion
1 tsp dried, minced garlic
5 Tbsp white sauce mix
1/8 tsp black pepper

1/2 tsp chicken bouillon
1/4 cup Parmesan cheese
1/2 cup real bacon bits
1 cup chicken, precooked, optional
1 1/2 cups Mozzarella cheese, shredded
Green onions, if available

Make a batch of the soft garlic breadstick recipe found in the bread section or use your favorite pizza dough recipe. After the first rise, punch it down and roll out on an oiled surface into a large circle. Place on pizza pan, prick multiple times with a fork, and bake at 425° F for 7–10 minutes or until lightly browned. While the crust is baking, whisk together warm water, onion, garlic, white sauce mix, pepper, and chicken bouillon in a saucepan. Cook over medium heat, stirring constantly until it boils. Cook for 2 additional minutes until it is thick. Remove from heat and stir in Parmesan cheese. Spread over the hot crust. Sprinkle on toppings. Bake at 425° F an additional 8–10 minutes or until cheese is melted.

Ham and Corn Chowder

This is a hearty soup that is great to serve company in the cold winter months.

1 cup chopped onions (1/2 cup dry)
1 cup diced carrots (1/2 cup dry)
2 1/2 cups cubed potatoes (1 1/4 cup dry)
1 can whole kernel corn, drained
2 tsp chicken bouillon
4+ cups water

1/2 cup + 2 Tbsp white sauce mix
2 cups hot water
2–3 cups shredded cheddar cheese
2 cups cubed fully cooked ham
10 bacon strips, cooked and crumbled

Cook vegetables in 4 cups water and bouillon until tender. Whisk white sauce mix and 2 cups hot water together in a bowl. Pour into soup. Stir until thickened. Stir in cheese, ham, and bacon bits just before serving. Using dehydrated vegetables may require more water. Add enough to make the consistency you like. I always use the precooked real bacon bits in this recipe to make it easy.

Potato Cheese Soup

I make this soup with dehydrated vegetables all the time—it is one my mom served growing up so it brings back memories every time I serve it.

2 potatoes, peeled and diced
3 cups water
1 carrot, chopped
1 celery stalk, chopped
½ cup onion, chopped

2 chicken bouillon cubes
½ cup + 2 Tbsp white sauce mix
2 cups hot water
Dash of pepper
1 cup cheddar cheese, grated

Cook vegetables in 3 cups water and bouillon until tender. Stir white sauce mix into remaining water and add to soup. Stir until thickened. Stir in the cheese until melted. You can very easily use dehydrated vegetables in this soup. You just may need to add some additional water.

Creamy Chicken Noodle Soup

We serve this when we have all the cousins over for a winter day of fun. Everyone loves it!

6 cups water
2 Tbsp chicken bouillon
1 ½ cups egg noodles
1 (12 oz) can chicken breast

2 cups hot water
½ cup + 2 Tbsp White Sauce Mix
4 Tbsp margarine (optional)
Pepper or lemon pepper to taste

Bring water and bouillon to a boil. Add egg noodles and boil until noodles are tender. Stir in chicken. Whisk white sauce mix and 2 cups hot water together in a bowl. Pour into soup. Stir until thickened. Add margarine and pepper if desired. I also drop in some dehydrated carrots and onions when I add the noodles to add a few more vitamins.

Broccoli Cheese Soup

Comfort food at its best! Serve in bread bowls to make it extra special.

2 potatoes, peeled and diced
3 cups chopped broccoli, fresh or frozen
1 carrot, chopped
1 onion, chopped
4 tsp chicken bouillon
Enough water to cover vegetables
½ cup + 2 Tbsp white sauce mix
2 cups hot water
1 cup grated cheese
Salt and pepper

Cook vegetables in water and bouillon until tender. You can very easily use dehydrated vegetables in this soup. You just may need to add some additional water. Whisk white sauce mix and 2 cups hot water together in a bowl. Pour into soup. Stir until thickened. Stir in the cheese until melted. Makes 2 quarts and fills 6 large bread bowls.

Clam Chowder

After a vacation on the Oregon Coast, my kids begged me to make clam chowder. This is what I came up with—another tasty experiment!

6–7 smaller potatoes, peeled and diced
½+ cup dried, minced onion
½+ cup dehydrated celery
6 cups water
2 Tbsp chicken bouillon
2 (6.5 oz) cans minced clams
1 (12oz) can evaporated milk
¾ cup white sauce mix
½ cup all-purpose flour
1 cup hot water
½ tsp dried dill
Salt and pepper to taste

Cook vegetables in water and bouillon until tender. If you choose to use fresh vegetables, saute in a little butter before adding to the broth. Pour in clams, juice and all. Add the evaporated milk. Whisk white sauce mix and flour with 1 cup hot water together in a bowl. Pour into soup. Stir until thickened. Stir in the dill and salt and pepper. This makes a large batch. Sometimes I make this without the clams for a delicious potato soup.

Creamy White Chicken Chili

We have a chili cook-off every fall at church. This one always receives rave reviews and has won more than once.

6 cups water
½ cup dried, minced onions
2 cloves minced garlic
2 (12 oz) cans chicken breast
2 Tbsp chicken bouillon
1 (4 oz) can diced green chilies
1 tsp ground cumin
1 tsp dried cilantro
¾ tsp red pepper flakes
5 (14.5 oz) cans white beans, rinsed
½ cup white sauce mix
1 cup hot water
1 cup grated Monterey Jack cheese

Simmer chicken and spices for 15–20 minutes so flavors can blend. Add beans. Whisk white sauce mix and 1 cup hot water together in a bowl. Pour into soup. Stir until thickened. Add additional water depending on how you like it. Top each bowl with shredded cheese. Feel free to double the spices if you prefer a spicy chili. You can also use 7–8 cups precooked dry beans in place of the canned beans.

Sausage and White Bean Soup

I had a good friend invite me over for lunch one day and she served me this soup. A few adjustments made it possible for me to make from my food storage.

6 cups water
½ cup dried, minced onions
3 cloves minced garlic
1 lb pork sausage, browned
2 Tbsp chicken bouillon
2 bay leaves
½ tsp thyme
½ tsp black pepper
¼–½ tsp cayenne pepper
5 (14.5 oz) cans white beans, rinsed
½ cup white sauce mix
1 cup hot water

Simmer sausage and spices for 15–20 minutes so flavors can blend. Add beans. Whisk white sauce mix and 1 cup hot water together in a bowl. Pour into soup. Stir until thickened. Add additional water depending on your taste. You can also use 7–8 cups precooked beans in place of the canned beans.

Pasta Carbonara

This is another meal that I often serve when company comes over. I use the bowtie pasta for a fancy look.

8 oz noodles, cooked
½ cup + 2 Tbsp white sauce mix
2 cups hot water
1–2 tsp chicken bouillon

½ cup Parmesan cheese
2 Tbsp real bacon pieces
Salt, pepper, garlic, onion

Cook noodles as directed. Whisk white sauce mix, water, bouillon, and Parmesan cheese together in a saucepan. Cook and stir over medium heat until thickened. Stir in bacon. Season with spices to taste. Serve over noodles. We love this with frozen peas and carrots stirred in. Just add them to your boiling pasta water the last few minutes of cooking and drain them along with the pasta. My kids love it when I use bowtie pasta or wagon wheels. I've also stirred in chopped, sundried tomatoes for a fancy flavored dish.

Homemade Mac and Cheese

Kids and adults alike can't resist this delicious version of the famous comfort food.

8 oz macaroni, cooked
½ cup + 2 Tbsp white sauce mix
2 cups hot water

1 ½ cups cheddar cheese
Salt, pepper, garlic, onion
Diced ham, optional

Cook noodles as directed. Whisk white sauce mix and water together in a saucepan. Cook and stir over medium heat until thickened. Stir in cheese. Add cooked noodles and stir. Season with spices to taste. For a more formal dish: Add diced ham. Pour sauce over cooked macaroni in a casserole dish. May be covered with buttered bread crumbs. Bake at 350° F until hot and bubbly. You can freeze this dish before baking. To use frozen casserole just thaw and bake as directed.

Scalloped Potatoes

Creamy and delicious—great as a side dish or add some chopped ham to make it a meal.

7–8 large potatoes, peeled and sliced
½ cup dried, minced onion
¾ cup white sauce mix
3 cups hot water
1 Tbsp chicken bouillon

3 Tbsp mayonnaise
1 tsp salt
¼ tsp pepper
Paprika, optional
Cooked ham, optional

Layer potatoes and onions in a greased 9x13-inch pan. You can use dehydrated potato slices that you have soaked in boiling water for 15–20 minutes. You can also add precooked ham pieces if you'd like. Whisk white sauce mix, water, bouillon, and mayonnaise together in a saucepan. Cook and stir over medium heat until thickened. Stir in salt and pepper. Pour sauce over potatoes. Sprinkle with paprika if desired. Cover and bake at 325° F for 2 hours or until potatoes are tender. I also cook this in the microwave. It always cooks faster on the edges so you have to stir it a few times when you use the microwave. You can also do it in the crockpot. Cook on high for 3–4 hours or on low for 6–8 hours.

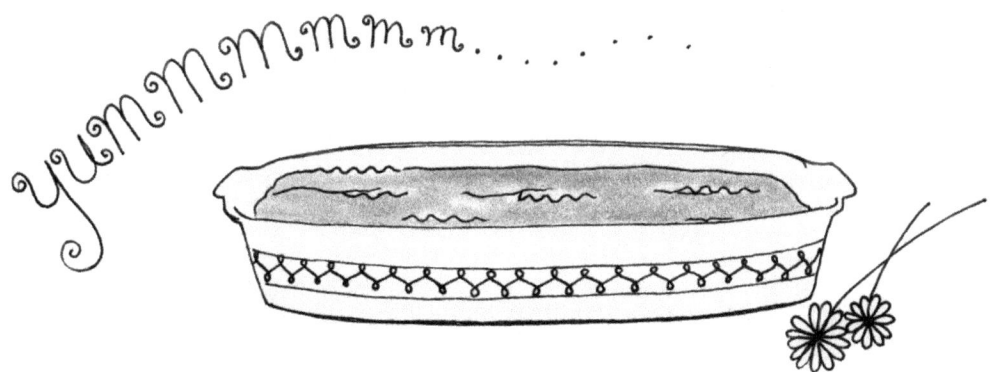

Using Garden Produce

Anyone who is concerned enough to be storing food usually grows at least a small garden. Gardens can provide us with fresh fruits and vegetables and give us extra to preserve for later use. Whenever I think about planting a garden, I remember the primary song that goes, "The prophet said to plant a garden so that's what we'll do." Children have such simple faith. They just do what the prophet says without taking time to reason about why it would be difficult.

Gardening doesn't need to be difficult and you can find ways to garden even in the smallest spaces. The website www.squarefootgardening.com has some great information for those of you who are just getting started. They suggest ways to garden in about any amount of space. My sister even planted tomato plants in 5-gallon buckets on her patio when she was in college.

We are not the greatest gardeners, but we are learning more every year. We love others who are willing to share their tips with us in our local climate. It has become a fun family adventure every summer. We do store seeds as part of our food storage plan to give us the option to grow produce regardless of the availability of fresh seeds.

This section shares recipes I've collected and developed over the years to use the fresh produce we grow. I hope you find some you and your family will enjoy!

Zucchini Casserole

We've cooked this in a Dutch oven on a camping trip. I mixed all the filling ahead of time to make preparations at the campground easier.

6 cups fine cubed zucchini
1 cup shredded or chopped carrots
½ cup chopped onion
½ cup butter or margarine

1 package Stove Top Stuffing mix
1 can cream of chicken soup
1 ½ cups sour cream (or plain yogurt)
2 cups cooked chicken, optional

Boil zucchini, carrots and onion in salted water for 5 minutes. Drain. In another bowl, melt butter and add stuffing mix. Mix well. Place half of stuffing in bottom of casserole dish. Add soup and sour cream to the vegetable mix. Spoon over stuffing in casserole. Top with other half of stuffing. Bake at 350° F for 25–30 minutes. I often make this substituting dehydrated carrots and onion for the fresh produce. Just rehydrate them first. It just depends on when everything from the garden is ready.

Chocolate Zucchini Cake

Don't hesitate to replace three-quarters of the oil with applesauce or black bean puree for a healthier cake.

1 cup vegetable oil
1 ¾ cup sugar
2 eggs
1 tsp vanilla
2 ½ cups all-purpose flour
¼ cup cocoa

1 tsp baking soda
½ tsp baking powder
½ tsp cinnamon
½ cup reconstituted powdered milk
2 cups shredded zucchini

Mix all ingredients except zucchini. Fold in zucchini and pour into greased 9x13-inch pan. Bake at 325° F for 45–50 minutes or until a toothpick comes out clean. Cool and frost with your favorite icing. I bake this in a 10-inch Dutch oven using 8–10 coals on the bottom and 14–16 coals on top for 60 minutes. It works out great. I also do it as muffins for breakfast and everyone loves them. Sometimes we add chocolate chips.

Crazy Zucchini Cake

Adapted from the crazy cake shared in a previous chapter, this is another fun way to sneak zucchini into our diet.

3 cups all-purpose flour
1 ½ cups sugar
1 tsp salt
2 tsp baking soda
¼ cup cocoa
2 tsp vanilla

2 Tbsp white vinegar
½ cup black bean puree
2 Tbsp oil
1 cup water
2 cups shredded zucchini

Mix all ingredients except zucchini. Fold in zucchini and pour into greased 9x13-inch pan. Bake at 350° F for 25–35 minutes or until a toothpick comes out clean. Cool and frost with your favorite icing.

Zucchini Enchiladas

The inspiration for this recipe came from a cookbook I found in the cupboard of a little home we rented one summer on the Oregon coast. Cook up a Rice Pilaf mix to serve on the side.

12 corn tortillas

Filling:
½ cup chopped onion
2 cups grated zucchini
2 cups grated cheese
1 cup shredded, cooked chicken
1 cup cooked navy beans

Sauce:
1 large can red enchilada sauce
1 cup reconstituted powdered milk
1 can cream of mushroom soup

Mix together all the filling ingredients in a large bowl. (You really can do any combination of these ingredients for the filling.) Mix together the sauce ingredients in another bowl. Dip tortillas in sauce. Fill with filling, roll up and place, seam side down in a 9x13-inch pan. Cover with extra sauce and shredded cheese. Cover pan and bake at 350° F for 30–40 minutes or heat through in the microwave.

Zucchini Burger Bake

One of my mother's friends shared this recipe with our family many years ago.

3–4 cups zucchini, chopped or sliced
1 ½ lbs hamburger
1 cup onion, chopped
1 cup green pepper, chopped
Chopped mushrooms, optional
1 ½ cups bread crumbs
1 Tbsp margarine, melted
1 ¼ tsp salt
1 tsp dry mustard
¼ tsp each pepper, thyme, oregano

Cheese Sauce:
¼ cup margarine
¼ cup all-purpose flour
2 cups reconstituted powdered milk
1 cup cheddar cheese, grated

Cook zucchini in boiling water just until tender. Drain. In a skillet, brown the hamburger with the onions. Add peppers and seasonings when meat is partially cooked. (I often use dehydrated onions and peppers. Just rehydrate them first.) Drain off excess fat. Remove from heat. Stir in ½ cup bread crumbs and zucchini. To make cheese sauce, melt margarine and stir in flour. Slowly add milk and stir until smooth. Stir in cheese until melted. Add cheese sauce to meat mixture. Combine remaining bread crumbs with 1 Tbsp melted margarine and sprinkle on top. Bake at 350° F 30–35 minutes. You can use the Basic White Sauce recipe to make the cheese sauce.

Grilled Zucchini and Summer Squash

A simple side to go with grilled meats.

Dice zucchini and summer squash and put onto skewers. Grill on medium heat for 10–15 minutes. Brush with Italian salad dressing every few minutes while grilling.

Zucchini Pie

My kids love to try and trick company with this pie. They serve them a slice and then tell them it is not apple and see if they can guess the main ingredient. No one believes it isn't apple and they certainly don't believe it is zucchini! Sometimes I drop in a few blackberries as well. It is always delicious!

8 cups chopped zucchini
¾ cup sugar
2 Tbsp tapioca
¼ cup lemon juice
½ tsp salt

1 ½ tsp cinnamon
¼ tsp nutmeg
2 tsp cornstarch
1 pie crust

Peel, seed, and chop zucchini to resemble sliced apples. Place in a pan with some water and boil for a few minutes until just barely soft. Drain and set aside. Combine remaining ingredients and cook until thick. Stir in zucchini and place in pie crust. Top with additional crust or do a crumble top. (I use the topping from the apple crisp recipe that you'll find in the dessert section.) Bake at 400° F for 25–30 minutes.

Zucchini Brownies

This makes 2 large pans of brownies so it is great to make for a potluck or BBQ.

1 cup oil
2 cups sugar
3 eggs
1 Tbsp vanilla
½ cup cocoa
1 tsp salt
¼ tsp baking powder
2 ½ cups all-purpose flour
1 tsp baking soda
1 tsp water

½ cup reconstituted powdered milk
2 cups zucchini, grated

Frosting:
½ cup margarine
4 Tbsp cocoa
6 Tbsp reconstituted powdered milk
1 tsp vanilla
4 cups powdered sugar
1 cup chopped nuts (optional)

Mix all ingredients and pour into two 9x13-inch greased pans. Don't hesitate to replace most of the oil with mashed black bean puree. Bake at 350° F for 30–35 minutes. To make frosting, combine margarine, cocoa, milk, and vanilla in a pan. Bring to a boil. Add powdered sugar and nuts if desired. Pour over brownies.

Rhubarb Crumble

Rhubarb freezes very well so I try to keep some in the freezer year round to be able to make this crumble whenever we are in the mood.

Filling:
4 cups rhubarb, cubed
⅓ cup sugar
1 Tbsp all-purpose flour
½ tsp cinnamon
1 Tbsp water

Topping:
¾ cup quick oats
¼ cup all-purpose flour
¼ cup brown sugar, packed
¼ cup sugar
¼ cup butter, melted

Place rhubarb in a pie pan. Mix the dry ingredients for the filling and sprinkle over the top of the rhubarb. Mix the topping ingredients until crumbly. Sprinkle over the filling. Bake at 350° F for 20–25 minutes.

Scrumptious Rhubarb Cake

Even my husband who is not a fan of rhubarb loves this cake! We've also baked it in a Dutch oven before when we were camping. Delicious!

5 cups chopped rhubarb
1 (3 oz) pkg raspberry jello
1 cup sugar
3 cups mini-marshmallows
1 white cake mix

Place rhubarb in greased 9x13-inch pan. Sprinkle jello powder and sugar over the top. Spread marshmallows over rhubarb. Mix cake according to package directions. Pour evenly over the top. Bake at 350° F for 50–55 minutes.

Fresh Salsa

The bowl is always empty when we take this to a BBQ.

Tomatoes
Onions
Green peppers
Small amount of minced garlic

1–2 Tbsp lemon juice
1–2 Tbsp chopped cilantro, optional
Salt to taste

Chop tomatoes, onions, and peppers until it looks like the right mix. Add other seasonings. Enjoy with tortilla chips.

Black Bean and Corn Salsa

You can add pasta to this salsa for a fun southwest salad. Just increase dressing amounts as needed.

2–3 large tomatoes, chopped
½ cup chopped green onion
½ cup chopped green pepper
3 cups cooked black beans
1 ½ cups frozen corn, thawed

2–3 Tbsp lemon or lime juice
4–5 Tbsp chopped cilantro
Salt to taste
⅛ tsp cayenne pepper
1–2 tsp minced garlic

Combine all ingredients, adjusting amounts to your liking. Serve with tortilla chips or as a taco salad.

Garden Pasta Salad

After eating a lot of canned or frozen items during the winter, we look forward to the fresh vegetables that gardens bring.

8 oz colored spiral pasta
½ cup chopped green onion
3 medium tomatoes, diced
½ cup chopped green pepper
2 medium cucumbers, diced

½ cup sliced black olives
2 Tbsp white vinegar
1 ½ cups salad dressing (mayo type)
2 tsp paprika
Salt and pepper to taste

Boil pasta until tender. Rinse in cold water. Stir in chopped vegetables. Mix remaining ingredients and stir into salad. Chill before serving.

Tomato Cucumber Salad

My sister taught me how to make this salad after serving her mission in Brazil. It is so simple to make and very refreshing on a hot summer evening.

3 large tomatoes, cut in wedges
3 large cucumbers, sliced
2–3 Tbsp chopped onion

1–2 Tbsp lemon juice
Salt to taste

Combine all ingredients in a large bowl and toss. Chill until serving.

Tomato Feta Bruschetta

This is the perfect appetizer to serve at a summer BBQ with friends. You can't beat the flavor of a garden tomato!

1 loaf Crusty French Bread
1 Tbsp olive oil
2 ½ cups diced tomatoes
¼ cup chopped onion

1 Tbsp chopped fresh basil
4 oz feta cheese
Salt and pepper to taste

When making the Crusty French Bread recipe found in the bread section, shape the loaf into a thin baguette before baking. When loaf is cool, slice and place on a baking sheet. Toast under the broiler on both sides until bread is lightly browned. Brush bread with olive oil. Combine all remaining ingredients in a large bowl and toss. Top each slice of bread with a generous spoonful of the tomato mixture just before serving. Feta cheese stores for quite a few months in the refrigerator so you can purchase enough to enjoy this appetizer the entire growing season.

Preserving Your Harvest

Once you plant a garden, you'll learn quickly that you very easily produce more than your family needs to eat fresh (and you may not be able to find any more neighbors to share that extra zucchini with.) Research suggests that produce preserved at its peak of ripeness contains as many or more vitamins than fresh produce picked too early or out of season. By learning how to preserve what you have grown, your family can enjoy the fruits of your labor all year long and eat very nutritionally. We eat from our garden all summer long and then preserve the extra to pull us through the winter months.

Garage or Pantry Storage

Some of your produce will store in your garage or pantry for quite some time. Here in Idaho, it is cold and dry enough through the winter that onions, potatoes, carrots, and winter squash will store just in cardboard boxes in the garage for many months. I just used my last garden onion for Easter dinner this year! If you have an extra fridge you can also use it to store your fresh items even longer.

Dehydrating

One tool I use to preserve fruits and vegetables is a dehydrator. This is a fun way to have your kids help you make some snacks. We love dried fruits and homemade fruit rolls or "fruit leather" as I grew up calling it. They are much more healthy for you than what you can purchase at the store because you control the amount of sugar. They are also very quick to grab and store in the car or diaper bag. You can dehydrate foods in the oven at a very low temperature, but it is usually more difficult to have your food dry evenly since your oven has hot spots.

When you are looking to purchase a dehydrator, watch for one that has a fan and a thermostat. This helps the fruit dry more evenly. There are a few options. We went with a basic model that cost around $50 and gave us the option to add trays as our family grew. This has worked very well for us. We especially use it a lot in the fall when all the fruit is ready in our area. Dried orange slices make beautiful Christmas ornaments. We also make Christmas presents by combining a dried orange slice with some cinnamon sticks and cloves in a cute little baggie. We give this to neighbors and friends with a jug of apple cider so they can simmer it together for a delicious spiced cider treat on a cold day! Every dehydrator comes with some suggested recipes. Don't hesitate to try some. The internet is also a great resource for additional ideas.

Freezing

Your freezer is another great tool for preserving your harvest. Anything you've seen in the freezer section of the store you can figure out how to freeze. Search online for specific directions. I have included tips on how I have frozen items over the years.

Bananas - When your bananas are too ripe for wanting to use fresh, just peel and freeze in freezer bags. Actually, you can freeze them in their peels and just peel them when you are ready to use them if you want to. We use frozen bananas in yogurt smoothies all the time. I also thaw them out for use in banana cookies, muffins, and breads. Remember to include all the water that is with them when you defrost them. It was originally in the bananas to begin with and your recipe will need that moisture.

Peaches - Peel and slice or chop. Place in ziplock bags and freeze. These work great in smoothies and muffins. We prefer the O'Henry variety for freezing.

Pears - Peel and slice or chop. Place in ziplock bags and freeze. These work great in smoothies and muffins.

Berries - Wash and place in a single layer on a baking sheet. Freeze. When frozen, use a spatula to loosen the berries and transfer to a ziplock bag for long-term storage.

Green beans - Wash and snip the ends off the beans. Blanch in boiling water for 3 minutes. Drain and transfer to ziplock bags and freeze.

Broccoli - Wash and cut into desired sized pieces. Blanch in boiling water for 3 minutes. Drain and transfer to ziplock bags and freeze.

Corn - Husk and wash corn on the cob. Blanch in boiling water for 3 minutes. Drain and transfer to ziplock bags if you want to leave the corn on the cob. You can cut the corn off the cob and place in ziplock bags and freeze, also.

Pumpkin/Squash - Cook pumpkin, sweet potato, or any winter squash in the oven or microwave until soft. You can also chop and cover with water in a large pot. Boil on the stove until soft. Allow to cool. Remove all skin and seeds. Puree in a food processor or blender. (Sometimes I have to add just a little water.) Put in freezer containers (sour cream and cottage cheese cartons work well) and use it in pancakes, muffins, and cakes all year long. You can interchange pumpkin, sweet potato, or any winter squash in all of your recipes. I measure my pumpkin in 1 and 2 cup portions before freezing so it is ready to use in my favorite recipe. If your recipe calls for canned pumpkin, one 15 oz can is equal to 1 ¾ cups and a 29 oz can is equal to 3 ½ cups.

Zucchini - Slice or grate your zucchini or summer squash and place directly into freezer bags—no cooking required. I usually freeze the grated zucchini in the amount of cups I need for my recipe. When I am baking, I just thaw it all out in the microwave and dump the entire bag (including the water) into my bowl.

Onions - Chop or slice onions and place directly into freezer bags—no cooking required. When ready to use, thaw just enough to break out the amount you need and return the rest back to the freezer for using later.

Green peppers - Chop or slice green peppers and place directly into freezer bags—no cooking required. When ready to use, thaw just enough to break out the amount you need and return the rest back to the freezer for using later.

Tomatoes - Cut the stem out of the tomatoes and then place in freezer bags. When ready to use, pull out the number of tomatoes you will need. Run them under water and the skin should just slip off. Now you can slice or dice them and toss into sauces or salsas.

Potatoes - I just recently experimented with freezing potatoes. Peel and cut into desired shape. Boil in water just long enough to make them barely tender. Drain. Spread out in a single layer on a cookie sheet to freeze. Once frozen, transfer to a freezer bag. When ready to use, cook as desired. I cubed some before freezing and then fried them in a little oil just as I do the frozen hash browns from the store. They were delicious. I also boiled a few of them to turn into a potato salad. No one would have ever known they had been frozen first. So if the potatoes in your garage begin to sprout or start going soft, peel them up and freeze them to preserve them a little longer. You can easily store enough potatoes to include them in your 3-month supply of meals.

Canning

The internet is a great resource for learning the specifics for canning your produce. There are many kind individuals who have put tutorials online so those of us who are visual learners can see just what to do. (Be careful when using the internet to find canning recipes. Not all of them have been tested to be sure they meet current safety recommendations.) I refer to the *Ball Blue Book of Preserving* to remind myself just how to it. It has long been the reference of choice for many home canners. It will also help you know you are following the most recent safety guidelines. You can look up your County Extension Office as well. They are an extension of your state's agriculture college and they keep a list of people on hand who can help answer your individual questions. They have helped me track down safe recipes and learn just what is causing my tomato plants to whither more than once over the years. They also may know of classes in your area that would allow you to learn home canning skills.

The remainder of this section is a collection of recipes I have used, adapted or developed over the years. I do not include the very basic instructions for canning applesauce, peaches, pears, etc. These can easily be found online or in the *Ball Blue Book of Preserving*. If you want to begin canning, find someone in your area who does it. Most home canners love an extra set of hands in the kitchen and you will learn so much more quickly by doing. Once you understand the basics, you can follow any recipe.

Strawberry Rhubarb Jam

I love that this jam doesn't require any thickener so when our rhubarb plant has an especially plentiful year, this is what I make for Christmas gifts for all our friends and neighbors. Watch thrift stores or yard sales to find inexpensive pint or jelly jars.

1 cup strawberries (or additional rhubarb)
4 cups rhubarb, chopped

¼ cup water
2 ½ cups sugar
3 oz box wild strawberry jello

Combine chopped fruit, water, and sugar in a large saucepan. Bring to a boil and simmer on low for 10 minutes to develop the natural pectin. Add the jello powder and mix well. Pour into warm jars. Process for 10 minutes. I usually do this without any strawberries. Chop the rhubarb very small or use a food processor.

Chunky Applesauce

This is delicious served warm with a scoop of ice cream or whipped cream. We also love it served over waffles.

Apples
Vitamin C
Water

Sugar
Cinnamon
Vanilla

Fill a large pan half full with water. Dissolve 3–4 vitamin C tablets into the water (or use Fruit Fresh to keep apples a light color.) Peel and chop your apples. (Choose a good cooking variety that will hold its shape when cooked. My parents have red and golden delicious trees so I usually use these varieties.) Add to the water. Make sure your apples stay covered with water. Bring to a boil. Simmer a few minutes until apples are tender. Remove from heat and drain most of the liquid off into another pan. I reserve the liquid to use with another batch of apples or to add a little back to my batch to get the right consistency. Mash warm apples just a bit with a potato masher. Add a little juice back in with apples, if needed to obtain the desired consistency. Sweeten to taste with sugar and cinnamon and just a touch of vanilla. Ladle into warm jars and process quarts for 20 minutes. Adjust time for elevation as needed.

Flavored Applesauce

Whether you use store-bought applesauce or make your own, the kids love this!

Make applesauce like you usually do. Before adding sugar, stir in some unsweetened Kool-Aid powder. (We have also used Crystal Light or any store brand equivalent.) This gives the applesauce a fun flavor and some color similar to the little packets you can purchase at the store. We use one packet of Kool-Aid for every 8–10 quarts of applesauce. Sweeten as needed and then process as you would regular applesauce. You can do this with store-bought applesauce also. It is just something fun to change things up a bit and keep the kids happy.

Dehydrated Apple Slices

Cut the core out of the apples. Slice your apples very thin and uniform. You don't even need to peel them. We were given a great slicer tool as a wedding gift that is great for this. It is called a mandoline. You can use an apple/peeler/corer/slicer as well. And if you have a steady hand, a good sharp knife works great. It is just more difficult to get the slices uniform which is helpful so they dry evenly.

Once your apples are sliced, dip them in lemon juice, orange juice, or pineapple juice to keep them from going brown while they are drying. We love them dipped in pineapple juice and dried without anything else being sprinkled on them. Spread them out on the drying trays and set the thermostat for fruits. My apples are usually done in about 4 hours. Try dipping them in lemon juice and then once you have them spread out on the drying trays, sprinkle them with cinnamon and sugar or use jello powder (any flavor). We do red jello for Valentine's Day parties at school all the time to take in a healthy snack the kids just love! You could do green jello for St. Patrick's Day. It really is a unique, healthy snack. Store in ziplock bags.

Dehydrated Peaches

Peel and slice your peaches, trying to keep them uniform in thickness. We prefer the O'Henry variety of peaches for drying. They seem to have the best flavor. Spread them out on the drying trays and set the thermostat for fruits. Check them after 3–4 hours. Store in ziplock bags.

Dehydrated Pears

Peel and slice your pears, trying to keep them uniform in thickness. Spread them out on the drying trays and set the thermostat for fruits. Check them after 3–4 hours. Store in ziplock bags.

Dehydrated Plums

Slice large plums, trying to keep them uniform in thickness. If you are using a smaller variety of plums, such as the Italian prunes, you can pit them and just turn them inside out. Set these on the drying trays, skin side down. Spread them out on the drying trays and set the thermostat for fruits. Check slices after 4 hours. If you have turned them inside out they take more like 20–24 hours to dry. Store in ziplock bags.

Fruit Rolls or Fruit Leather

The basic directions are to puree your fruit in the blender or food processor. You can also send your fruit through a Victorio strainer or "applesauce maker" as we call it in our family. Add a little lemon juice if desired to keep fruit from darkening. Sweeten fruit puree with corn syrup (using sugar will result in a brittle fruit roll.) Spread out as evenly as possible on fruit roll trays and then dehydrate. You can speed this up by using canned or bottled fruit. Drain it and then puree it and dry as described above. When dry, peel off trays and place on a piece of plastic wrap. Roll up and store in a gallon ziplock bag. You'll have to hide these from the kids or they won't last long!

You can play around to create some fun flavors. We stretch a lot of our fruit with applesauce since it is lots less expensive. Mix about 1 cup applesauce with 4 cups of other fruit puree and dry as above.

You can also flavor your applesauce to come up with lots of fun tastes. Use jello powder or Kool-Aid packets. Mix any flavor with applesauce to taste. You may not need the entire jello packet for the amount of applesauce you are using. Pear sauce works well also since it will take on the flavor of what you mix with it. Pears are usually more expensive though so I usually stick with applesauce.

Some of your fruits need to be cooked first to soften them enough to be able to puree them. This is definitely true for apples. Have fun experimenting. I'm sure you'll come up with some combinations that everyone will enjoy.

Ultra Gel

Ultra Gel is an instant thickener made from corn. It is lots less expensive per batch than pectin when you use it in your freezer or cooked jams, and it allows you to use far less sugar or even Splenda or honey in your jams and syrups. It is available online from Carnet Foods. It also works well to thicken sauces and pie fillings. Carnet foods sells two products: Ultra Gel and Thick Gel. The Ultra Gel can be used in hot or cold liquids. The Thick Gel must be heated to allow it to thicken.

I don't usually worry about purchasing special products. After years of using these thickeners though, I haven't found anything at the regular grocery store that can compare. Flour and cornstarch break down in the freezer and in the canning jar. Ultra Gel and Thick Gel hold up nicely for years and they store forever, so don't hesitate to order the large container. I received permission from Carnet Foods to include some recipes here that I use regularly. There is a fun cookbook available that includes many more recipes and ideas for freezer meals using these thickeners. It is *The Ultra Gel Answer Book* by Carma Christensen and Janet Stocks.

Ultra Gel is also available under some other names. Some places sell Ultra Sperse and others sell Ultra Maxigel. All of these products are the same and can be used interchangeably in the following recipes. Thick Gel is also the same as Clearjel. Check your area for what is available locally or use the internet to purchase what you need. I always keep some on hand because it makes home canning so easy. I also end up using the Ultra Gel to thicken many items in my everyday cooking. If my spaghetti sauce is a little too thin, I add a bit of Ultra Gel, for example. I also use it often to thicken the homemade yogurt that you can learn how to make in the powdered milk section of this book. The Ultra Gel is so easy to use since it is an instant thickener. Adjust the amount of ultra gel according to how thick you want it.

Fresh Pie Glaze

A fresh fruit pie can be on the table in a matter of minutes when you use this recipe.

1 pkg Kool-Aid, any flavor
2 cups water
1 cup sugar

10 Tbsp Ultra Gel*
4–5 cups fresh berries

Combine all ingredients and mix well. Fold in berries and pour into baked pie shell.

Freezer Jam

Use just about any kind of fruit or berry in this delicious recipe.

4 cups mashed fruit
1 cup applesauce
¼ cup light corn syrup
2 Tbsp lemon juice

2+ cups of sugar depending on tartness of fruit
½ cup Ultra Gel* (add more if you like it thicker)

Combine all ingredients and mix well. Sprinkle the Ultra Gel in gradually to avoid lumps. Pour into freezer safe containers and freeze.

I love this recipe because it works with every kind of fruit or berry. The applesauce takes on the flavor of the other fruit and allows you to stretch your berries or more expensive fruit. You really just need 5 cups of fruit so if you have 4 ½ cups of berries, add ½ cup of applesauce, etc. This is a recipe my mom got years ago and our family has used it every year since. I make strawberry, raspberry, blackberry, peach and apricot freezer jams every year. The apricots I put in the blender, the strawberries I put in the food processor, all the other fruit I mash with a potato masher. This jam never needs to be cooked so it retains its fresh fruit flavor. You can also use frozen berries if you'd like. I save my sour cream and cottage cheese containers to freeze my jam in. They really work well. One note of caution, because this jam has far less sugar than many recipes it will spoil faster once it is thawed out. Knowing this, choose containers the appropriate size for your family so that it can be eaten in a week or two once it is thawed out. Enjoy!

Soft Set Jelly/Syrup

I played with this a little and made syrup by not adding as much Ultra Gel. It is fun to have fruit syrup all ready to go.

8 cups fruit juice or puree
½ cup lemon juice
4 cups sugar
1 cup corn syrup
1 ½–2 cups Ultra Gel*

Combine all ingredients except Ultra Gel and bring to a boil. Remove from heat and whisk in Ultra Gel gradually. Return to heat and boil 1 minute. Ladle into jars immediately and process for 35 minutes in hot water bath. Makes 5 ½ pints.

Apple Pie Filling

My parents have lots of apple trees on their property. We get all the grandkids together to pick apples one day and then return a couple of weeks later to make pie filling, cider, and applesauce. Many days we process over 100 quarts before we are finished!

6 quarts, fresh apples, peeled, sliced
5 ½ cups sugar
1 ½ cup Thick Gel*
1 Tbsp cinnamon
1 tsp nutmeg (optional)
2 ½ cup cold water
5 cups apple juice
¾ cup bottled lemon juice
7 drops yellow food coloring (optional)

Blanch apples in the microwave or on the stove top. Combine sugar, thick gel, and spices in a large pan with water, apple juice, food coloring, and lemon juice. Cook over medium high heat until thick and bubbly. Fold in apples. Fill jars, leaving headspace. Boil in hot water bath for 35 minutes. Makes 7 quarts.

You can use this recipe with zucchini instead of apples. No one can ever tell it isn't an apple pie! It works especially well when a zucchini hides in the garden and grows to monster size. Peel, seed, and chop zucchini to resemble sliced apples. Place in a pan with some water and boil for a few minutes until just barely soft. Drain and set aside. Mix and cook filling ingredients as above and fold in the zucchini as you would the apples. Place in ziplock bags and freeze instead of processing in jars.

Cherry Pie Filling

Cherries are always ripe around the 4th of July in our area. I have fond memories of driving out to the orchards to pick cherries with my family and then returning home for a BBQ, homemade ice cream, and fireworks.

6 quarts fresh or thawed cherries, pitted
7 cups sugar
1 ¾ cup Thick Gel*
9 ⅓ cups water

½ cup bottled lemon juice
1 tsp cinnamon (optional)
2 tsp almond extract (optional)
2 tsp red food coloring (optional)

Combine sugar, thick gel, and water in a large pan. If desired, add the optional ingredients. Cook over medium high heat until thick and bubbly. Add lemon juice and boil 1 minute. Fold in cherries. Fill jars and boil in hot water bath for 35 minutes. Makes 7 quarts.

Fruit Syrup

Use this recipe if you only want to make a small batch of syrup for breakfast and you don't want to worry about processing it.

1 cup fruit juice
½–¾ cup light corn syrup

2 Tbsp Ultra Gel*

Combine all ingredients and mix well. Serve with pancakes or waffles. You could use honey or sugar as the sweetener in this recipe if you prefer.

Sweet and Sour Sauce

We love this with chicken or meatballs over rice. It is a true convenience item at our house and uses our garden produce!

8 cups tomato puree
4 cups chopped onion
4 cups chopped green pepper
2 (20 oz) cans pineapple chunks
6 cups sugar

½ cup soy sauce
3 cups white vinegar
1 cup water
2+ cups Ultra Gel*

Put tomatoes through a Victorio strainer to make tomato puree. Chop onions and peppers into desired size pieces. Combine all ingredients in a large pan except for the Ultra Gel. Do not drain the pineapple; add juice and all. Bring to a boil and very gradually add Ultra Gel, stirring constantly until thickened. Ladle into warm pint or quart jars and process immediately. Process jars for 35 minutes (sea level). Adjust for altitude if needed. Makes about 12 pints or 6 quarts.

Salsa

I love collecting new recipes. This one was passed to me by a friend who plants a "salsa garden" every year just so she can make this recipe.

3 gallons quartered tomatoes
30 large Anaheim peppers
26 jalapeno peppers
10 medium onions
8 green peppers

1–2 bunches cilantro
¼ cup garlic powder
4 cups white vinegar
½ cup salt
3 cups Ultra Gel*

Cut out stems and remove the skin from the tomatoes. Dip tomatoes in boiling water so the skins will slip off easily. Use a gallon ice cream bucket to measure the tomatoes. Pack it tightly. Cook your tomatoes in a large pot while you are chopping everything else. Stir occasionally. Use gloves when working with peppers and avoid getting any oils into your eyes. (I use a food processor to chop my onions and peppers.) You can trade the pepper varieties around to play with the spice level. We use more green peppers and less jalapeno. Mix everything except the Ultra Gel with the tomatoes. Bring to a boil. Gradually add the Ultra Gel, stirring until thick. Bring to a boil again. Ladle into warm pint or quart jars and process immediately. Process jars for 20 minutes (sea level.) Adjust for altitude if needed. Makes about 18 quarts. I chop peppers and onions as we pick them from the garden and store them in the freezer a little at a time until I have enough. I also cut the stem out of the tomatoes and freeze them in gallon bags. To use the frozen tomatoes, just run under cold water and the skins will slide right off. No need to dip them in boiling water and then wait for them to cool. This makes salsa day go much faster and not feel like as much of an ordeal.

*Ultra Gel and Thick Gel are registered trademarks of Carnet LLC, Boise, ID.

Just for Kids

Kids need fun activities often. There are so many possibilities that don't need to stretch your budget and they can be done with storable items. Here are a few ideas that we have done repeatedly over the years. I also keep plenty of paper and crayons along with other craft supplies in a drawer for my kids to access. A few fun games or activities can turn a crisis into a fun memory. I still hold fond memories of playing cards by candle light during a power outage. Many times we are safe within our homes and we just have to wait the situation out. Fun activities for the kids makes the waiting not so difficult.

Play Dough

We often make batches of this to give as birthday gifts for young children. You can pick the color of Kool-Aid that matches their favorite color.

1 ¼ cups all-purpose flour
¼ cup salt
1 pkg unsweetened Kool-Aid
½ tsp cream of tartar
1 cup water
1 ½ Tbsp oil

Combine the dry ingredients in a large glass or metal bowl. Combine water and oil and bring to a boil. Pour the water over the dry ingredients and mix well with a wooden spoon. Add a little food coloring at this point if desired. The Kool-Aid usually colors it well and gives it a fun smell. We do add yellow food coloring when we use lemonade Kool-Aid packets to make it a little more bright in color. Continue to mix with a spoon until it cools enough that you can knead it with your hands. Knead until you have a good, smooth texture. Store in ziplock bags once it cools down. It will keep for many months this way.

Salt Dough

We like to use this dough to create shapes the children can paint. It is something I turn to often when it is my week to teach preschool.

2 cups all-purpose flour
1 cup salt
Water
Food coloring, optional

Combine the flour and salt in a bowl. Start by adding ½ cup water and knead until it forms a dough. Add a little more water, as needed, to create a smooth dough. Roll out and cut into shapes using cookie cutters or mold into other shapes. Allow to air dry for a few days, turning as needed, to allow it to dry on all sides. To speed up the drying process, you can place items on a baking sheet and bake at 200 ° F until dry. Again, flip items over if needed to dry completely. Once items are dry, they can be painted with acrylic paints.

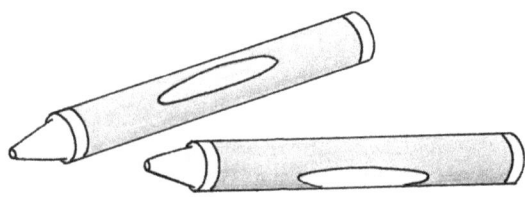

Mummy Dogs
When it's not Halloween time, we call these pigs in a blanket.

Hot dogs   1 batch basic bread dough

Roll dough into very thin snakes. Wrap each hot dog so it resembles a mummy, remembering that the dough will rise as it bakes and fill in the gaps. Place on a greased baking sheet and bake at 425° F for 10–12 minutes or until golden brown. Brush with melted butter while hot.

Ghost Treats
Doctor up some store-bought ingredients to create these ghostly treats.

1 pkg Nutter Butter Cookies   Mini chocolate chips
White almond bark

Melt almond bark according to package directions. Dip cookies in the melted almond bark and place on waxed paper to harden. While the almond bark is still soft, place two mini chocolate chips to be the eyes.

Breadstick Bones
These are the hit of the school Halloween party!

1 batch breadstick dough

Roll breadsticks into short, stubby snakes. Knot each end so they look like a bone. Place on a greased baking sheet. Allow to rise for 20 minutes and bake at 425° F for 10–12 minutes or until golden brown. Brush with melted butter while hot. Dip in vampire blood (pizza sauce.)

Octodogs and Seaweed

Our kids request this meal when they have friends over for lunch. It is easy and it pleases everyone at the table.

Hot dogs
Ramen noodles
Food coloring

Boil hot dogs until they swell and puff up as my kids say. Remove from the water and cut them to resemble an octopus. Leave the top 1 inch of the hot dog intact to be the head and then cut the remaining hot dog into the legs. It is difficult to get 8 legs. We usually settle for 6 even though we know an octopus actually has 8 legs. While the hot dogs are boiling, cook ramen noodles according to package directions. Stir in a little blue or green food coloring when done. This creates the seaweed. Serve the octodogs on a bed of seaweed and the kids will love it!

Shaped Empanadas

We make these for themed parties. We've made jack-o-lanterns and footballs.

1 recipe Breakfast Empanada dough
1 recipe Sloppy Joe filling

Roll out the dough and cut with large cookie cutters or a knife into the desired shapes. We've done pumpkins and footballs. You really can do anything. Place one shape on a greased baking sheet, put a teaspoon or two of filling in the center and then place another shape on top. Use a fork to crimp the edges together. Use a knife to cut vent holes in the top. For the pumpkins, we cut jack-o-lantern faces in the top and for the footballs, we cut the laces. Bake at 375° F for 15–20 minutes or until golden brown. **To freeze:** Wrap cooled empanadas in paper towels and then place in ziplock bags. Reheat in microwave. You can also freeze these before baking. Just thaw and bake as above.

Cinnamon Ornaments

Heat from the Christmas tree lights really helps the cinnamon smell come out. It gives our home such a fun scent during the holidays to have these ornaments hung on our tree. They are also fun to attach to gifts.

Cinnamon   Applesauce

Combine equal parts cinnamon and applesauce. Work with your hands until you have a dough ball that is not too sticky. You may have to add extra cinnamon depending on how thick your applesauce is. Roll out the dough and then cut with cookie cutters. Use a straw to make a hole at the top so you can thread ribbon through later or poke a thin piece of wire through the top of each ornament that you can use to hang it once it is dry. Allow to air dry for a few days, turning as needed, to allow it to dry on all sides. To speed up the drying process, you can place items on a baking sheet and bake at 200° F until dry. Again, flip items over, if needed, to dry completely. Once the ornaments are dry, they can be painted with acrylic paints. It is also fun to paint them with glitter glue.

Homemade Baby Wipes

Anyone with children will understand the need for wipes. We keep the ingredients on hand to make these as part of our emergency toiletry supplies.

1 big roll paper towels   2 Tbsp baby oil
2 cups warm water   1 Tbsp baby shampoo

Cut the paper towel roll in half with a serrated knife. Carefully remove the cardboard tube by pulling it out of the center. Place the remaining ingredients in a plastic container with a lid that is the right size for the paper towel roll to fit in. (Rubbermaid makes a container that has a #9 on the bottom that has worked perfectly for this.) Mix the ingredients and drop the paper towel roll in. Cover the container and then tip it upside down for the towels to able to absorb the moisture. After a few hours, they are ready to use. They pull up out of the center and you can tear one off at a time. Store them tightly covered.

Egg Yolk Paint

Kids love to paint on just about any surface. This paint is edible so when they are done creating, they can enjoy eating their art work.

Egg yolks   Food coloring

Separate the eggs so you only have the yolk. Save the egg whites to use in another recipe (¼ cup egg whites can substitute for 1 egg in most recipes.) Choose the number of eggs you use by how many colors of paint you want to make. Place one egg yolk in each small container. We always use small custard cups. Add a few drops of food coloring to each yolk to reach desired color. Remember that yellow and blue make green. The yellow of the egg yolk will mix with the blue food coloring and give you green. Have fun creating some interesting colors because of this principle. These paints are used when you are baking sugar cookies. Have the kids help you cut out their favorite cookie shapes and then paint before baking. Place painted cookies on baking sheets and bake according to the cookie recipe's instructions. The paints give the cookies a stained-glass look. They don't add any sweetness like frosting would so choose a sweeter cookie recipe for the tastiest results. You can also paint bread with these for some very fun results. Try making pizza dough, push it out on a greased pizza pan and then bake at 425° F for 10–12 minutes. It should just feel a little firm to the touch. Let your kids use it as a fun art canvas. After painting, bake at 425° F for an additional 5–10 minutes or until golden brown. We baked rolls this year for Thanksgiving and I pulled them out of the oven about 5 minutes early. The kids helped to paint pumpkins on them and then we popped them back in the oven for 5 minutes. They were the hit of the table!

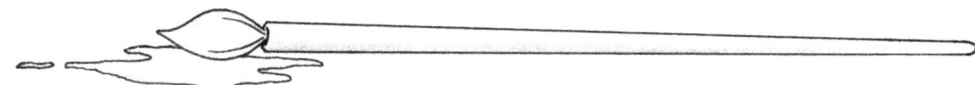

Corn Syrup Paint

Fun, non-toxic paint for kids! Dries with a shiny appearance.

2 Tbsp light corn syrup   3–4 drops food coloring
1 tsp water

Mix a few colors of this paint in separate paper cups or plastic yogurt cups. Use paint brushes or fingers to paint a fun design or picture. Set picture aside to dry. It may take a few days to completely dry.

Organizing Your Family's Finances

In D&C 109:8 we read, "Organize yourselves; prepare every needful thing, and establish a house, even a house of prayer, a house of fasting, a house of faith, a house of learning, a house of glory, a house of order, a house of God."

In order for your house to be in order, you have to spend some time reviewing your finances and determining if your financial choices are in line with what prophets have been teaching for generations. It takes time each month to keep these in order.

Many prophets and apostles have spoken on this topic over the years. One particular talk that I appreciate was given by Elder Joseph B. Wirthlin in the April 2004 General Conference. It is titled "Earthly Debts, Heavenly Debts."

In this talk, he reminds us of an important teaching of the Savior found in Luke12:15: "And he said unto them, Take heed, and beware of covetousness: for a man's life consisteth not in the abundance of the things which he possesseth."

Many of the choices we make regarding our spending are driven by feelings of covetousness, selfishness, and pride. Another well-known teaching of the Savior is, "Lay not up for yourselves treasures upon earth, where moth and rust doth corrupt, and where thieves break through and steal." (Matt 6:19 or 3 Ne 13:19) We know that the stuff we collect here on earth is just that—stuff, yet we still get caught in the race of trying to "keep up with the Joneses" as the popular saying goes.

Elder Wirthlin warns us, "Brothers and sisters, beware of covetousness. It is one of the great afflictions of these latter days. It creates greed and resentment. Often it leads to bondage, heartbreak, and crushing, grinding debt. The number of marriages that have been shattered over money issues is staggering. The amount of heartbreak is great. The stress that comes from worry over money has burdened families, caused sickness, depression, and even premature death." (Joseph B. Wirthlin, "Earthly Debts, Heavenly Debts," Ensign, May 2004, 40.)

Here are a few other thoughts shared by Elder Wirthlin in the same talk:

"Remember this: debt is a form of bondage. It is a financial termite. When we make purchases on credit, they give us only an illusion of prosperity. We think we own things, but the reality is, our things own us.

Some debt—such as for a modest home, expenses for education, perhaps for a needed first car—may be necessary. But never should we enter into financial bondage through consumer debt without carefully weighing the costs.

We have often heard that interest is a good servant but a terrible master. President J. Reuben Clark Jr. described it this way: 'Interest never sleeps nor sickens nor dies; it never goes to the hospital; it works on Sundays and holidays; it never takes a vacation…Once in debt, interest is your companion every minute of the day and night; you cannot shun it or slip away from it; you cannot dismiss it; it yields neither to entreaties, demands, or orders; and whenever you get in its way or cross its course or fail to meet its demands, it crushes you.'"

"May I suggest five key steps to financial freedom. …

"First, pay your tithing. …

"Second, spend less than you earn. …

"Third, learn to save. …

"Fourth, honor your financial obligations. …

"Fifth, teach your children to follow your example."

I'm sure these thoughts from Elder Wirthlin have caused you to think about some of your own choices and habits. Now that you are thinking a little more about your finances, take some time to reflect even more by asking yourself the following questions. The Holy Ghost will help you recognize the true answers to these questions. Often the answers don't come all at once. They may be questions you need to ask yourself again and again over the years as your family situation changes. The answers to these questions can help you chart a course of action. Sometimes it just means getting a little more creative with the income you do make so it can stretch farther. The other chapters in this section will help you in this area.

Hard questions to ask as you evaluate your financial habits:

1. Does the standard of living I have chosen require that I spend more than I earn each month?
2. Do my required expenses force us to spend so many hours working each week that our family and church responsibilities are neglected?
3. Are both parents required to work outside the home in order to meet our financial obligations?
4. Does my job stop me from keeping the Sabbath Day holy?
5. Is my pay so low that I am hindered from meeting my long-term financial goals such as saving for college, missions, or retirement?
6. Does my lack of employable skills require that I complete additional education so I can increase my earnings?
7. Have we made choices as a family that have gotten us into too much debt? If so, what habits do we need to change?
8. Do we need to reevaluate our expectations of what standard of living is acceptable to allow us to live well within our means every month?
9. We are doing a good job of living within our income, but do we plan ahead for bigger expenses?
10. Do we have enough cash in savings to cover emergencies that arise so we do not rely on a credit card?
11. Do I have a concrete plan on how I am going to pay my debt off?
12. Am I managing my resources well enough to be of service to others when called upon to give assistance?
13. Are my relationships with others strained because of some of my spending choices?
14. Am I constantly relying on others to bail me out financially?
15. Are we in control of our finances or are they controlling us?

We all have room to improve—don't get discouraged. Pledge to do better!

Paying Your Tithing

Tithing helps us qualify for temple blessings - As members of The Church of Jesus Christ of Latter-day Saints, we know that being a full-tithe payer is required for us to be worthy of a temple recommend. Blessings come into our lives immediately when we begin to live the law of tithing. There is great power that comes from being obedient.

Tithing helps us develop selflessness - Heavenly Father has given us all that we have. He asks for 10% back to help accomplish His righteous purposes. As we learn to enjoy giving, we forget ourselves and recognize the good that is being done around us.

Tithing shields us from want - A sister shared this thought during a Relief Society Lesson in one of my wards years ago. I have reflected on it again and again. When we are full-tithe payers, Heavenly Father helps us not miss the money. He somehow reduces our wants so it is not difficult to pay our tithes or our offerings. Our "want" list is reduced and we just don't worry about the things we must wait a little longer for or never have.

Tithing allows our feelings of gratitude to grow - When we focus on being grateful for what we have, our desire to help others increases and we somehow forget about ourselves. We begin to watch for ways that we can serve those around us. By serving, we lose ourselves and feel more fulfilled in the long run.

Tithing helps us become self-disciplined in financial matters - There are many financial experts who are not necessarily religious but they advocate giving 10% of your income to the charity of your choice. They have found that families are more careful with how they spend the other 90% when they give to a charity first.

Spending Less Than You Earn

Everyone will agree that spending less than you earn is definitely what we *should* be doing. Credit has become so available that it is very easy to find ourselves overshooting our incomes each month. This is an area that requires great self discipline.

James and I discussed money issues while we were dating. I knew he wasn't driven by wanting to impress other people because he had graduated from college, had a great job and still drove an old Ford LTD boat of a car! I actually appreciated his decision. I knew that he had finished school without any debt and that he was committed to living below his means no matter how meager. I am hard wired to be a saver which makes our personalities work well together regarding money. Still, we set a good rule when we first got married that has really helped us communicate about money. We committed that neither one of us would spend more than $20 without talking to the other one about the purchase or the desire we had for something. This got us talking often about money since you can't do much of anything for less than $20. It really helped us get into good habits.

Money can't buy happiness, but being in control of your money will bring happiness!

The other thing we did at the very beginning was set up a budget. James was paid a salary each month so we set up our budget based on what we knew would be coming in. We wanted to discipline ourselves to live on just his income so it would be much easier for me to stay home once children arrived. My income from teaching school went straight to savings.

I realize that "budget" is a negative word in some households. James and I look at a budget as a plan for our spending. It isn't restrictive. It actually frees up funds for us to do fun things with. We both grew up in households where income was tight. We are thankful that our parents were great examples of living within their means even when those means didn't stretch very far. These same lessons apply when money isn't as tight. The gift of prosperity comes with great responsibility. We want to be sure we are managing our funds wisely and saving for all our future needs. This intense desire to be self-reliant drove us to develop a budget so we could know there was enough money to meet all of our needs before purchasing new furniture, going on vacations, or even eating out every now and then.

Before you can set up a good budget, you must gather some information on your spending by recording what you spend each month. Use the Family Expense Record found in the Appendix of this book to help organize your expenses into categories so you can use this information later when you are planning for future expenses. If you don't know where your money is going, you can't make choices to spend it differently. It took James and I an entire year of recording our expenses to catch everything since some items are only paid once every six months, like car insurance, or once a year, like school registration fees. Also, by recording expenses for the entire year, you can see just what you are spending on some of the extras such as vacations, gifts, holiday expenses, etc.

As I mentioned before, we have always lived on less than we earn, but we still went through this process so we could better determine how much we could plan to put away for future goals. We tried to put together a monthly budget after recording just a month or two of expenses. We thought we had remembered everything. It seemed like each month brought a different "surprise" that we hadn't remembered. By keeping a record of our expenses for the entire year, we were confident that we had caught everything. We also came to realize that sometimes true surprise expenses come up. As an example, one time my eyeglasses got sat on and they needed to be replaced. One day we woke up with no heat in the house because the furnace had broken during the night. These surprises happen and we need to be able to cover these expenses without turning to a credit card. We determined that we needed to add an "other" section of our budget to catch all these surprises.

Here are the categories of our monthly budget:

Tithes and Offerings
        Tithing
        Fast Offerings
        Other Offerings
House
        Mortgage payment

    Extra principal payment
Utilities
    Phones
    Natural Gas
    Power
    Water/Sewer/Garbage
    Internet
Yearly Bills (These are those bills that come due once or twice a year. We determined what we needed to save each month to be ready when they came due.)
    Property Taxes
    Subdivision Fees
    Home Owner's Insurance
    Life Insurance
    Car Insurance
Long-Term Goals
    College Savings
    Retirement Savings
    Mission Savings
    New Car fund
    Home Improvements
Other
    Home Maintenance
    Automotive Repair/Gas
    Travel/Entertainment
    Gifts
    Household items and food
    Clothing/shoes
    Medical Expenses
    Other (We put some aside each month to catch those surprise expenses.)

It seems like a lot of categories, but it works well for us. You can change it up as you need to in order for it to match the way you think. Our budget for utilities is based on a monthly average. This took recording everything for the year and then dividing the categories by 12. We did this with other categories also.

One of the oldest ways of budgeting is referred to as the envelope method. This method requires you to put so much cash in each envelope at the beginning of each month. Once the money is gone, you have to be done spending in that category. If there is money left over, leave it in the envelope so when your expenses are higher in that category you have the extra to put towards them. We essentially follow this method, we just do it electronically. Mint.com is a free internet site that will do this for you. After getting things set up, we can quickly login and check where we are in each category. Some families have "yours," "mine," and "ours" accounts to give each other a little more freedom in choosing how to spend a portion of the income. Others load debit cards every couple of weeks with household and food money. When the debit card is empty, the spending is done. Some use a combination of these methods. There are many ways. What is vitally important is that you find the way that will work for your family. It has to work well enough that it will keep you motivated for years and years!

> *We must not allow our yearnings to exceed our earnings.*
>
> Thomas S. Monson

I will say that if you are struggling to stay within your budget, you need to go to a strictly "cash only" system for all the categories that are not set amounts each month. We have an emotional connection to cash and studies show that we spend less when we actually have to hand over those dollar bills. When the cash is gone you have to be done. This way you don't end up having to pay overdraft fees or late fees on top of everything else.

After setting up a budget (i.e. plan for your spending,) you need to review this each month and determine how well you did at staying within the set amounts. Utilize the Family Spending Plan form found in the appendix of this book to help you plan your spending each month. Be very honest with each other on just how much money needs to go to which expenses. Set some goals, stick to them, and then follow up with each other.

We sit down the first Sunday of every month when our children are in bed and review the finances. It has been good to create a set time each month to do this. It took a little while to get into a good habit with it, but now it is what each of us expects and we can go over things quite quickly. Determine what will work for your household and move forward with your plan.

In the beginning, recording expenses and planning where the money will go seems cumbersome and time consuming. Don't lose sight of your goal to be self sufficient and debt free. Any goal worth achieving will take concentrated time and effort. Be good about reminding each other what you can and can't afford as your family makes changes to your lifestyle so that you can more quickly achieve your goals.

Learning to Save

We learn from the story of Joseph in Egypt that seven years of plenty will be followed by seven years of famine. My husband, James, uses this phrase often to remind him and I that we need to be careful during our times of prosperity to be sure we are planning properly to survive our tough times that will surely come. We must prepare our families to weather the periods of famine in our lives.

We all know that emergencies happen. A job layoff, unexpected medical issues, a car accident, etc. can send us into debt at a frightening speed. The prophets have taught for years that it is important to save for these unexpected emergencies. Financial experts advise building an emergency fund of 3 months to a year of your expenses. If you have a two-income household then a layoff would not be as devastating to the family income so you may feel it is okay to stop at the 3-month level. For those in single income households and for jobs that are less secure, you are going to want to save 6 months to a year of expenses.

Now before you sink into despair because the amount seems so unrealistic to ever save, let's consider a couple of things. I didn't say a year of your salary. I said a year of your bare minimum expenses. By determining how to lower your expenses you end up receiving two blessings: You can save more since you are spending less and your emergency fund will be completed sooner since the total won't be as much. For example, if a family is spending $3,500 each month then they will need to save $42,000 to cover a year of expenses. If they can figure out reducing their spending each month to $2,500 then they will only need $30,000. If they are saving at the rate of $1,000 a month, they will reach their goal an entire year earlier!

If the emergency fund still feels too out of reach then you need to find a creative way to follow this counsel. First, squeeze every little bit of savings you can out of your regular earnings. (You'll find lots of suggestions in the next section.) Second, consider an additional part-time job that will help you fund your emergency goal. You will feel the added stress that working additional hours requires, but the peace you will feel once you have those emergency funds in place will far outweigh the relatively short time of added stress. Plus, once you have sacrificed and worked so hard to fill your emergency fund, it is going to take an emergency of epic proportions to make you take money out of it knowing that you'll have to fill it all over again if you do. James laughs at the idea that our emergency fund has an emergency fund. I just want to keep that money so safe that I still squeeze savings out of our earnings to give us additional cushion.

You have probably heard the idea of paying yourself first. This is the idea that you put some aside into savings each month before you begin spending. I have learned that I save far more each month by controlling my spending. This takes a lot of discipline, but it is part of learning to "bridle all your passions" as we are taught in Alma 38:12. Then out of what we save each month, we assign some to each of our savings goals before we determine the amount that is "leftover for fun."

As you begin this process, ask yourself some questions to start the brainstorming.

Questions to ask

1. Are my needs truly *needs*?
2. Can I reduce my fixed expenses by canceling unused memberships, reducing phone options, price checking insurance, etc?
3. In what ways can I get creative with my flexible expenses to spend less each month?
4. How can I have fun on a dime?
5. Is there a way that we can do _____ for less?
6. Over the years, James and I have asked ourselves these questions many times. We almost always come up with at least one thing we could do differently.

Insurance

It can really make a big difference to check with multiple companies for your insurance needs. This year alone we found a difference of over $600 annually for our homeowner's insurance! That adds up to thousands of dollars of savings over the time that we will own our home. Health insurance is another area that you need to check into. Sometimes the plan available through your employer at work is not the best plan to add your family to. It may be better for you to purchase a private plan for your spouse and children through another source. Once you have your emergency savings in place, you can increase your deductibles on all your plans which can really reduce your monthly costs for insurance.

Life insurance is also very important to purchase to make sure your family's needs will be taken care of if you were to die. Both the husband and the wife need to have life insurance. Term life insurance is the way to go. It is relatively inexpensive and will cover your needs. It is suggested that you purchase a policy big enough to cover your debts and replace your income for as long as you feel it is needed. For our family, since I stay home with the kids, we use 5–8 times James' salary as our guide. We want enough that I wouldn't have to go back to work until all the kids are in school. For me, we carry enough that James could hire a nanny and a housekeeper to replace what I do each week. Check the internet for price quotes on life insurance policies.

Disability insurance can also bring great peace of mind. Medical advances have made it possible for many to survive accidents that would have taken their lives in years past. Just because you survive doesn't guarantee you'll be able to work in your current field though. Disability insurance will replace a portion of your income for a certain number of years. Especially if you are the only income for the family, you will want to check into buying a disability policy. Also, talk through your plans so you already know what you'll do if a disability occurs. I keep my teaching certificate current as part of our disability plan. With current skills and training, I could more quickly enter the work force if James were to be disabled. My teaching salary would be less than we are making now but because we have learned to limit our spending, we could live on it and we'd have disability insurance coming in to help us through the transition.

> *Wisdom from a fortune cookie: You shouldn't overspend at the moment. Frugality is important.*

Grocery Costs

Grocery expenses are another area that many people spend far more than they need to. Here are a few suggestions for shrinking this area of your budget.

1. The first thing you need to do is begin cooking from scratch. Many families these days have not taken the time to learn to cook. It really isn't difficult and can actually be fun once you have collected some good recipes. Start by asking friends and family members to share favorite recipes with you. If you are a family that buys many prepared items each week from the freezer or deli section, you will notice a drastic drop in grocery spending by increasing your cooking talents.

2. Start tracking the cost of items you buy regularly in a grocery notebook. You will begin to recognize patterns in their pricing. Set some rules for yourself on how low an item has to go before you will buy it. I do this with all the items that can store either in the freezer or in my pantry or food storage areas. I have created my "Stock up Price List" and I only buy these items when they hit this low price. I buy enough to get me through the next 3–6 months so I can wait for another good deal. This has saved our family hundreds of dollars each month. Grocery prices vary so much from region to region that you really need to track it in your area. If you live in the Boise, Idaho area, check out my blog at www.allthingsprovident.blogspot.com for an updated copy of my list.

3. Use coupons only if this brings the item down to the low price you determined by following the previous step. Do not end up buying something you really don't *need* just because it is a great deal with a coupon. Even if it only costs you $.25, for example, and you buy 12 of them that adds up to $3 that could be put towards "needed" items.

4. Don't assume that buying the large bulk items at warehouse stores will be the better deal. You have to figure out the price per ounce or pound.

5. Do your best not to raise picky eaters. Help your children be willing to eat different brands and different dishes. This will allow you to shop for the lowest priced items by watching the ads each week and then plan your meals around what you have at home and what is on sale. Many of the grocery stores have their ads online so you don't even need to take the newspaper.

6. Be creative with your use of leftovers. I read once in *Money* magazine that on average people throw away 14% of what they buy each week! This shocked me and motivated me to do better at cleaning out the fridge in creative ways. We have leftover nights sometimes. We call them "Clean out the fridge parties" or "Choose your own adventure nights." I also freeze many in single serving sizes for James to take in for lunch. Another thing I do is reuse the leftovers in a new dish. For example, leftover sloppy joe meat makes a great shepherd's pie. I layer the meat in the bottom of a 9x13-inch pan, add a layer of green beans, a layer of mashed potatoes, and top with grated cheese. Heat through and you've got an easy new meal a few days later. You get the idea—stop throwing so much away!

7. Plan ahead for nights that you know sports, music lessons, or church meetings are going to make dinner time tight. Prepare your meal early to heat in the microwave or crockpot. You can also have a few homemade dinners in your freezer to pull out for nights like this. (See my freezer section for ideas.) A fast-food stop will easily triple your food costs for the night.

8. Reduce trips to the store. Research suggests that we can easily spend $20 on impulse buys every time we go shopping. Create a good list. Type one on the computer that includes items you usually purchase and organize it according to the aisles of the store where you traditionally do your shopping. (Check out the appendix for a copy of the one I use.) Print this off and leave it in a drawer or cupboard in the kitchen. When you realize you are low on an item, check it off or write a little number off to the side of the item to indicate just how many to purchase. Challenge yourself to stretch out the days between trips to the store. Your well-thought-out list will help you avoid running for just that one ingredient you neglected to pick up.

9. Plant a garden. This can save $40 dollars or more a week through the summer months for our family. It also reduces the cost through the rest of the year since we freeze or preserve all our extra produce. Gardening is not difficult. Talk with people in your area about what grows well. Most gardeners love sharing tips and tricks they have learned over the years. Even if you live in an apartment you can have a container garden on your patio or possibly find another family who has extra garden space who is willing to let you plant and help take care of the bigger space. Check out www.squarefootgardening.com for great information on gardening in any space.

I probably haven't shared anything new here. I do need to let you know that these methods really work. This is how my Mom taught me to shop as I watched her do it over the years to feed all eleven of us on a shoestring. I spend about half of what the average American family spends according to reports I've read. I feel confident that this is a good system to follow, especially considering that I feed twice as many people as the average family!

Money Saving Snack Ideas

When you do your grocery shopping, you can very easily spend $20–30 a week or more on pre-packaged snacks. (That adds up to over $1,000 a year!) As a family, this is one area of the food budget that can be tightened quite easily. The money you save can be used to pay down debt, increase emergency savings, or purchase additional food storage items. Talk through some of these suggestions as a family and decide which ideas you'd like to try. Many of these recipes and ideas would be great for school lunches also. You'll find plenty of fun recipes in the food storage sections of this book.

Muffins

Dried fruit

Homemade trail or snack mix

Chex mix – using store brand cereal

Popcorn/caramel corn

Homemade granola bars

Cookies or brownies

Homemade Lunchables

Rice Krispie treats/no-bake treats

Cinnamon toast or toast and jam

Boiled eggs/deviled eggs

Yogurt smoothies

Cheese ball with homemade crackers

Garden vegetables and ranch dip

School Supplies

Stores begin having school supplies on sale beginning in July in our area. You will save hundreds of dollars each year by stocking up during these sales. Our local schools have started sending supply lists home with final report cards. I hold on to these and then grab what my kids will need when the prices hit their low mark. We have a place set aside at home for extra supplies. I always purchase extra paper, crayons, markers, glue, pens, and pencils. I know the kids will need more of these before the year is through and I don't want to pay full price. We have also used new markers or crayons for birthday gifts for cousins or friends. Everyone loves crayons with new tips!

Use it up, wear it out, make it do, or do without.

We have our kids re-use what they can from year to year. Scissors, big pink erasers, school boxes, and backpacks can all last more than one year. Teach your children to take good care of their items and they will always last longer.

Trade Services

My brother and sister-in-law have traded babysitting for years. They found a family who had similar ages of kids and worked out a schedule. Every Friday night they are either on a date or watching the other family's kids. It has really helped them feel they can afford those date nights that are so important to a relationship.

I teach piano lessons and trade for yard work or house cleaning services. Many people want to work something out if you let them know you are willing. In the summer, I put together a rotation with other moms in the neighborhood to help teach skills to our older children. One of us teaches sewing, another mom does art, and another mom sets up science experiments. This gives our kids a day camp experience without the cost. It also helps build lasting friendships for the moms and the kids!

Preschool/ Play Groups

Once my kids reach about age 2 ½ they are ready to play with other kids on a regular basis. I have helped to set up playgroups in the neighborhood to help meet this need. It is a great part of their preschool experience. I have found the blessings are two-fold. The kids make friends and learn to be comfortable around other moms and at other homes. I also make friends with the other moms and have a support group I can rely on when I need a babysitter for a doctor's appointment or a friend to go with us to the park. It also gives me one morning a week to do my visiting teaching or go grocery shopping with one fewer child which most of the time fills my need for a break. We have always set up the playgroup one day a week for 1½–2 hours. Each mom takes a turn of hosting and we all just drop our kids off. We work out a rotation and then just follow the schedule. We are tempted to put in some sort of a lesson time, but research suggests that play time at this age is the most important use of a child's time. As the kids get older, we have allowed the playgroup to grow into a preschool group.

The preschool program is similar to the playgroup in that we rotate houses each week. Each mom takes a turn at being the teacher and helping all the kids work through the curriculum to help them as they prepare for kindergarten. It really isn't difficult to put together a program. Begin by interviewing kindergarten teachers in your area to determine what students need to know as they enter school. Use these guidelines to create a list of areas to focus on . (For those who are interested, I have included some handouts in the appendix that describe the program I put together. Use these as a guide to put together your own program.) The internet is a great resource for classroom ideas. I figure that by doing preschool this way, I have saved our family thousands of dollars over the years considering the going rate for preschool in our area. All the children who were involved in the preschool groups we participated in have been ready to enter kindergarten and all of us as moms feel the experience was well worth it.

Family Fun

You are only limited by your imagination in this category. Here is a list of some of our favorite things to do.

1. Go for a family walk or bike ride.
2. Hold a ping-pong/air hockey tournament complete with a bracket. Invite a few other families to join in.

3. Go on a picnic. We keep our eyes open for new parks as we drive around town. It is fun to explore a new place.

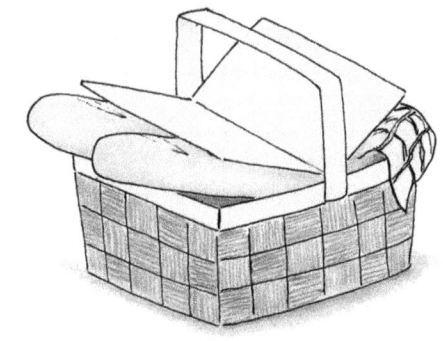

4. Set up a backyard carnival and invite the neighborhood kids over. We've recruited other moms to help man the stations. All the games are homemade for little or no cost.
5. Play kickball, hide-and-seek, tag, etc. Check out the internet for rules to some of these old-fashioned games.
6. Have a pizza party where everyone brings toppings to share. Check out the bread making section of this book for a great pizza dough recipe!
7. Host a potluck game night where families bring treats or dinner to share and then everyone plays games together.
8. Have a campout in the family room. The kids all sleep in sleeping bags on the floor after watching a movie together. This tradition began when I was on bed rest with my third child. My husband wanted us to have a fun family activity. He decided to carry the kids' mattresses downstairs to be next to where I was camped-out on the couch. The kids loved it and we've done it off and on ever since!

You'll notice that many of these activities are held at our home. Home is an inexpensive place to be. Start brainstorming and you'll come up with some fun ideas too. If you need some help, you should look at the Family Fun website at familyfun.go.com or check out the book *Great Kids are Homemade* by Shelley Wille. Both of these are endless sources of ideas for fun things to do.

Vacations

Vacations can be low cost and fun. Camping is a great option, especially if you can borrow the equipment from someone or go with a group so your family doesn't have to purchase every needed item. Once you purchase camping equipment, you are more prepared for emergencies since all the equipment can be part of your 72-hour kit. We have purchased a little equipment each year and borrowed the rest until we built a complete set for ourselves.

Plan a vacation around where family or friends live so you can stay with them and save on hotel and food costs. The other way to save on food costs is to book a hotel that has a microwave or kitchenette so you can prepare your own meals. We've also rented vacation houses over the years to have the option of cooking our own food and doing laundry. Sometimes we determine where we are going on vacation by where we can find inexpensive options for accommodations. We then frequent local parks for free entertainment with our children while we are away.

Set a vacation budget and save a little each month to help you reach your goal. Then discipline yourself to stick within your budget—it's really the time spent together in a new place that builds the memories not the amount of money you spend.

Home Value

Your home will retain its value if you keep things looking as new as possible and in good repair. It is so much easier to do a little at a time to keep things looking nice instead of waiting and having to do major renovations later. When you need to pay someone to help you do a project always solicit at least three bids for the job and ask for references. You'll be amazed at the difference in cost for the same job!

Clothing

1. Organize a neighborhood "Swap Meet." Everyone cleans out their closets and brings their items to the swap meet. People are then free to sort through and take home whatever items they can use. Any items remaining at the end of the swap meet can be taken to a local thrift store.

Don't trade what you want most for what you want now!

2. Purchase clothing from the clearance racks whenever possible. Definitely set a rule for yourself to never pay full price for any item. Just as you track grocery prices, you can track clothing prices also and set some rules for how low items have to go before you will purchase them. I have found that January and February are the best months for clothing clearance prices. It is especially good for men's dress clothes so I always buy James' work clothes then. I also find deals in other departments and I buy ahead for the kids. We stock pile our clothing budget money to give me a larger amount to spend this month since in the long run we save hundreds of dollars. You

will find clearance deals at the end of each season as well. Just start watching and changing your buying habits.

3. Purchase clothing items that are traditional or classic in their style so you aren't having to replace your wardrobe every season.

4. Pay attention to how many items you or your children actually wear. Don't over buy just because. Serving a mission helped me realize how little clothing I truly needed. Somehow we made it with just a few outfits.

5. Keep your clothing looking nice and in good repair. One of the greatest cleaning secrets I ever learned about is a bar of soap called Fels-naptha. It has been around for many years. It is just a yellow bar of soap you can purchase in the laundry aisle of many stores. It usually costs about $1. It is a rare thing to find a stain it won't remove! You don't even have to treat the stain immediately, you can wait a few days until you are ready to run a wash load. Just get the item wet, rub the Fels-naptha over the stain and then toss it in the washing machine. Every now and then I have to wash an item twice to get the stain out. Usually it comes out in the first washing. It will save your kid's clothing! Another suggestion to think about is that drying your clothes in a dryer can wear them out more quickly. If you need to stretch your clothing to last longer, hang it to dry. You'll save on energy costs and clothing costs since you won't have to replace items as quickly.

6. Learn some basic sewing skills to help you save money. You may find a great pair of pants on sale but if you have to pay someone to hem them you just lost the savings the sale gave you. I have to take in some of my kid's clothing since they are all tall and skinny. The other thing I've done is add an extra ruffle to the bottom of skirts to extend the time my daughters can wear them. All of these things can be learned quite quickly. If you don't have a sewing machine, borrow one from a friend. They will probably help you with your project as well while you are gaining confidence in your own abilities.

Cell Phone/Cable TV

We are not big cell phone users. We knew we weren't using many minutes so even at the lowest rate plan of $20 a month this was more than we needed. As we checked into options, we decided to pre-pay minutes through T-mobile. This gives us the cell phone for when we do use it for our long distance calls and keeps it available for when the kids need to reach me. We usually spend $100–$120 a year now this way which is half of what we were spending before.

When it comes to television, there are many inexpensive options for having something to watch when we feel like it. The television in on probably far too many hours in most American households if we paid attention to what research suggests. Cutting cable channels or television all together can save a few dollars each month. If you've never had it, you can choose not to add it to what is available in your home and your family will probably not miss it. You'll have to decide what to do in your home. I cite these as just a couple of examples of finding ways to save and changing your mind set.

Use the Library

Most communities have a library. You can save hundreds of dollars a year just by checking out movies and books instead of purchasing them. Maybe you could even find another book that would give you additional ideas on saving money.

There are many, many ways to save money. Decide on what is important to you as a family and what you are not willing to give up. If there is something you just have to have, then figure out a way to either afford it in your budget or trade for it in some way. As you make saving money a goal and include Heavenly Father in the process, you will begin to notice how many little hints the Spirit shares with you along the way. Heavenly Father wants us to be wise stewards of our income and have enough and to spare so we can help build His kingdom with our surplus. He will guide us as we ask for assistance. You'll also come to realize that when we are striving to do the right thing, blessings come. It seems like "surprise" money will just show up one day once you are doing things right. The bill for your car repair will be half of what you were first told or your husband will be given an unexpected bonus at work. Whenever you put Heavenly Father to the test, He always comes through. So "experiment upon the word" as we are taught in Alma 32 and you will quickly begin to see and feel the fruits of your new found determination to live on less.

Honoring Your Financial Obligations

When you make a commitment, you need to be ready to hold to your promise. Be wise with the amount of debt you take on in the form of loans. There will come a day of reckoning and you will need to be ready to pay it all back plus interest. Don't trust the banks or the credit card companies to tell you what you can afford. Determine what payment you could very easily afford after you have kept a good record of all your obligations as discussed earlier in this section. You are the only one who truly knows what you need money for and you only know this after keeping a very careful record.

Once you have established good habits and are living below your income every month, you must be careful about committing to new purchases. It becomes very exciting to think about driving a new car or purchasing a larger home or some new furniture. Do not commit your family to a new payment because the bank thinks you can afford it. Take some time to plan out what your new budget would look like with this new payment. I do not encourage anyone to go into debt for a new car or furniture or even home improvements. If you discipline yourself enough, then you can be saving a little each month until you have enough to pay for these items outright.

When you are thinking about purchasing a larger home, it is very difficult to save enough to pay for it outright. A new mortgage requires that you have saved enough for a down payment and then your payment will most likely be higher. You will also have increased costs for home owner's insurance, utilities and maintenance. Don't let the excitement of a larger home take over and destroy the careful planning you have been working so diligently on. When James and I were dreaming of a new home, we pushed the numbers and really felt we could afford it. We decided to put ourselves to the test. We set aside each month the added costs we had been able to calculate. These additional funds went into a savings account. We did this for an entire year while we watched the housing market in our area and tested out how we could live without this money for other expenses. After a year, we decided that we truly could afford the new purchase and not have it stretch us too far. The added savings we had built up gave us two blessings—a sizeable down payment and the confidence that we could honor our new obligation.

As a general rule of thumb, you should limit the loans you take out so that your debt payments are no more than 25% of your take home pay. This means that if you bring home $4,000 a month, you should not have debt payments of more than $1,000. Divide your take home pay by 4 to determine the maximum amount that your debt payments should be. Once you have established good money habits, you should work to accelerate your debt payoff as soon as possible by increasing your payment. You will save thousands of dollars in interest just by increasing your payments by even just a little. For example: If you have a 30-year mortgage of $100,000 at 6% and you increase your payment by just $50 a month, you will pay off your loan 5 ½ years early and save nearly $25,000 in interest! If you have credit card debt at a higher interest rate, your savings will be even better. My advice is to never carry credit card debt. It can get out of hand quickly, and when it does, it will crush you! Search for a mortgage calculator online to put in your specific situation and play with the numbers a little. By tightening the belt a little more now, you win huge rewards in the end. The feeling of being completely debt free is amazing!

You should set a goal to be completely out of debt (including your mortgage) by the time you are 45. This will give you the time you need to focus your savings towards retirement. Depending on where you are in life, this may seem impossible. We know it is possible. We watched our parents do it and we are well on our way. Break your goals down into smaller pieces and you will be able to see your progress.

Many families can tell you of the stress they have felt as they have fallen short on their financial obligations. Careful planning and lots of discipline can help you steer clear of this stress. Keep your dreams and expectations in line with what you can truly afford. Heavenly Father will bless you with joy and contentment as you ask for His help in this huge mortal endeavor.

Teaching Your Children to Follow Your Example

Your children need to know you are working hard at living within a budget and that you have a plan. Don't be afraid to tell them that what they want is not in the budget. As they get older, include them in some of the planning for how you are spending money. For example, we set a vacation budget before taking a family vacation. With the help of the internet, we check out options of things we could do and then the kids help us decide what will fit in the budget. We encourage them to get creative with some ideas of how we could save money in one area so it can be available to do something else. They often opt to eat a picnic at the local park instead of eating out so money can be available for other fun things. We have discovered some very fun parks doing this and many times the night at the park has become one of our favorite memories of the entire trip!

The Parenting Breakthrough by Merrilee Browne Boyack is a wonderful book about teaching children how to work and how to manage money. I appreciate the approach she suggests and we have found success using many of her ideas with our own children. Ask around among the parents you know who seem to be making progress in this area. We have learned many lessons by talking with those who are just a few years ahead of us in the parenting realm.

Another author I appreciate is Neale Godfrey. I heard her speak once on financial challenges facing families and was very impressed with her knowledge and emotional drive. She has written many books on teaching children about money that are helpful and well worth the reading time.

There are many activities to do with your kids to teach them these important principles. Here are a few things we have done.

Play "Report for Duty" - Have the kids stand at attention and salute you while saying, "Reporting for duty." At this point, assign each kid to do something different such as pick up all the toys that have yellow on them, pick up all the books, put away your clean laundry, etc. Be sure they count how many items they put away. Each time they finish the task, they report back and you pay them a penny for each item. This game works especially well with young children. After playing, I always pull out a few snack items and assign an amount to each one. They can then use their pennies to buy their snack of choice from Mom's store.

Fill a Vacation Savings Jar - For Family Night one week, have the children help decorate an empty jar that can be used to save towards a vacation or some other fun family event. Discuss how much money will be required to do what is planned. Make a list of odd jobs that kids can do around the house or in the neighborhood to help earn money towards this event. Make a big deal out of it whenever someone is able to put money in the jar. Celebrate as a family when you reach your financial goal.

Yard Sale Stand - We have a community yard sale every year in our neighborhood. Our kids sell homemade caramel corn and maple bars each time. They always sell out and learn a little bit in the process. I always keep a record of their expenses for supplies so they can determine their true earnings.

Create a "Family Fun" Envelope - As the children get older, they can help to make some of the decisions about where the family money is spent. Once you have decided on the amount of money that will be available for fun activities during the month, place this amount of money in an envelope or jar. Allow the children to have a say in what activities the family decides to do. Help them realize that when the money is gone, it is gone, and all fun activities from this point on will have to be free. You can also help them realize that if they choose to save some one month, they can add it to the total for the next month and end up being able to do a more expensive activity this way. It is an eye-opening experience to listen to the children try and decide what to do. Their personalities about money will begin to come out. As time passes, you will also be able to see their reasoning skills mature. Depending on how your family runs, you may choose to set an amount each week instead of for the entire month to make it a little easier for the kids to grasp the concepts you are hoping to teach.

Family Budgeting - With teenagers, you can use monopoly money to actually demonstrate where all the family income goes each month. Have the children join you in dividing the money into the different categories and realize what is left over. (You need to have tracked your spending for a few months and created a budget on your own before involving your children.) It is usually an eye-opening experience for the youth of the family to realize just how much it takes to live each month. They begin to understand why you tell them there just isn't money in the budget for what they would like to do sometimes.

Create a Small Business - As your children get older, it is important to begin requiring them to earn some of their own money. They can mow lawns, babysit, clean houses, teach piano lessons, etc. Get creative with what they can do to learn the principle of work. One family in our area runs a science camp each summer for elementary age children to attend. The older children work together to get the word out about the camp and plan activities. Through this experience, they have been able to save money to cover the cost of participating in the sports activities that they enjoy and would not fit within the regular family budget.

Open a Savings Account - Anytime your children earn money, you need to help them understand the importance of saving for future expenses just like you are doing. Help them set up a savings account where they can put money away that will eventually help pay for their college or mission expenses.

Pass Some Expenses to Your Kids- Car insurance, sports fees, summer camp registration fees, etc. can all be passed over to your children once they are earning some income. This will help teach the importance of saving for future expenses.

Discuss Money Often - When your children begin considering colleges and trying to decide where they want to go, help them push some numbers so they can understand more fully the true cost of attending each school. If they won't be attending college, but are at a point where they feel ready to move out, help them set up a budget with the amounts that you feel are realistic for your area. They need to know what expenses they will have to be responsible for beyond just basic rent. If you have kept them involved in your family budgeting all along, this should not be an awkward conversation.

I feel like my children help keep me diligent in my money management. I know I need to be a good example to them and teach them through my actions. Many children leave home thinking they can live the same standard of living as their parents. This is not the case in most situations. (They don't stop and realize that it took their parents 20 years or more to reach this level.) I want my children to know that they can have fun without spending money. I also want them to understand how important it is to be able to honor their financial obligations and not commit to more than they can truly afford. It does take vigilance and consistent reminding, but children begin to get it. My nine-year-old is finally catching on. She's our oldest so we have hope that the others will catch on also here pretty soon.

Emergency Preparedness

Preparing For Emergencies

No book on provident living would be complete without a section on emergency preparedness. This section is not intended to be a handbook with all the specific information you need on how to be ready for everything. There is plenty of that kind of information online or printed in other books. (One great resource is www.ready.gov.) Plus, depending on where you live or the phase of life you are in requires very different planning. The purpose of this section is to get you thinking about possible hazards and questioning what you would do in certain situations. What is important is that your family has a plan.

As you read through this section, set some goals focusing on small things your family can do to be just a little more ready. If your mind gets wrapped around a certain idea or concern that seems to grow within you, allow this energy to be channeled into reading more about it and actively doing something to prepare your family. I have found that when I hear of challenges others are facing such as a big earthquake, a blizzard, a job loss or a sudden death in the family, I begin to wonder what we would do in that situation. Would we be okay or would it feel like a HUGE crisis? These thoughts have led to more questions and then I have done some research and my husband and I have worked together to do what is required to feel prepared.

He has told me more than once that he has no problem channeling our savings to preparedness items. He just isn't the one to think about these worries so he's grateful my mind turns that way so we can all feel a little more secure. Find ways you can work together to get these things accomplished. It is more than one person can do. I promise that as you work as a family, whether that's a husband and a wife or a parent with children, you will feel a synergistic effect. That means that 1+1 will feel like 5. You will accomplish far more than you thought possible when everyone works together.

I learned long ago that if you give yourself a deadline, you get it done. If I write it on the calendar, I leave time available to do it. Sometimes my deadline gets pushed back a little, but it still happens. I've also developed a system over the years that works well for me. I have a whiteboard that hangs in the kitchen so I see it multiple times a day. This is where I keep my to-do list. Once I write an item up there, it stays there until I've completed it. The more kids we've had, the harder it's been to keep track of everything I should be helping with. I'm sure you all relate. This system helps me remember to do the extra things that are not in our daily routine. I include our preparedness goal on this board. For example: I write the word "heater" up on the board. As I see it every day for a few weeks, I'm reminded to research heaters so we can choose one that would heat a portion of our home during a severe winter storm that takes out the power. This whiteboard system really helps me get more accomplished. I'm not having to rethink all the time, "Now what was I going to do with these few spare minutes?" I just look up at the board and it keeps me focused. Hopefully, you can figure out a system that works for you. Thinking a little about preparedness every day helps you to change the way you do things. Over time, you will become the provident person you are striving to be.

72-Hour Kits

It is a rare occasion that an emergency of such proportions occurs requiring us to have to evacuate our entire family. We seem to be hearing of more and more of these events though. If, for some reason, an event like this occurs in your area you will want to be ready. Every family should have a very basic 72-hour kit. There are many ideas online about what to include. I have included the list of what we came up with. The square bullets mark the items that we felt were essential and then we worked to add the other items until our kits were complete. The family kit includes items that can be shared by family members. Each member of the family will need a personal kit and a food kit. What you really need to include is what it will take to actually survive for 72 hours. We aren't talking about being comfortable; we are just planning for survival.

There are options for packaging your kit also. We still have young children who cannot be expected to carry their own kits so we have chosen to store our supplies in two Rubbermaid bins in the garage. I have taped to the inside of the lid a list of essentials that I need to quickly grab to complete my survival supplies. These are items that are harder for me to keep rotated or are season specific such as prescriptions meds, winter coats, etc. It also includes the camping gear we would need to grab. Most families have 20–30 minutes of warning before having to evacuate so this would give me time to quickly go down the list and grab what I need. The list just insures that I have thought of everything because I know my mind would not be able to stay focused if we were truly in an emergency.

Our bins are stored with our camping gear in the same area of the garage so at a moment's notice we could load it all in the van and get out of town. Other families have each member keep a backpacking backpack packed at all times with their individual survival kits, dividing the family items among themselves. The important thing is to have a kit and a plan as to how you are going to get your family out of town fast if the time comes that you will need to leave. The food, water and batteries in your kit need to be rotated every 6 months to a year.

The other item you need to change your thinking on is the amount of gasoline you always keep in your car. Many of us drive our cars until the tank is empty or very close anyway. Change your thinking to always keep about a half a tank of gas. At our house, when the needle on the gage registers half full it is time to head to the gas station. If you have to evacuate very quickly, you don't want to find yourself needing to go to the gas station. You'll run into long lines and even gasoline shortages. You can get quite a few miles from home on half a tank and then you should be far enough away from the dangerous situation. Having some gas in your tank at all times provides you with some fuel storage as well. Even if you don't need to evacuate, you can siphon the gasoline out of your tank to use in your generator if you needed to.

What happens far more often than a calamity that requires us to leave our homes is an emergency that allows us to stay at home, but not receive any comforts such as clean water, heat, or electricity. Your 72-hour kit will help you through this sort of emergency as well. Very few Americans can go more than three days without having to go to the store for some basic need such as diapers, medicine, food, etc. We need to change our thinking and our habits so we don't panic when these emergencies occur. By changing our thinking and planning ahead, these emergencies become inconveniences and not true emergencies. They become the adventures that everyone talks about and remembers for years to come.

72-Hour Kit Contents

Family Kit - build 1 per family

- ☐ Duct tape
- ☐ Toilet paper
- ☐ Soap
- ☐ Toothpaste
- ☐ Matches
- ☐ Fuel for cooking
- ☐ Water purification tablets
- ☐ Comb
- ☐ Can opener
- ☐ 2 flashlights w/batteries
- ☐ Pocket knife
- ☐ Zip lock bags
- ☐ First aid kit
- ☐ Hand sanitizer

Items to consider adding:

- o Small stove
- o Mess kit or small saucepan and utensils
- o An AM/FM battery or hand crank radio
- o Scriptures
- o Tent or tarp for shelter
- o Card game of your choice
- o Cash and coins
- o Photocopies of credit and identification cards
- o Family pictures (To show around if someone is missing so others can help your family reunite)
- o Candles
- o Hand warmers
- o Sewing kit
- o Rope
- o Have enough sleeping bags, blankets, coats, hats gloves, etc. that you could pack these on a moment's notice if evacuating in the winter or use at home if you are without heat.

Personal Kit - build 1 per person

- ❑ Whistle
- ❑ Toothbrush
- ❑ Lip balm
- ❑ Moist towelettes
- ❑ Drinking cup
- ❑ Plastic utensils
- ❑ Emergency blanket
- ❑ Large garbage bags

Items to consider adding:

- o A change of clothes and shoes
- o Extra eye glasses, if needed
- o Contact cleaning supplies, if needed
- o Any necessary prescription and non-prescription medications
- o Feminine hygiene supplies
- o Baby items
- o Sunscreen
- o Hand towel
- o Personal identification information and a family picture to aid in finding each other if your family is separated

Food Kit - build 1 per person

- ❑ 2 granola bars
- ❑ 1 fruit snack
- ❑ 2 oatmeal packets
- ❑ 1 beef stick
- ❑ 1 tube of nuts
- ❑ 3 apple cider packets
- ❑ 1 juice packet (Crystal Light)
- ❑ 2 ramen soup
- ❑ 2 cracker packets
- ❑ 3 applesauce
- ❑ 1 can pork & beans
- ❑ 1 can chili
- ❑ 12 pieces candy
- ❑ 1 package gum
- ❑ Add: 1–2 gallons of water

72-Hour kit menu

This tells you how to ration your food kit over 3 days.

	Day 1	Day 2	Day 3
Breakfast	1 granola bar 1 fruit snack 1 apple cider	1 oatmeal 1 apple cider	1 oatmeal 1 juice packet
Lunch	Ramen soup Crackers	Beef stick Applesauce Nuts	Chili Crackers
Dinner	Pork & beans Applesauce	Ramen soup Crackers	1 apple cider 1 applesauce 1 granola bar
Snacks	4 pieces candy 1 piece gum	4 pieces candy 2 pieces gum	4 pieces candy 2 pieces gum

Add to your kit:
1–2 gallons of water

Be sure your family kit contains:
Small stove and fuel w/matches or another way to heat your food
Mess kit or small saucepan and utensils
Can opener

You can put together a different menu if this one includes items your family members would not eat. Just keep in mind you need high protein foods to provide energy and also food that requires little or no cooking. Searching online will give you other menu ideas.

Preparing for an Emergency at Home

The majority of all catastrophes that occur allow us to stay in our own homes. The big question we have to ask ourselves is, "Am I prepared at home so we could live through the crisis?" The remainder of this section will cover some basic information and ideas about how to stay calm through a crisis because you are prepared. I'm going to assume that you've already read through the sections on food storage. Hopefully, this means you are changing your thinking about buying in bulk or stocking up when items go on sale. This means the food needs that your family will face during a crisis will be taken care of. We will address the other areas that will need some attention.

Water

The recommended basic amount to store is 14 gallons per person. When calculating how much you need, check the size of your water heater. It may be large enough to hold what you need without worrying about other containers. You will still want to store enough in portable containers with your 72-hour kit in the event that you need to evacuate. You will also want to learn how to drain your water heater in case you need to access the water.

If your family is large enough that you need additional water than what your water heater will hold, there are many options for containers. Some families choose to go with larger containers such as a 55-gallon drum. Other families opt for smaller containers that are easier to move and deal with. We actually have some water in both of these types of containers. I appreciate the small 2-liter pop bottles or juice jugs I've saved, cleaned out and filled with water. Sometimes the emergency is not a huge deal, like when the water must be turned off for a certain amount of time to do repairs. By having a few small containers, we can easily make it through these short-lived emergencies even when they coincide with potty training or the stomach flu.

When saving plastic containers, check the bottom of the bottle. If you see in capital letters "PETE" then you know it is made of food grade plastic and is safe for storing both food and water. It is recommended that any container used to store water be cleaned then rinsed with a diluted bleach solution of 1 part bleach to 10 parts water before filling. Fill these clean containers using tap water. If you are on city water, then you will not need to treat your water in any way before storing it. The city treatment plants have already done so for you. If you are on a well or using some other untreated water source, you will want to add a few drops of bleach to your water. Add 8 drops (about $\frac{1}{8}$ tsp) of unscented bleach to 1 gallon of water.

Store your water containers away from direct sunlight in a location where possible leaks won't be a problem. If freezing may occur, remember to allow head room for expansion. Storing water in plastic milk containers is not a good option. The plastic is biodegradable and will develop leaks easily.

Don't forget about other sources of emergency water. Some of these include liquid from canned fruits and vegetables, melted snow or ice cubes, or the water in the back of your toilet tanks (not the bowls). Reserve the water from the toilet tanks for sanitation purposes instead of drinking since it may contain cleaners that you have added. I mentioned hot water heaters before as a source for storing water. During an emergency, you will want to turn off the water entering your house to not contaminate the water already in your hot water heater.

There are some other preparedness items to consider when you are thinking about water storage. You should have some way of purifying water in case you run out of your clean water sources. Boiling always works, but this may require you to use a lot of the fuel you are conserving to cook your meals. You can purchase a water filter or water purifying tablets from sporting goods stores or online to give you a way to purify water. They also sell water bottles that have a filter built right in so as you drink from them the water is automatically filtered. You may also want to consider storing a bunch of coffee filters. Boiling your water will purify it but it won't take the "floaties" out. By running your water through a coffee filter after purifying it, it will look clean and you will have an easier time swallowing it.

Food and Other Essentials

You should store two week's worth of very easy to prepare meals. These could be just "heat and eat meals" such as canned chili or "just add water" dishes like some of the freeze-dried meals that are available. If you are cooking without power, you will want to conserve your fuel and not have to spend all day cooking since you will have plenty of other worries on your mind. Additionally, you need to store 3 month's worth of food that you eat on a regular basis and a year supply of basics such as wheat, rice, and beans. See the sections on food storage for more specific information.

In addition to storing food, you should build a stockpile of other essentials that could last at least 3 months. These are items such as toiletries, medications, dish and laundry detergent, household cleaners, etc. To determine my list, I opened cupboards and drawers to see what I had and what I wouldn't want to run out of. I created my shopping list and then watched for deals on what I needed. Now I just replace an item when I finish one container and rotate through my stockpile similar to rotating my food storage.

A note on storing medications: The pharmacist will tell you that just because a medication has reached its expiration date does not mean that it will not work. It just may not be as potent. It doesn't hurt to have pain killers and cold medicines on hand so when they are needed you will be ready. Store them in a cool, dry place. If you take any prescriptions on a regular basis, talk with your physician about your goal to have enough at your home to make it through 3 months. Many doctors can write a prescription for a 90-day supply. My doctors have praised my efforts to be prepared and they have given me the prescription for what I needed.

Here is a list to get you going. Add any items specific to your likes or needs.

Shampoo	Toothbrushes
Conditioner	Feminine supplies
Shower gel/soap	Dishwashing soap
Deodorant	Dishwasher detergent
Toilet paper	Laundry soap
Paper towels	Stain remover
Kleenex	Bathroom cleaning supplies
Q-tips	Bleach
Cotton balls	White vinegar
Hairspray	Cold medicines
Hair gel	Pain medicines
Make-up supplies	Prescription medications
Face washing supplies	Trash bags
Toothpaste	Ziplock bags of all sizes

Cooking

A cook stove that does not require electricity is a must. You can purchase a simple camping stove or choose one of the bigger models. Don't forget that you will also need to store the fuel that is needed to allow your stove to work. A Dutch oven and charcoal are other cooking options. Be sure and store plenty of charcoal. There are many books and websites that share information on Dutch oven cooking. There are some very simple ovens you can make with a box and some aluminum foil. Search online for solar oven, apple box oven, hay box oven, or paper box oven. None of these options are difficult or expensive. You could even do it as a family activity and then try it out the next day to cook your dinner. It helps to make "getting prepared" a fun thing to do.

Cooking with a Dutch Oven

To achieve a 350° F temperature inside the oven, follow the Rule of Four. Take the diameter of the oven (10-inch, 12-inch, 14-inch, etc) and add four to it. This tells you the number of hot charcoal briquettes to place evenly spread out on top of the oven. Subtract four from the diameter of the oven to determine how many hot charcoal briquettes to place evenly spread out under the oven. This will heat the oven to approximately 350° F.

Any recipe you bake in a regular oven can be cooked in a Dutch oven. You can place the ingredients directly in the pot or you can use a separate oven proof pan and place it inside the Dutch oven. We usually just put the ingredients in the pot, but I have used a bread pan when baking bread loaves and a pie pan when baking a pie. I just place the item in the Dutch oven as if I were placing it in my oven at home. To adjust the oven temperature, add one coal on the top and bottom to increase the temperature by 25° F or subtract one coal from the top and bottom to drop the temperature by 25° F. Feel free to try any of your regular recipes in a Dutch oven.

Shelter

A tent large enough to accommodate your family is all you need. You may consider a few smaller tents to make them easier to fit into your 72-hour kit.

Heat

If you live in a climate that gets cold, you need to think about the best way to heat your home in the event that your furnace stops working. There are options. You may have a wood burning fireplace. Keep in mind that this will heat only a small portion of your home directly in front of the fireplace unless you have an insert with a good fan or it is somehow connected to your duct system. Be sure and store plenty of wood. If you don't have a wood burning fireplace, there are different propane and kerosene heaters available. Again, the important thing is to store enough fuel to run these. Different sizes are available that heat different size rooms. Talk about which room you could close off and heat. We plan to heat the master bedroom since it is large enough for all if us to sleep on the floor and we would have access to a bathroom. Do some research to determine which heater is your best option for what you decide you need. Be sure to test it periodically so it is ready when you need it. Also store extra blankets, sleeping bags, coats, hats, mittens, etc. to help you stay warm.

Generator

If you count on a freezer to store some of your food, you will want a generator. You may also want to consider one large enough to run a lamp for a few hours if needed or some small cooking appliances such as a hot plate or a microwave. A generator could also be used to run an electric space heater for a short time. You must store enough fuel to keep your generator going. One friend always fills up the gas tanks in her family's boat and travel trailer before parking them for the season so she could use the fuel to run a generator in the case of a severe winter storm. Check on the regulations for storing fuel in your area before deciding for sure how to do it.

Shopping for Supplies

Spring and early summer are the times of year to watch for sales on camping and survival equipment. You may also find the items you need at yard sales or thrift stores. Remember that a little bit at a time will add up so don't feel like you need to get everything all at once. Decide on what is most important to you and figure out a way to fit it in the budget. James and I have always tried to focus on one thing a year. First, we built our 72-hour kits then we bought our propane stove. The next year we purchased our kerosene heater and began saving for a generator. Each year we are just a little more prepared and would have to rely less on others if a true emergency occurred.

You can also pair up with a friend or family member who lives close and divide the list knowing you would share items if the need arose. This way one of you can buy a generator and the other family can purchase a heater or stove for cooking. By dividing the list, you can know that between the two families you will have the bases covered quicker than you could afford it by yourself. Then, eventually, you can work to accumulate the items over time so you have a full complement of emergency supplies.

First Aid/CPR

Basic first aid and CPR training is very important in feeling prepared to act quickly during an emergency. Many local hospitals and Red Cross chapters have information on classes for you to learn these skills. The Young Women's Camp Manual or the Boy Scout Handbook are also great places to refer to so you can review basic first-aid skills as a family. It is also important to have a first aid kit at home, at work, and in the car. These first aid kits should contain more items than just simple band-aids. If there was a true emergency, you would be very grateful to have large bandages, burn cream, antibiotic ointment, etc. Check sporting good stores or online to purchase a few well-stocked kits.

"CPR Anytime" offered by the American Heart Association is a program that allows you to learn and review the steps of CPR in your own homes. You can purchase a kit online for a small fee and then have the ability to train your entire family over and over again. You are not able to become CPR certified with this program, but you will gain knowledge and confidence that will be invaluable if needed. Since reviewing these steps regularly allows you to retain your knowledge of CPR, purchasing one of these kits could be very helpful.

"Just in Case"

Will/Living Will - Do a little research to learn what is required in your state. If you have children, you need to have at least a basic will in place so they will have legal guardians upon your death that you choose for them instead of a judge. A Living Will helps medical personnel understand if you desire to have life support left on or not. If you have specific wishes, you need to make them known. There are many sites online that can give you direction in how to go about writing a will. There are also free forms available. Depending on your situation, you may want to visit with a lawyer to receive specific advice. This is one item that I highly suggest you give yourself a deadline to get done. It is something that many of us know needs to be done, but we never quite get around to it. It is important enough that my husband and I set aside a few date nights to discuss it in particular. We don't get date nights very regularly so it was difficult to use this precious time for paperwork, but we are so very thankful we did.

Child Identification Kit - In the event that one of your children is kidnapped or missing, a child identification kit can help law enforcement officers more quickly understand who they are looking for. Look online to find a source for free kits that you can complete. In the least, be sure you have a current picture of what your children look like so you can show it to the police. We take weight and height measurements every January to document how much the kids have grown. This information would be very useful to police. If your children really went missing, you would be so very stressed out. It would be difficult to remember all the information that the officers would like to know. Having a Child ID kit filled out and filed in a safe place would be very helpful. This is a great activity to do during a Family Night. It is something that you need to update each year so the information can be current.

Car Emergency Kit - We spend so much time in our cars these days that we need to carry some emergency supplies with us. We keep a few things in the car at all times. These include water, a flashlight, basic medicines, jumper cables, gallon zip-lock bags (for when stomach flu hits) and a few basic tools. Depending on the season, we add some additional items. These include snow chains, jackets, sunscreen, and bug spray. I also always have a spare diaper bag in the car since we still have young children. We carry extra diapers, baby formula, an extra bottle, snacks, and a change of clothes for the baby. This has saved us on many occasions.

You will need to customize your car kit to your family's needs. There are lists online to help you brainstorm what you feel is important. Before leaving on a long road trip, I always review what is in the car and add what is needed. It is a good idea to carry extra water and snacks anytime you are going on a longer trip. We've heard too many stories of families who end up stranded somewhere and survive on one bag of chips and melted snow. With a little planning ahead, many hardships can be avoided.

Computer Back-up - In our computer driven society, it is important that you count backing up your computer as part of emergency preparedness. Much of the vital information that we may need to refer to is saved on our computers. There are ways to make backing up your computer automatic. This is one area that I have turned over to my husband. He works on computers all day and he is much more aware of just what needs to be done. I rely on him to make sure it is happening. I'm sure someone you know could help you figure out just what to do if you need some help. Our medical history, tax information, family pictures, and all my recipes are on the computer. We also store all our contact information for family and friends. The few times we have had a computer crash over the years have been devastating. Taking a few steps periodically to prevent this has brought me great peace of mind.

Fireproof Safe - One of the main reasons families in our area have to evacuate is an individual home fire. Once I learned this, I took steps to prepare for it. We practice fire drills as a family a couple of times a year. It is one of our kids' favorite family night activities! The other thing we did was purchase a small fireproof safe. It contains copies of our insurance papers, bank account information, family pictures, computer back-up disks, etc. We hope a fire never hits our home, but we all know families that this has happened to. Taking steps to have a plan and to prepare can lessen the fear we carry.

Getting It All Done

It can be so overwhelming to tackle all of these things. We just have to remember the old saying, "How do you eat an elephant? One bite at a time." It is in the little changes that we make day after day that we end up making the big changes in our lives. We can't expect to be fully ready in a week or a month or even a year. It takes a lifetime, one day at a time.

There are a few habit changes I have made over time that help me accomplish a lot more than I used to be able to do. I hope some of these tips can inspire you to set some goals and reach for a new level of provident living.

I determined what was draining my time - For me, I turned the TV off. I learned as a missionary how to be very effective without the TV or radio. We still need to have some down time, but it can be had in many other ways. I found that I would get sucked into a program and lose 1–2 hours quite frequently. It's amazing what I can accomplish in that amount of time after my kids are in bed.

Maybe you have something else that is draining your time. It could be book reading or spending time online. Whatever it is, even if you are only involved in good things, it may be keeping you from getting the best things done. Steal back a few hours each week by setting some new goals in this area.

I stopped redoing the same things again and again - As a mom, there are many things we have to repeat out of necessity. There are others that, if we organize ourselves, we don't end up having to rethink over and over again. As an example, there was a period of our lives that we were traveling more frequently. I found I was constantly packing and unpacking a bag of toiletries. I realized that if I just packed my extra toiletries that I keep at the house as part of our emergency preparedness plan I could be ready for a trip so must faster.

I now have a bag that is fully packed all the time. I quickly refer to my packing list and look through it to make sure nothing has run out and I add my curling iron and blow dryer and I'm done. It makes packing for a trip so much easier. I did something similar with our camping gear. We have a bin that stays packed all the time. This was especially helpful when my husband, James, worked with the Boy Scouts and was camping every month.

Another thing that I found myself doing again and again was making lists. I would make a shopping list, a camping list, a trip packing list, etc. every time we were headed somewhere. James used to tell me I needed to print a book of my lists one day. I decided to put these lists on the computer and now I just print them off and check off what we need. (I've included these lists in the appendix for you to refer to if you are interested. Hopefully they will inspire you to develop one for your own needs.)

Take some time to think through what you are doing again and again. Develop a list or system that will make it faster for you. You will be amazed at how much time you reclaim! Put it to good use and you will make great progress on your goals.

I realized it wasn't just up to me - Living providently is an entire family affair! Everyone in the family needs to understand the importance of living these principles. Start small and get others involved. James and I would split the list up on items we needed to research. He is always so willing to lift the heavy boxes and make trips to the cannery or the orchards. His willing attitude has been the best support. The kids are getting old enough now that they have a hand in things as well.

Canning day is an extended family affair that everyone looks forward to. My parents and siblings join together for a day or two and help put up over 100 quarts of applesauce each year. The kids all love taking a turn picking and then squishing the apples. We join together again when the peaches are ready. It has become part of our fall tradition.

Family Night is another great way to motivate others to want to live these principles. We dedicate a few family nights a year to the topic of Emergency Preparedness. This is a good time to include your children in the preparing process. Here is a list of topics you could cover at family night:

- Fire/escape drills

- Building or rotating your 72-hour kit

- Completing or updating Child ID kits

- Basic first aid/CPR training

- How to turn off the water or gas at the main shut-off valve

- Rotating your water storage
- Planting/caring for a garden
- Cooking with your emergency stove

Get creative as you plan these nights. Our kids actually request to do our Fire Drill night where we time ourselves at getting out of the house and redo the drill two or three times to see if we can do it faster. They also love it when we empty the 55-gallon water drum, put in a few drops of bleach and let them roll it around the yard so the bleach can swish around. These are fun memories that teach important lessons. Even a little bit of training can lessen the fear during a true emergency.

I decided I would focus on one thing a year - This helped me break the big picture down into small steps. One year we built our 72-hour kits. One year I focused on putting our meal plan together. One year I learned all I could about using powdered milk. One year we really focused on organizing our finances. One year I figured out cooking with dry beans. Even if I only had one day a month that I did something towards my goal, this means I spent 12 days that year learning or doing something. This is 12 more days than I would have done before setting this goal.

> *Focus on one area a year and little by little you will make it.*

By having an area decided on each year, it really gave me a focus. It helped keep the idea in the back of my mind so that during those rare snippets of free time, I could do a little research. I found myself feeding a baby in front of the computer and using the internet to learn so many things. I developed lists of things we needed to purchase and we chipped away at it a little at a time. If I found a recipe that sounded worth trying, I would print it off and take it to the kitchen and then try it out sometime over the next couple of weeks.

I found that as I committed to do something regardless of how small, Heavenly Father helped me figure out a way to get it done. It's amazing what I have learned in the eleven years I have been married.

I made my time at the grocery store and in the kitchen count - When I go shopping, I try to plan two weeks out and stock up when I see a good price. With 5 kids and no one old enough to be a babysitter, shopping trips can be an ordeal. With a little planning and a good list, I can get through the store in record time. Less time at the store means more time to get other things done. (See the appendix for the shopping list I use.)

When you are cooking, don't be afraid to cook in bulk or make a bunch of mixes at a time. Growing up in a large family helped me realize that it doesn't take much more effort to cook for 12 than it does to cook for 4. Most of us are not cooking for 12 on a daily basis, but if we do this every now and then, we save hours in the kitchen another day. Triple the batch of something that freezes well and you have dinner for that night and two other nights also. You already have the recipe and the ingredients out. It really is so simple to do a large batch.

Use your freezer to your advantage. Precook meat in large batches to make dinner prep most nights a breeze. Bake bread or rolls in mass and you are good to go for later. Cook up a large pot of dry beans when you will need some for dinner and freeze the extra. Little changes in how you think in the kitchen will save you hours down the road. Put that new found time to good use!

I developed an "I can do it!" attitude - Perhaps the greatest habit change is in the way I think about challenges. Many of us are born with the attitude that we can do it. We see this come through very clearly at about age two with our toddlers when they tell us, "I do it, Mommy!" They are very determined to figure out doing it without relying on us. Somewhere between age two and twenty-five we lose some of our confidence and aren't ready to tackle a challenge with as much gusto.

I've learned over the years that in order to become like Heavenly Father, we must be able to know and do *all* things. This is definitely an overwhelming thought. All things includes food storage, finances, and emergency preparedness. We have been given spiritual gifts to help us in these efforts. The gift of a willing heart, the gift of learning from others, and the gift of organization can all be ours if we desire them enough. Alma teaches us to "let this desire work in you" (Alma 32:27). If these gifts were not given to you from the beginning, they can still be yours. As you increase your desire to follow the counsel we've received, you'll grow in your understanding of where you are lacking. I have found that when I get specific with my prayers, I often am better at seeing the blessings.

Don't hesitate to ask for help in organizing your food storage. I remember when I was first putting together my meal plan, I knew it would take a certain amount of focused thinking time. At that point, I had three children under the age of four. I was a very busy mom. I prayed that the children would overlap their nap times long enough each day to give me the time I needed. I committed that any time I had them all asleep, I would focus on my food storage. It was a very specific request, but I saw the results. As soon as I had them all asleep at the same time, I pulled out all my notes. I stayed dedicated to using that time that was given to me on the project I knew I needed to complete. It was an amazing testimony builder of the importance of provident living principles! Heavenly Father knows challenges will come, but He wants to limit our discomfort as we live through them. He has given us the ability to plan ahead and provided us with plenty of resources, but in the end, we just have to "do it." Put these skills into practice now, don't wait for a crisis, and don't forget that you can call on Him for help.

Appendix

Family Spending Plan Instructions

This is a long budget form. It will only take a few times of filling it out to get the hang of it though. It is long on purpose so you don't leave anything out and end up with surprise expenses you haven't planned for. You'll soon figure out that you don't end up listing something on every line every month, but by having all the categories it will get you talking together about upcoming expenses and planning just how your income will be distributed.

At the beginning of each month, list the budgeted amount for each necessary category. Every single dollar of your income should be accounted for in some area of this form. At the end of the month, record the amount you actually spent. It is recommended that you use a cash-only envelope system for the categories marked with an asterisk *. If after a few months you are consistently budgeting too low or too high for certain categories, you will have to make the necessary changes to your budgeted amount.

During the middle of each month you may find that one area's expenses are quite a bit higher than you expected. You will need to call an emergency budgeting conference to decide which category you will pull money from in order to cover these higher expenses.

In planning your savings goals, remember that you should build up an emergency fund of at least $1,000 before putting extra money towards debt pay down. You don't want to have to turn to credit cards ever again, if possible. Once you are out of debt, except for your mortgage, you should build your emergency fund to cover 3–6 months of your family's needs. (If your job is seasonal, less secure, or you have only one source of income at home, you will want to save 6+ months of expenses.) Once your emergency fund is in place, then you can begin paying down your mortgage and saving for additional goals such as vacations, home improvements, a new car, etc. If, for any reason, you determine that you have to pull from your emergency funds then your family has to enter a "spending freeze" mode and only buy the bare essentials until you have the fund built back up. As you are paying down debt, be wise in the extra expenses for things such as vacations or activities. You still need to do these things, you just can't let them drive you deeper into debt.

This form works very well for those who earn a consistent salary each month. It can still work for those who earn an irregular income. With an irregular income, you have to prioritize your spending to cover what is most important first. Fill out the form using a color code system. Fill the amounts in using a red pen for the items that are bare essentials. These items will be paid with the first money that comes in. Fill in all other areas using a blue or black pen and add a small number off to the side to indicate which order they will be paid in. As additional income is made, pay these areas off in the order you planned. Anytime you have a great month, you need to fill your savings to make up for the months when income is especially tight. Anyone making irregular income needs to try to have an emergency fund that could cover 6 months to a year of your family's expenses.

As with anything you do consistently, talking about money will become a habit. You will recognize the great blessings of peace that come as you figure out a system that works for you and helps you feel on top of all of your obligations.

Family Spending Plan Form

Category	Planned Amount	Actual Amount
Tithes & Offerings		
Tithing		
Fast Offerings		
Other		
Housing		
Rent/Mortgage (Include PMI)		
2nd Mortgage		
Mortgage Pay Down		
Property Taxes		
Homeowner's Insurance		
Subdivision Fees		
Home Maintenance		
Home Improvement		
Other (Curtains, furniture, appliances, etc.)		
Utilities		
Power		
Water		
Gas		
Phone		
Trash		
Satellite/Cable TV		
Internet		
Other		
Food & Household Goods *		
Groceries *		
School Lunch *		
Dinners Out *		

	Misc. Household Goods (TP, diapers, cleaners, etc.)*		
	Food Storage *		
Clothing & Shoes *			
	Kids *		
	Adults *		
	Cleaning/Laundry *		
Personal *			
	Toiletries *		
	Cosmetics *		
	Hair Care, etc. *		
	Other (Spending allowance, etc.) *		
Car			
	Car Payment 1		
	Car Payment 2		
	Gas & Oil *		
	Repairs/Tires *		
	Car Insurance		
	Car Registration		
	Parking Fees		
	Public Transportation Costs *		
	Car Replacement (Amount you are saving each month for this)		
	Other		
Medical			
	Health Insurance		
	Disability Insurance		
	Doctor		
	Dentist		
	Vision		
	Prescription Drugs		
	Over-the-Counter Medication *		

Veterinarian			
Other			
Education/Work Related Expenses			
Tuition/Fees			
Books			
Activity Fees/Lessons			
School Supplies *			
Magazines/Newspapers			
Child Care			
Recreation			
Vacations *			
Hobby Supplies *			
Gym Memberships			
Other Memberships			
Athletic Events *			
Activities (Movies, etc.) *			
Babysitter *			
Gifts *			
Birthday *			
Christmas *			
Other (Mother's Day, Anniversary, etc.) *			
Additional Charitable Donations *			
Savings			
Emergency Fund			
Retirement			
College			
Investments			
Life Insurance			
Other (List your specific goal.)			
Debt Payments			
Credit Card 1			

Credit Card 2		
Dept. Store Card 1		
Dept. Store Card 2		
Student Loan		
Alimony/Child Support		
Other		
Other		
Other		
Other Expenses (These don't fit in any other category.)		
List specific items.		
Leftover for Fun! (When all your obligations are met, you can have some fun and not feel guilty about it!)		

Family Expense Record Instructions

This form is to help you organize and keep a record of your expenses and your savings. To really be effective, you need to complete one of these for every month of the year. It takes an entire year to gain a good understanding of where your money is going. After collecting this information, you can make more accurate plans for future budget needs.

Suggestions on How to List Items

1. Tithes & Offerings - List all charitable donations here.

2. Housing/ Utilities - List mortgage payment or rent, home insurance, repairs, painting, and other improvements. Also include household items such as furniture, carpet, draperies, appliances, lighting fixtures, etc. Utilities should also be included, as well as cleaning supplies and lawn care expenses. Really any cost for something for the house or apartment falls in this category.

3. Food - Include all groceries, fast food, restaurant meals, and school lunches in this category.

4. Clothing - Include all clothing, sewing materials, shoes, and accessories in this category. Also add clothing repair or alteration costs, laundry, and cleaning.

5. Personal - List personal allowances, haircuts, cosmetics, etc. in this category.

6. Car, Other Transportation, and Insurance - Include car payments, gas, oil, repairs, tires, parking fees, public transportation expenses, licenses, registration, and auto insurance in this category.

7. Medical - Include doctor, hospital, dental, vision, and prescription expenses. List health insurance premiums in this category as well.

8. Education - List tuition, fees, books, magazines, newspapers, school supplies, and any lesson or sports fees here.

9. Recreation - Include hobby supplies, movies, gym memberships, athletic events, and vacations.

10. Gifts - List all gifts including birthday, graduation, Christmas, or "just because" in this category.

11. Savings/ Investments - List all money put into savings accounts, mutual funds, IRAs, or any other investments. Life or disability insurance payments should be listed in this category.

12. Credit Payments - List any payments for credit cards or other loans.

13. Other - List any purchase that does not fall in another category.

Family Expense Record

Date	List Items	1. Tithes & Offerings	2. Housing/ Utilities	3. Food	4. Clothing	5. Personal
	Amount Budgeted	$	$	$	$	$

6. Car	7. Medical	8. Recreation	9. Gifts	10. Education	11. Savings/ Investments	12. Credit Payments	13. Other
$	$	$	$	$	$	$	$

Trip Packing List

Toiletries - *Most of this stays packed all the time.*

Curling iron
Blow dryer
Brushes & clips
Deodorant
Toothbrushes & paste
Floss
Make-up
Glasses & case
Sunglasses
Contacts /solution
Sunscreen
Bug spray
Hairspray
Gel
Shampoo/conditioner
Razor
Q-tips
Vitamins
Prescription meds
Obuprofen
Kid's meds
Feminine needs
Mirror
Nail clippers/file
Scrunchie
Soap

Kids

Diapers/wipes
Plastic bags
Baby food/crackers
Formula
Bottles/cup
Snacks
Feeding towels/bibs
Spoons/bowls
Blankets
Clothes
Sunday clothes
Under clothing
PJs
Socks/shoes
Jacket or coat
Swimsuits/towels
Swim diapers
Backpack/front pack
Stroller
Bouncy seat
Night light

Adults

Clothes
Sunday clothes
Shoes/socks
Belt
Under clothing
PJs
Jacket or coat
Swim suit/towel

Miscellaneous

Phone/charger
CDs/DVDs
Activity bag
Pillows
Cash
Camera
Trash bags (for dirty laundry)
Scriptures
Journal/pen
Maps/trip info

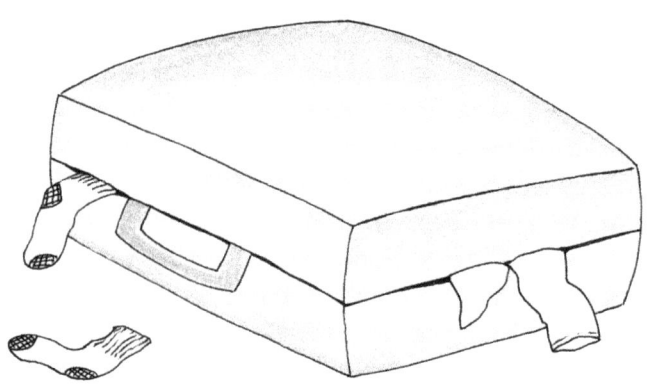

Camping List

Pack in plastic bin - *Check to refill at the beginning of each summer.*

Lantern
Flashlight
Work gloves
Foil
Hot pads
Paper towels
Wooden spoon
Spatula
Sharp knives & peeler
Cutting board
Can opener
Tongs
Roasting sticks
Leftover containers
Pans
Bowls
Garbage bags
Ziplock bags
Dish soap
Wash cloth
Dish towels
Cooking oil
Newspaper
Matches
Rope
Bug spray

Sunscreen
First aid Kit
Toilet paper
Duct tape

Picnic box - *This is a separate smaller bin that stays packed so we can go to a park on a moment's notice. Store it near the camping bin.*

Paper plates
Cups
Utensils
Napkins
Tablecloth
Wipes
Hand sanitizer

Pack in car - *Add to car as needed for specific trip plans.*

Pillows
Sleeping bags
Sleeping pads
Blankets
Tent
Chairs

Camera
Toiletries
PJs
Jackets
Hats
Clothes
Swimsuits
Towels
Stroller/backpack
Diaper bag
Water
Cook stove
Propane
Griddle
Grill
Dutch oven
Lid lifter
Chimney
Firewood
Charcoal
Cooler

Food - *Be sure to include any specialty items needed to prepare food that is planned*

Grocery Shopping List

Produce
___Apples
___Bananas
___Fruit
___Tomatoes
___Lettuce
___Carrots
___Celery
___Broccoli
___Potatoes
___Onions
_____
_____

Snacks
___Corn chips
___Pretzels
___Wheat Thins
___Snack crackers
___Cheese crackers
___Saltines
_____
_____

Canned Goods
___Mayo
___Ketchup
___Pickles
___Ranch dressing
___Green beans
___Black olives
___Pineapple
___Juice
_____
_____
___Pasta
___Spaghetti sauce
___Mac & cheese
___Ramen

___Rice
___Tuna
___Soup
_____
_____
_____

Baking
___Pudding
___Jello
___Sugar
___Flour
___Cornmeal
___Soda
___Powder
___Shortening
___Oil
___Syrup
___Pancake mix
___Pan spray
_____
_____

Cereals
_____
_____
_____

Bulk Foods
___Dried fruit
___Nuts
___Yeast
___Spices
___Dry hash browns
___Parmesan Cheese
___Pasta
_____
_____

Deli/Meats
___Cheese
___Cream cheese
___Lunch meat

___Hot dogs
___Chicken
___Sausage
___Ham
___Roast
___Hamburger
___Pork
___Salmon
_____
_____

Dairy
___Eggs
___Milk
___Yogurt
___Cottage cheese
___Sour cream
___Butter tub
___Margarine
_____

Frozen Foods
___Hash browns
___Tots/fries
___Broccoli
___Mixed vegetables
___Juice
___Cool Whip
___Ice cream
_____

Bakery
___Tortillas
___French bread
___Bagels
___Bread
___Rolls
_____
_____
_____

Preschool Program

Days and Time: Tuesdays and Thursdays

Daily Schedule: 9:30–9:55 Recess (outside or project inside)
Ring bell and have students line up for school
10:00–10:30 1st circle time
10:30–10:45 Snack time
10:45–11:15 Work time
11:15-11:30 Final Circle time: Calendar and story time
11:30 Pack backpacks and head home

Monthly Schedule: There will be a color and a shape assigned each month. All of us can work these into our lesson plans throughout the month.

Weekly Schedule: Preschool will be at the same home each week. There will be a letter assigned to each week. Incorporate these into your lesson plans along with the color and shape for the month as much as possible.

Curriculum: Language concepts
   Alphabet –upper and lowercase sounds, recognition and writing
   Rhyming words
   Name recognition (first name only)
  Math Concepts
   Patterns – such as ababab, aabaabaab, aabbaabbaabb, etc.
   Numbers 1-10 counting and recognition
   Shapes
   Sorting items
   Greater than and less than
  Other Concepts
   Colors
   Days of the week
   Months of the year
   Fine motor skills (coloring, cutting, sorting small objects)
   Body parts and senses

School Supplies: Backpack
Pocket folder and change of clothes (in backpack)
Old shirt or paint apron (in bin)
$10 to cover cost of additional supplies in bin

1ˢᵗ Circle Time: This is your instruction time. We will have a welcome song to add consistency and also teach patterns.

> (To the tune of "Here We Go 'Round the Mulberry Bush")
> This is the way we start the day, start the day, start the day
> This is the way we start the day so early in the morning
> Wave your hand at Kendra, Kendra, Kendra
> Wave your hand at Kendra so early in the morning
> Point your toes at Spencer, Spencer, Spencer
> Point your toes at Spencer so early in the morning
> Wave your hand at Alex . . .
>
> Additional ideas: Give each child a bead that will make a pattern
> See what color Alex has, Alex has, Alex has

At the end of the song, quiz the children on what would come next.

The rest of 1ˢᵗ circle time should be used to teach basic concepts and introduce work time activities. Dismiss the kids with a quiz. Example: Put a few letter cards down in front of you and say, "Spencer, point to the letter R" then direct him to the work you want him to do.

Snack Time: Use every opportunity to teach basic concepts even during snack time. We will have place mats made in the color of the month with names on them. Have the snack helper lay these out just as work time ends and then have students find their name. Also, use this time to teach the children how to stand in a line as you have them wash their hands before going to the table.

Here are a few suggestions of snack ideas that teach:

> Have the children sort fruit loops into colors
> Cut cheese pieces into different shapes
> Crackers come in many shapes and colors
> Use canned cheese to write letters on crackers
> See what letters they can make with pretzel sticks
> Serve snacks that begin with the letter of the week

You get the idea. Be creative and make it fun.

Work Time: The kids can work independently or in small groups depending on what you have planned. The weather chart helper fills in the chart during work time.

Final Circle: This is the time to go over the calendar and weather chart. See the calendar lesson plan to understand how to do this. When the calendar is done, read a story that goes along with the monthly or weekly theme. Dismiss the kids to pack bags and get ready to go.

Rotating Bin: We will have a bin that rotates each week. It will hold school supplies such as scissors, glue, crayons, paints, etc. as well as carpet squares (or pillow cases), the calendar, weather chart, classroom helper chart, flashcards, lesson plan books, and any other activities you have put together and would like to share.

Student Helpers: We will have a classroom helper chart to keep the kids involved. This is also another chance to help the kids recognize their names in print. The following jobs will be on the chart: (These change depending on the number of kids.)

> Snack helper – Sets place mats out and passes out snack
> Bell ringer – Rings the hand bell to begin school
> Calendar helper – Places numbers on calendar
> Weather chart – Fills in the chart
> Line leader – Leads children in from recess time to circle
> Circle helper – Gets things the teacher needs, chooses a song to sing, etc.
> Pledge - Leads us in the Pledge of Allegiance

Field Trips: We will each be responsible for planning one field trip during the year. This will replace one of our regular school days.

Birthdays: Each child will get a special crown on their birthday or un-birthday if they have a summer birthday. Feel free to bring a special snack to be shared at snack time if you would like.

Holiday Parties: These will fall on the closest school day to the holiday. You will be responsible for planning the party if it falls on your week. Parties will be the last 30–60 minutes of preschool time depending on what is planned. Please let us know what we can do to help with activities and/or treats to simplify the party for you. All moms and siblings are invited to be there for the party.

Calendar Lesson Plan - Done during final circle

The teacher sits on the floor with the students facing her and the calendar between them. Place the calendar so it is right side up for the students. Have the calendar helper sit so he/she can reach the calendar easily.

Teacher: Can you tell me what month this is? Let's sing the months of the year song to help us figure it out.
> (To the tune of "Ten Little Indians")
> January, February, March, and April
> May, June, July, and August
> September, October, November, December
> Now we start again

Sing through the entire song once. The second time through is when you stop after singing the current month.

Have the helper place the month of the year word card along the top of the calendar.

Teacher: What year is it? Have the student place the year card at the top.

Teacher: Now let's figure out what day it is. Last time we had school, it was Tuesday, September 22nd. What day of the week is it today? Let's sing our song to find out.
> (To the tune of "Allouette")
> Sunday, Monday, Tuesday, Wednesday, Thursday,
> Friday, Saturday, now we start again.

Sing through the entire song once. The second time through is when you stop after singing the current day.

Teacher: So today is Thursday.
> Sing: Today is Thursday
> Today is Thursday
> Happy, happy Thursday
> Happy, happy Thursday
> Thursday! (Throw arms up in the air at the end.)

Now have the helper count out loud with you from 1 to the day that it is as you point at the numbers. Allow them to stick the missing numbers on the calendar.

Reiterate that today is Thursday, September 23, 2010 as you dismiss the helper to sit back with the circle for story time.

Recipe Index

A

Alfredo Pasta · 71
Angel Biscuits · 142
Angel Food Cake Roll · 47
Angel Hair Pasta · 86
Any "Old Fruit" Cake · 102
Apple Cinnamon Oatmeal · 80
Apple Crisp · 102
Apple Muffin Breakfast Cake · 81
Apple Pie Filling · 206
Applesauce Oatmeal Cookies · 103
Autumn Wheat Berry Salad · 119

B

Baked Chicken Strips · 61
Banana Cookies · 105
Banana Muffin Mix · 145
Basic Bread Dough · 128
Basic Muffin Mix · 144
Basic Pizza Dough · 132
Basic White Sauce · 178
BBQ Chicken Filling · 66
BBQ Pulled Pork · 67
Bean and Rice Burritos · 159
Beef and Barley Soup · 78
Beef Enchiladas · 40
Beef Stroganoff · 73
Biscuit Mix · 151
Black Bean and Corn Salsa · 193
Black Bean Brownies · 162
Black Bean Soup · 160
Braided Swiss Bread · 138
Bread Bowls · 128
Bread Dipping Herb Mix · 135
Bread in a Bag · 132
Breadstick Bones · 213
Breadsticks · 128
Breakfast Burritos · 38
Breakfast Danish · 141
Breakfast Empanadas · 38
Breakfast Sandwiches · 39
Broccoli Cheese Soup · 182
Brownie Marshmallow Bars · 99
Buttermilk · 168

C

Casserole Bread · 136
Cheese Ball · 93
Cheesy Garlic Breadsticks · 133
Cherry Pie Filling · 207
Chewy "Healthy" Chocolate Chip Cookies · 163
Chewy Caramel Corn · 107
Chewy Granola Bars · 96
Chicken and Broccoli Casserole · 57
Chicken and Veggie Pasta · 75
Chicken Bistro Twist · 62
Chicken Caesar Tetrazzini · 42
Chicken Dumplings · 40
Chicken Enchiladas · 41
Chicken Noodle Soup · 152
Chicken Pot Pie · 56
Chicken Salad · 67
Chicken Tacos · 50
Chocolate Chews · 175
Chocolate Chip Cookies · 92
Chocolate Crinkles · 103
Chocolate Oatmeal Bars · 91
Chocolate Zucchini Cake · 188
Chunky Applesauce · 200
Cinnamon Ornaments · 215
Cinnamon Twists · 128
Clam Chowder · 182
Coconut Bread · 104
Coconut Chex Mix · 90
Confetti Salad · 83
Corn Bread · 144
Corn Tortillas · 52
Cottage Cheese · 172
Crazy Cake · 105
Crazy Zucchini Cake · 189
Cream Cheese · 171
Cream Cheese Spread Options · 171
Cream of Chicken Soup Substitute · 179
Cream Pie · 114
Creamy Chicken and Rice Soup · 76

Creamy Chicken Noodle Soup · 181
Creamy Fruit Cups · 83
Creamy Italian Chicken · 58
Creamy White Chicken Chili · 183
Crustless Quiche · 175
Crusty French Bread · 135

D
Danish Dessert · 106
Dehydrated Apple Slices · 201
Dehydrated Peaches · 201
Dehydrated Pears · 202
Dehydrated Plums · 202
Dinner Rolls · 128

E
Easy Sloppy Joes · 68
Egg Yolk Paint · 216
English Muffin Bread · 137
English Toffee · 111
Evaporated Milk · 169

F
Fabulous Homemade Bread · 130
Fettuccine · 71
Flavored Applesauce · 201
Flour Tortillas · 51
Fluffy Fruit Salad · 84
Focaccia Bread · 131
Freezer Cinnamon Rolls · 139
Freezer Crescent Rolls · 140
Freezer Jam · 205
French Lentil Rice Soup · 153
Fresh Pie Glaze · 205
Fresh Salsa · 193
Fried Rice · 70
Frog Eye Salad · 84
Frozen Banana Snacks · 90
Frozen Pudding Pops · 90
Fruit Flavored Yogurt · 170
Fruit Leather · 203
Fruit Pandowdy · 114
Fruit Rolls · 203
Fruit Syrup · 207
Funeral Potatoes · 47
Funnel Cakes · 98

G
Garden Pasta Salad · 193
Ghost Treats · 213
Gourmet Oatmeal · 147
Granola · 80
Greek Style Yogurt · 170
Green Pea and Crisp Corn Salad · 86
Green Sauce Enchiladas · 41
Grilled Salmon · 61
Grilled Zucchini and Summer Squash · 190

H
Ham and Corn Chowder · 180
Hamburger Buns · 128
Hamburgers · 45
Harvest Snack Mix · 98
Hash Browns · 82
Hays' Special · 72
Hearty Bean Soup · 162
Hearty Whole Grain Pancake Mix · 151
Hobo Stew · 77
Hockey Pucks · 108
Homemade Baby Wipes · 215, 216
Homemade Baked Beans · 158
Homemade Crackers · 94
Homemade Ice Cream · 174
Homemade Kettle Corn · 97
Homemade Mac and Cheese · 184
Homemade Refried Beans · 158
Homemade Yogurt · 169
Honey Butter · 131
Honey Graham Crackers · 95
Hot Dog Buns · 128

I
Ice Cream Crunch · 48
Instant Oatmeal Mix · 147
Instant Pumpkin Pudding · 106

J
Jello Marble Pie · 109

K
Kid-Friendly Fruity Yogurt · 170

L
Lasagna · 44

Latkes · 81
Lentil Soup · 77

M

Macaroni Salad · 85
Magic Fruit Dumplings · 104
Manicotti with Cheese Stuffing · 42
Maple Bars · 128
Maple Icing · 128
Mashed Potato Casserole · 59
Meatballs · 45
Meatballs in Mushroom Gravy · 46
Meatloaf · 45
Mediterranean Chicken · 73
Medium Cheddar Cheese · 173
Mexican Lasagna · 50
Mexican Rice · 161
Mexican Sweet Pork · 54
Microwave Caramel Chex · 91
Mint Hot Cocoa Mix · 148
Moist and Delicious Cornbread · 160
Mountain Man Breakfast · 79
Mummy Dogs · 213

N

Nachos · 179
Navy Bean Soup · 161
No Bake Chocolate Cookies · 109
No-Bake Cereal Bars · 93
No-bake Granola Bars · 97
No-bake Yogurt Cheesecake · 174

O

Oatmeal Waffles · 149
Octodogs and Seaweed · 214
One Hour Hot Rolls · 137
Orange Chicken · 69
Orange Julius · 98
Overnight Whole Wheat Pancakes · 120

P

Pancake Mix · 150
Panquecas · 65
Parmesan Cheese · 172
Party Meatballs · 44
Pasta Carbonara · 184
Pasta Primavera · 72

Pasta with Sour Cream Sauce · 74
Peanut Brittle · 111
Peanut Butter Balls · 112
Peanut Butter Chocolate Chip Cookies · 108
Peanut Butter Yogurt Dip · 99
Pepperoni Pizza Twists · 63
Pie Crust · 113
Pineapple Cheese Ball · 93
Pinto Bean Fudge · 163
Pita Bread · 128
Pizza Carbonara · 180
Pizza Dough · 128, 134
Pizza Pasta · 73
Pizza Pinwheels · 64
Play Dough · 212
Popcorn Balls · 110
Popcorn Cake · 110
Poppyseed Chicken · 58
Pork Chop Supper · 59
Potato Casserole · 56
Potato Cheese Soup · 181
Potato Dish · 47
Potato Pancakes · 81
Potato Wedges · 87
Pumpkin Braid · 136
Pumpkin Muffin Mix · 145
Pumpkin Oatmeal Cookies · 107
Pumpkin Yeast Rolls · 136

Q

Quiche · 39
Quick and Easy Chili · 159

R

Raspberry Cream Pie · 113
Restaurant Style Refried Beans · 159
Rhubarb Crumble · 192
Rice · 88
Rice Casserole · 59
Rice Haystacks · 62
Rice Krispie Candies · 110
Rice Pilaf · 152
Ricotta Cheese · 172

S

Salmon Cakes · 60
Salmon Salad · 66

Salsa · 209
Salt Dough · 212
Saucy Tarragon Chicken · 74
Sausage and White Bean Soup · 183
Sausage Gravy · 178
Sausage Spaghetti Pie · 43
Scalloped Potatoes · 185
Scotchies · 164
Scrumptious Rhubarb Cake · 192
Seafood Pasta Salad · 85
Shaped Empanadas · 214
Simply Delicious Potatoes · 87, 88
Slick Rock Chicken · 60
Sloppy Joes From Scratch · 68
Snickerdoodles · 48
Soft Garlic Breadstick · 134
Soft Set Jelly · 206
Soft Shell Tacos · 54
Sour Cream Substitute · 171
Sour Milk · 168
Spaghetti · 71
Spiced Orange Drink Mix · 149
Split Pea Soup · 78
Stir Fry Noodles · 70
Stove Top Lasagna · 72
Stovetop Rice Pudding · 79
Strawberry Rhubarb Jam · 200
Stuffed Burgers · 65
Surprise Pancakes · 82
Sweet and Sour Chicken · 43
Sweet and Sour Sauce · 208
Sweetened Condensed Milk · 169

T

Taco Cups · 53
Taco Filling · 53
Taco Nests · 53
Taco Soup · 51
Tamale Casserole · 55
Tater Tot Casserole · 56
Tomato Basil Bruschetta · 194
Tomato Cucumber Salad · 194
Tortellini Soup · 76
Tortilla Roll-ups · 92
Tortilla Soup · 55
Tuna Noodle Supreme · 75
Tuna Salad · 66
Turtle Delights · 112
Twice Baked Potatoes · 46

U

Ultimate Chocolate Chocolate Chip Cookies · 164

W

Warm Bean Dip · 53
Wheat Berry Chili · 119
Wheat Berry Fruit Salad · 119
Wheat Berry Pilaf · 120
White Sauce Mix · 178
Whole Wheat Baking Powder Biscuits · 122
Whole Wheat Bread · 130
Whole Wheat Brownie Mix · 121
Whole Wheat Flour Tortillas · 52
Whole Wheat Muffins · 122
Whole Wheat Sugar Cookies · 121

Y

Yogurt Cheese · 171
Yogurt Smoothie · 171

Z

Zucchini Bread · 146
Zucchini Brownies · 191
Zucchini Burger Bake · 190
Zucchini Casserole · 188
Zucchini Cookies · 146
Zucchini Enchiladas · 189
Zucchini Pie · 191
Züpfa · 138

About the Author

Tamara Price (known as Tammy to her friends and family) lives in the Boise, Idaho area with her husband and five children. She holds a bachelor's degree in Education from Boise State University and taught school before her children were born. Now she is thankful she is able to be home with them. Her biggest challenge has been complications with all five pregnancies, which required that she spend many months in bed–a little over a year of her life in all.

It was during this period of her life that she turned to her food storage and learned firsthand the importance of having it organized in a manner that even her eight-year-old could help with the cooking. Facing the staggering medical bills that come with having children born prematurely, she and her husband figured out ways to be in control of their finances so they could meet all the demands placed on them. Through these and other experiences, she has gained insights that she hopes will help others in their quest to be prepared. She has taught preparedness classes for many years and has finally compiled her knowledge into a book.

About the Illustrator

Katie Ormond recently returned to the Boise, Idaho area now that her husband finished his graduate degree. They have three young children. She holds a bachelor's degree in Political Science from Boise State University along with a Minor in Art. She has loved art since her middle school years and has worked to fine tune her own style ever since. She has enjoyed trying every kind of art medium there is, but her favorite is charcoal portraits. It was exciting for her to try book illustrations and be a part of this project.

> For new recipes, additional tips, and tutorials check out:
>
> ## allthingsprovident.blogspot.com

Printed in the USA
CPSIA information can be obtained
at www.ICGtesting.com
CBHW062326201024
16153CB00019B/1847